IMAGES of America

# MOUNT VERNON

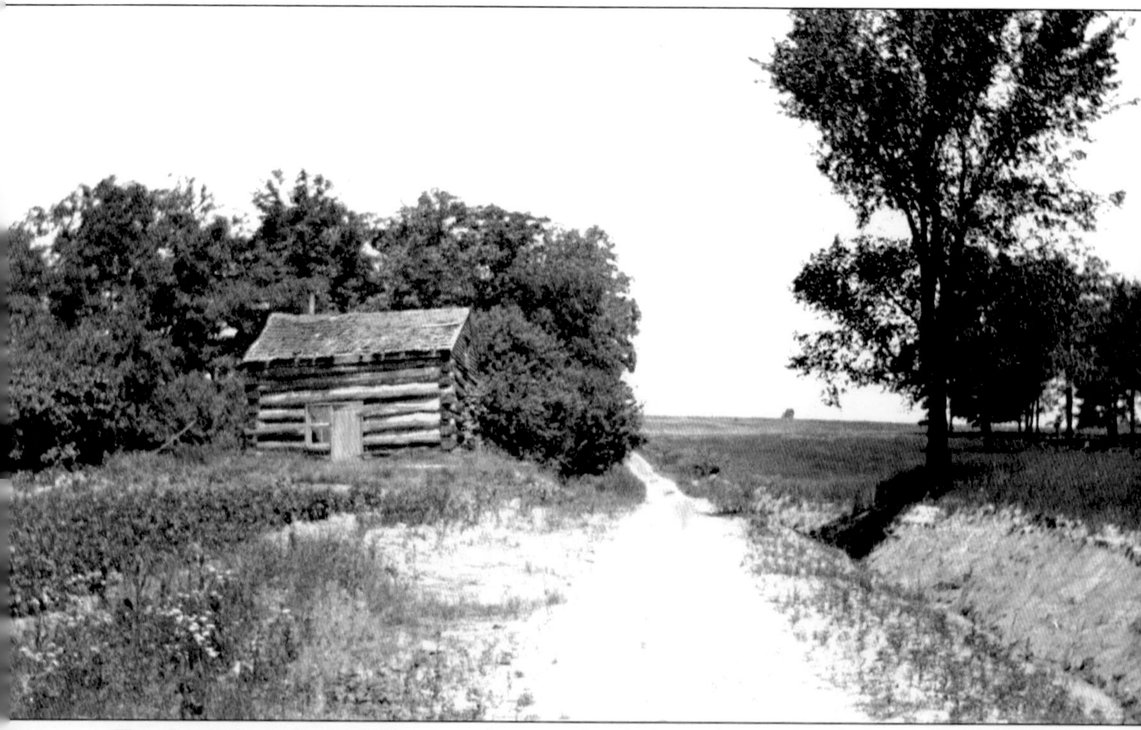

**THE LAST LOG CABIN?** This is a photograph of a log cabin in Gambier, *c.* 1917. It is similar to the early log cabins in Mount Vernon. It is rare to find photographs of original log cabins in Knox County, such as this one, that had not been restored or relocated. (Photograph courtesy of the Olin Library, Kenyon College, Greenslade Special Collections and Archives.)

IMAGES
*of America*

# MOUNT VERNON

Donald Edgar Boyd

ARCADIA
PUBLISHING

ISBN 978-0-7385-3321-6

Published by Arcadia Publishing
Charleston, South Carolina

Printed in the United States of America

Library of Congress Catalog Card Number: 2004107552

For all general information contact Arcadia Publishing at:
Telephone 843-853-2070
Fax 843-853-0044
E-mail sales@arcadiapublishing.com
For customer service and orders:
Toll-Free 1-888-313-2665

Visit us on the Internet at www.arcadiapublishing.com

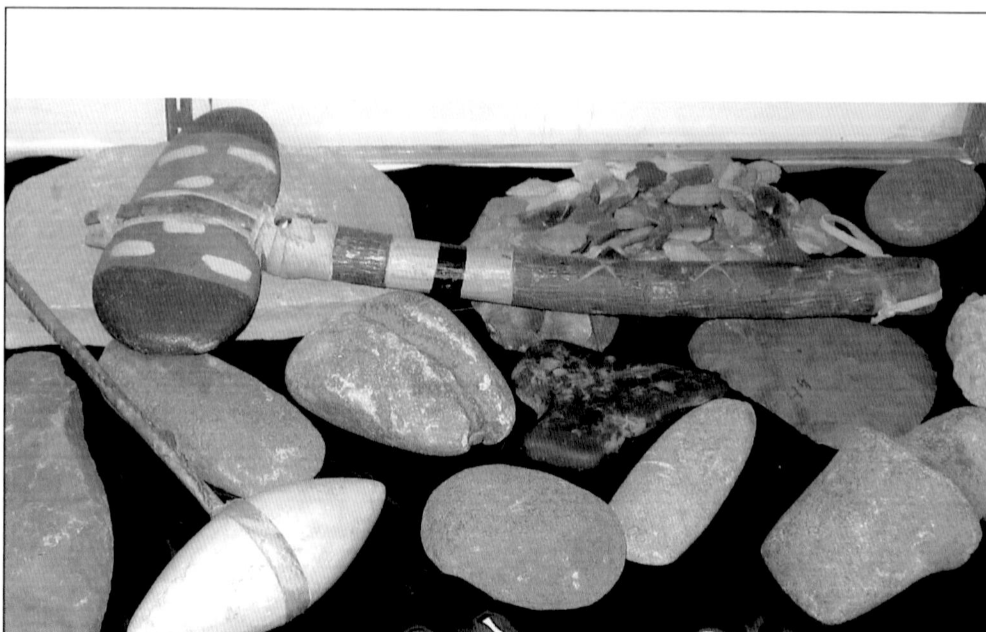

**NATIVE AMERICAN ARTIFACTS.** These were found in various mounds in Knox County during investigations by early settlers. (Photograph by D.E. Boyd.)

# Contents

Introduction 7
1. The Early Settlement 9
2. Progress 19
3. Buildings, Businesses, and Street Scenes 29
4. Transportation 69
5. World War I and the Depression Era 77
6. World War II and Beyond 87
7. People, Places, and Events 109
Acknowledgments 127
Bibliography 128

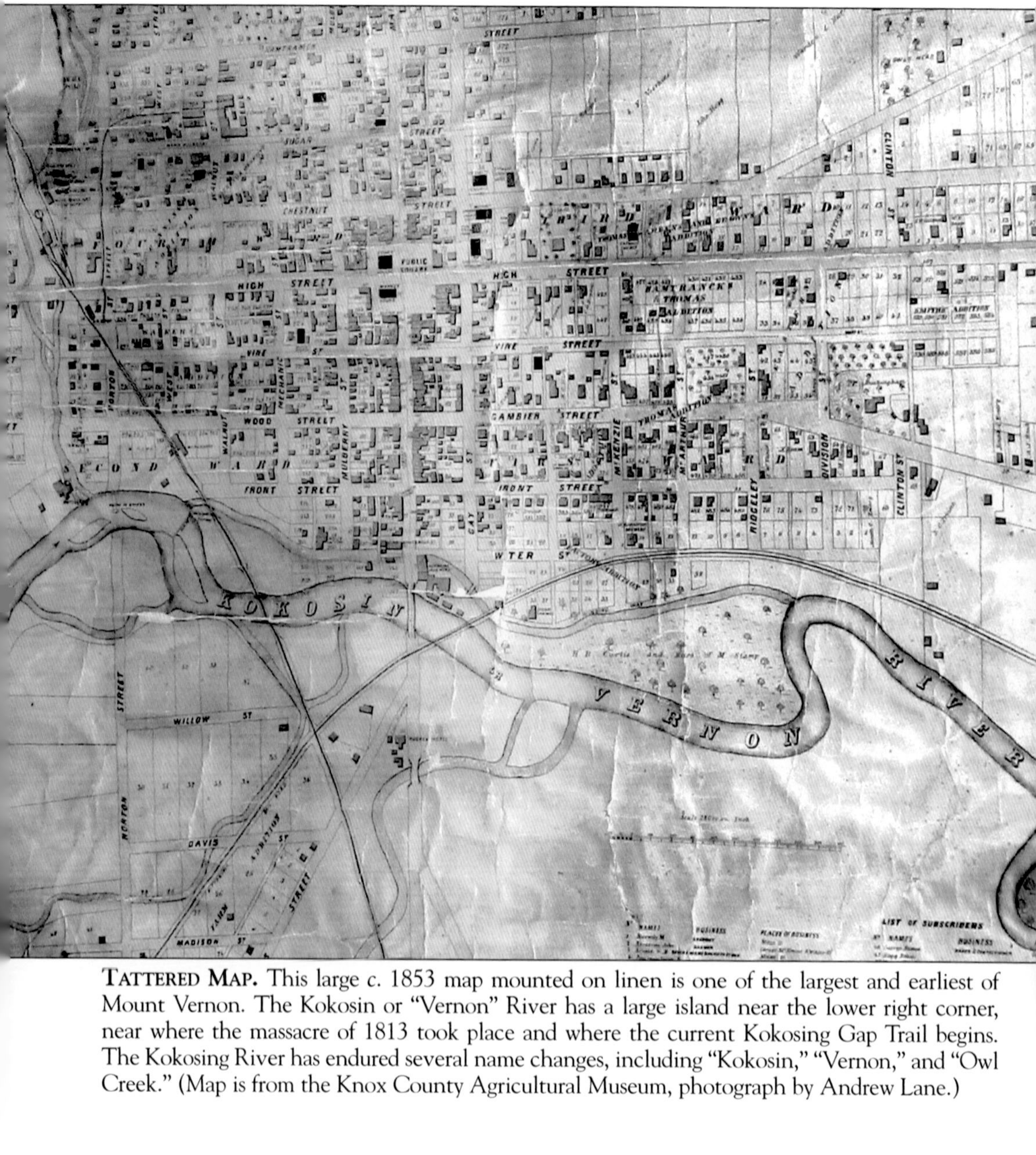


**TATTERED MAP.** This large *c.* 1853 map mounted on linen is one of the largest and earliest of Mount Vernon. The Kokosin or "Vernon" River has a large island near the lower right corner, near where the massacre of 1813 took place and where the current Kokosing Gap Trail begins. The Kokosing River has endured several name changes, including "Kokosin," "Vernon," and "Owl Creek." (Map is from the Knox County Agricultural Museum, photograph by Andrew Lane.)

# INTRODUCTION

The area of North America where Mount Vernon now sits was inhabited thousands of years ago by a people identified as the Moundbuilders and later, the Adena and Hopewell Cultures, names given them by William C. Mills, an early Ohio archaeologist. Many of the mounds built by these people have been lost due to agricultural use or development, but a few remain in Knox County.

Before there was a Knox County, Mount Vernon was located in what was known as the United Military Lands, established to satisfy claims of officers and soldiers of the Revolutionary War. Virginia claimed most of the land west of it, to the east side of the Mississippi River. In 1787, Massachusetts, Connecticut, New York, and Virginia ceded lands to establish "the territory of the United States northwest of the river Ohio." Marietta was named the capital. Connecticut kept some land in the northern part near Lake Erie known as the Western Reserve. Virginia retained 4.2 million acres to award to Revolutionary War soldiers. When the first six counties were established in what was to become Ohio in 1798, Mount Vernon was in Ross County. The Ordinance of 1787 had established that when 60,000 citizens over the age of 21 lived in a certain geographical area, they could apply for statehood, which happened for Ohio in 1803. Settlers poured into Ohio from Virginia, Maryland, Pennsylvania, and New Jersey. Mount Vernon was established as a town in 1805 and named the county seat of Knox County in 1808.

The early settlers could travel easiest via the various rivers and streams. William Chapman, known as Johnny Appleseed, came to Mount Vernon, and it was one of the many places he stopped to buy land. He owned two lots on the north bank of the Kokosing River on the south edge of town. Chapman later moved on to Mansfield, 20 miles north. Native Americans did not always welcome the white settlers to their area, and Johnny is purported to have run all night from Mansfield to Mount Vernon warning settlers in each cabin along the way of a Native American uprising in Mansfield during the War of 1812. The Native Americans had objected to being removed from Greentown and marched to a holding area near Sandusky in northwest Ohio.

When Mount Vernon was named the county seat of Knox County, according to A. Banning Norton's History of Knox County (1862), the three leading choices in order were as follows: Clinton, Fredericktown, and Mount Vernon. Norton's book explains how Mount Vernon came to be chosen as the county seat in a story told by Benjamin Butler, a tavern keeper and one of the founding fathers of Mount Vernon. Butler met with three other citizens, Sam Kratzer, Thomas Bell Patterson, and Joseph Walker, to devise a plan to get Mount Vernon selected over the other two towns. The four men chipped in $10 a piece to hire local rowdies to get drunk and act up in the other two communities on the day the commissioners visited. They also encouraged Mount Vernon residents to clean up the town on its visitation day. The plan worked.

This pictorial history will attempt to deal primarily with the last 200 years of development in Mount Vernon and Knox County. Photography was not developed or popularized until 1839, but we have included several photos by some of the most prominent inventors and innovators of the medium. Hamilton Smith and Peter Neff in nearby Gambier worked with the tintype, a photographic process popular in the last half of the 19th century. Fredericktown native Stanley J. Morrow studied with Mathew Brady, the nationally prominent Civil War photographer.

Mount Vernon and Knox County have produced numerous important citizens, most of whom will be discussed in this book. There have been movie stars and inventors and entrepreneurs of every degree. Politicians from Mount Vernon helped shape our democracy. Through the times, agriculture has been a major feature of the area, the land rich and productive, managed by excellent stewards. Major industries have rooted down here to use the natural resources. Military and sports heroes abound. If we could imagine Mount Vernon as a modern space ship, we are on the launching pad, filled with enthusiasm and community spirit as our rocket fuel, eagerly anticipating our flight into the 21st century.

Mount Vernon has won many awards, the most prestigious being the Look Magazine designation of "All American City" in 1965. In 1994, Ohio Magazine named Mount Vernon "Ohio's Most Liveable Community." Mount Vernon has long held the title of "Ohio's Colonial City" and has been designated a "Tree City" for the past 10 years. Hal Holbrook once said, "If you want to discover what America is all about, you should go to Mount Vernon."

This bicentennial pictorial history of Mount Vernon will attempt to give a glimpse into our past glory and to serve as a valuable memento of our 200th anniversary!

# *One*

# The Early Settlement

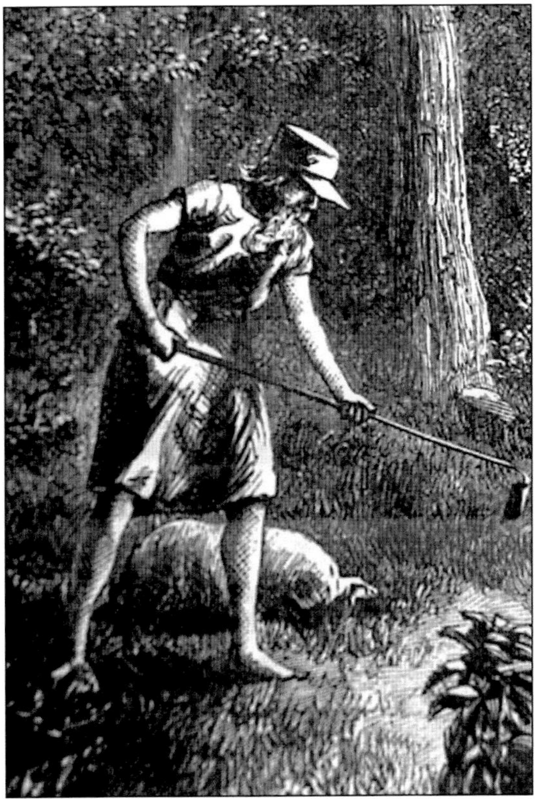

**John Chapman, also known as "Johnny Appleseed."** Johnny was a Swedenborgian missionary, kind to animals, insects, and all humans, and a friend to settlers and Native Americans alike. His good deeds became legend throughout the nation. He owned two plots of land in Mount Vernon near the Kokosing River, where he planted an apple nursery c. 1800. (Line art from a local publication courtesy of the Fredericktown Historical Society.)

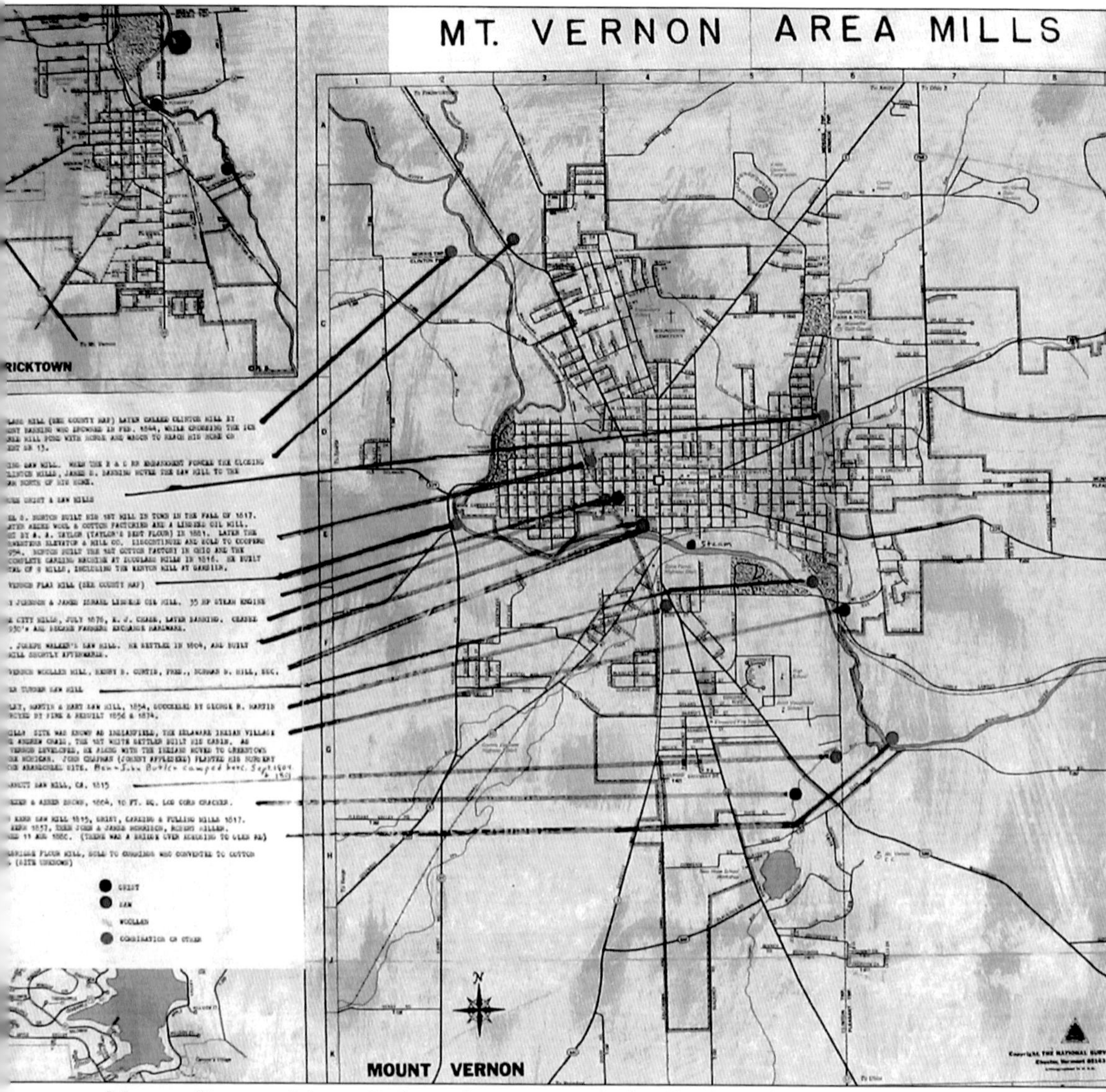


**MOUNT VERNON MILLS.** Early settlements required mills. One of the oldest in Mount Vernon is considered to be at "Indianfield," where Andrew Craig, the first white settler, built his cabin among an encampment of Delaware Indians, near the confluence of Center Run and the Kokosing River. When more white settlers moved in, Craig and the Delaware Indians moved 30 miles north to Greentown in Richland County. Early Mount Vernon developed along West Vine Street , then Main Street. (Map courtesy of the Knox County Agricultural Museum, photograph by Andrew Lane.)

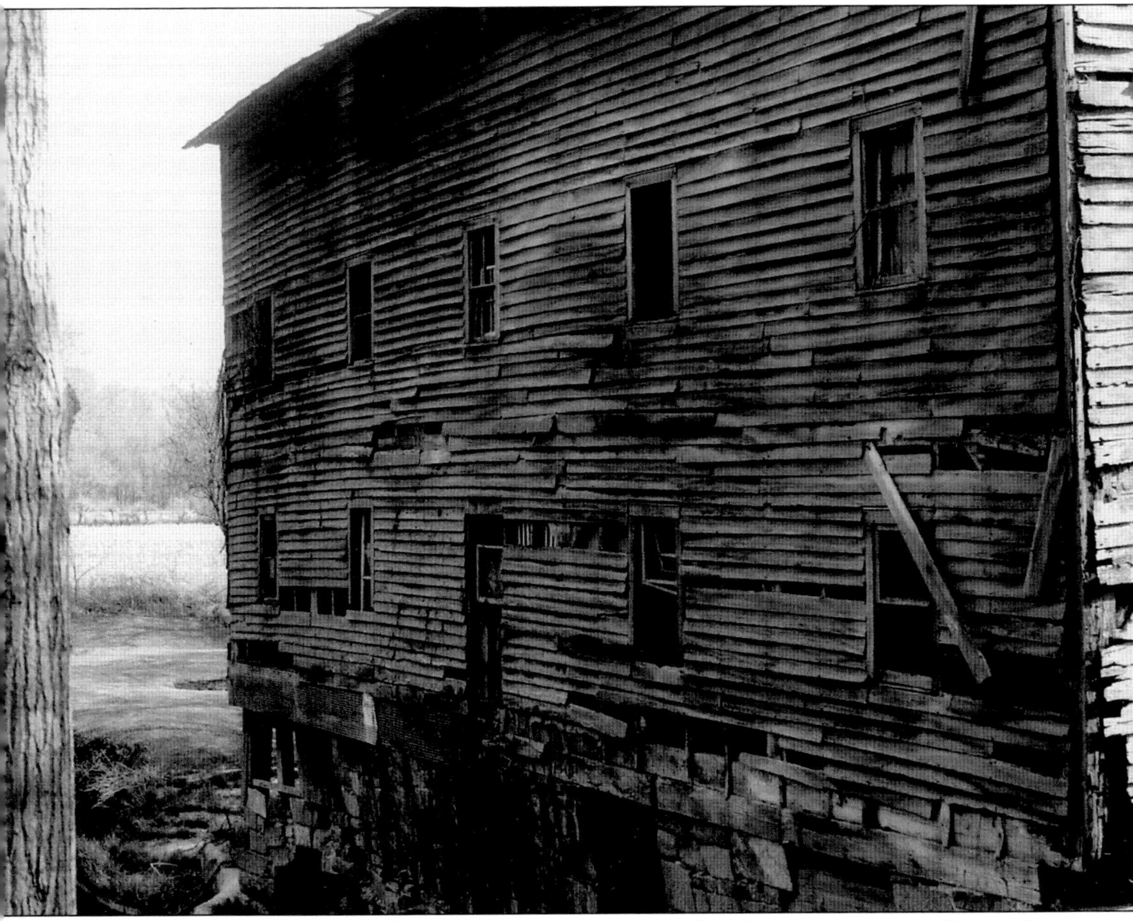

**UNKNOWN MILL.** Ebenezer and Abner Brown had a 10-square-foot log corn-cracker mill east of Route 13 on Delano Run between Dixie Drive and Ames Street in 1804. (Photograph courtesy of the Knox County Agricultural Museum.)

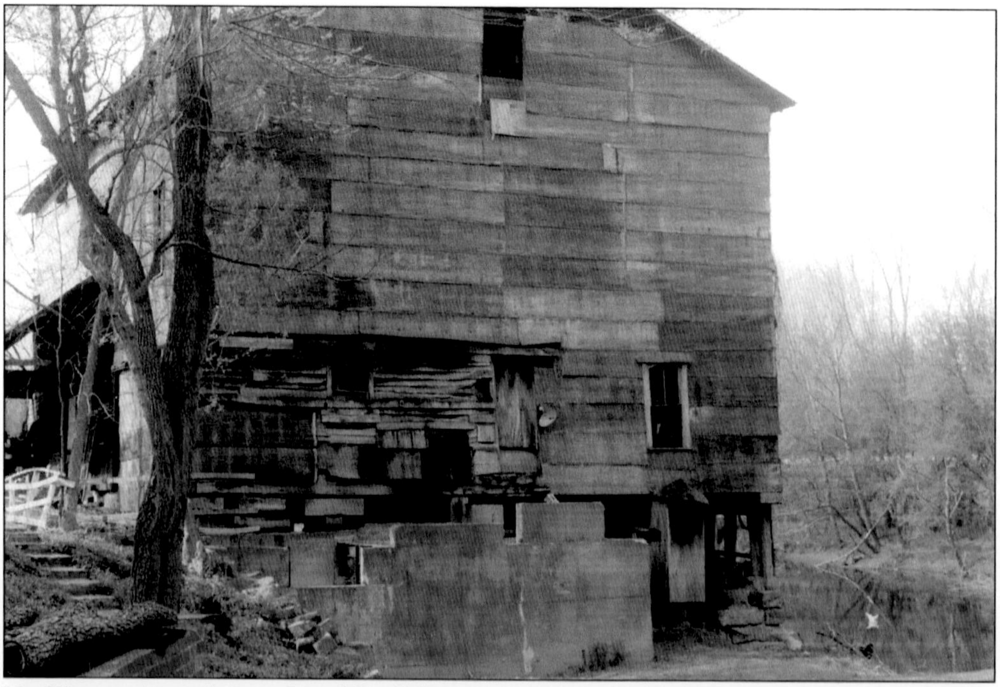

**NO WATER.** An end view of an old mill that is no longer in use is shown in this photograph. John Kerr had a sawmill in 1815, but expanded it to a fulling, carding, and gristmill by 1817. His mill was near where Delano Run joins the Kokosing on Glen Road, the site of the current Mount Vernon Nazarene University. (Photograph courtesy of the Knox County Agricultural Museum.)

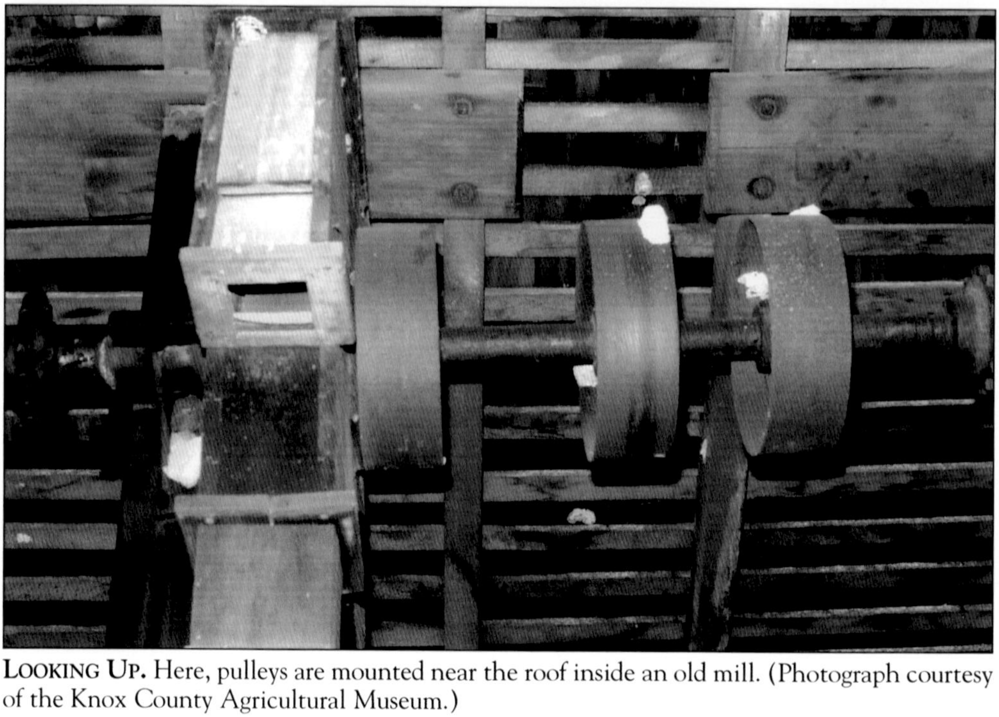

**LOOKING UP.** Here, pulleys are mounted near the roof inside an old mill. (Photograph courtesy of the Knox County Agricultural Museum.)

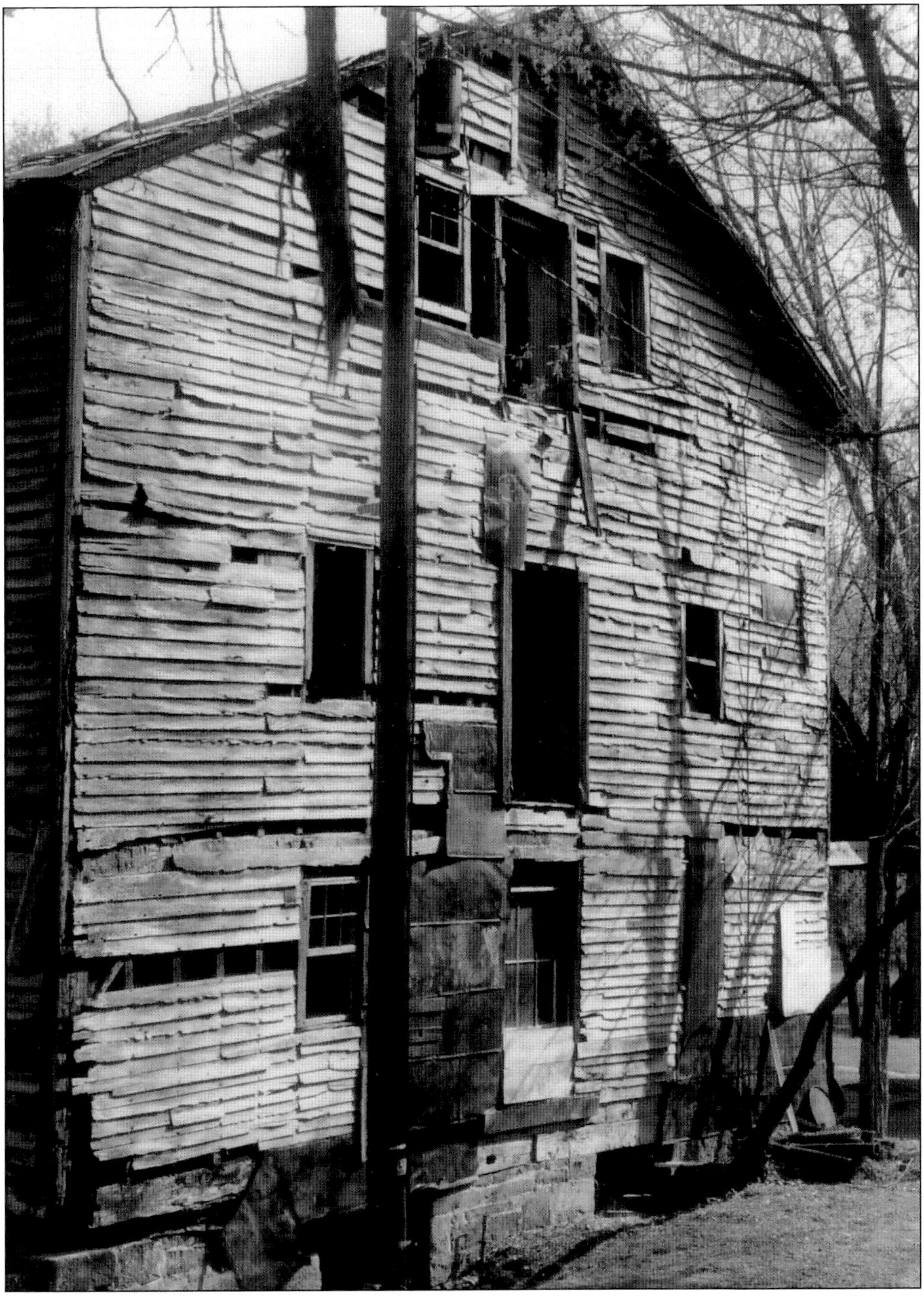

**MILL END.** Mills, blacksmith shops, and nurseries were essential to the settlement of Mount Vernon. Many early mills from the 1800s remained in Knox County up until 1970 and beyond. Some are now being restored. Charles Whitney of Mount Vernon is well known for his expertise in preserving and restoring old barns and mills in the region. (Photograph courtesy of the Knox County Agricultural Museum.)

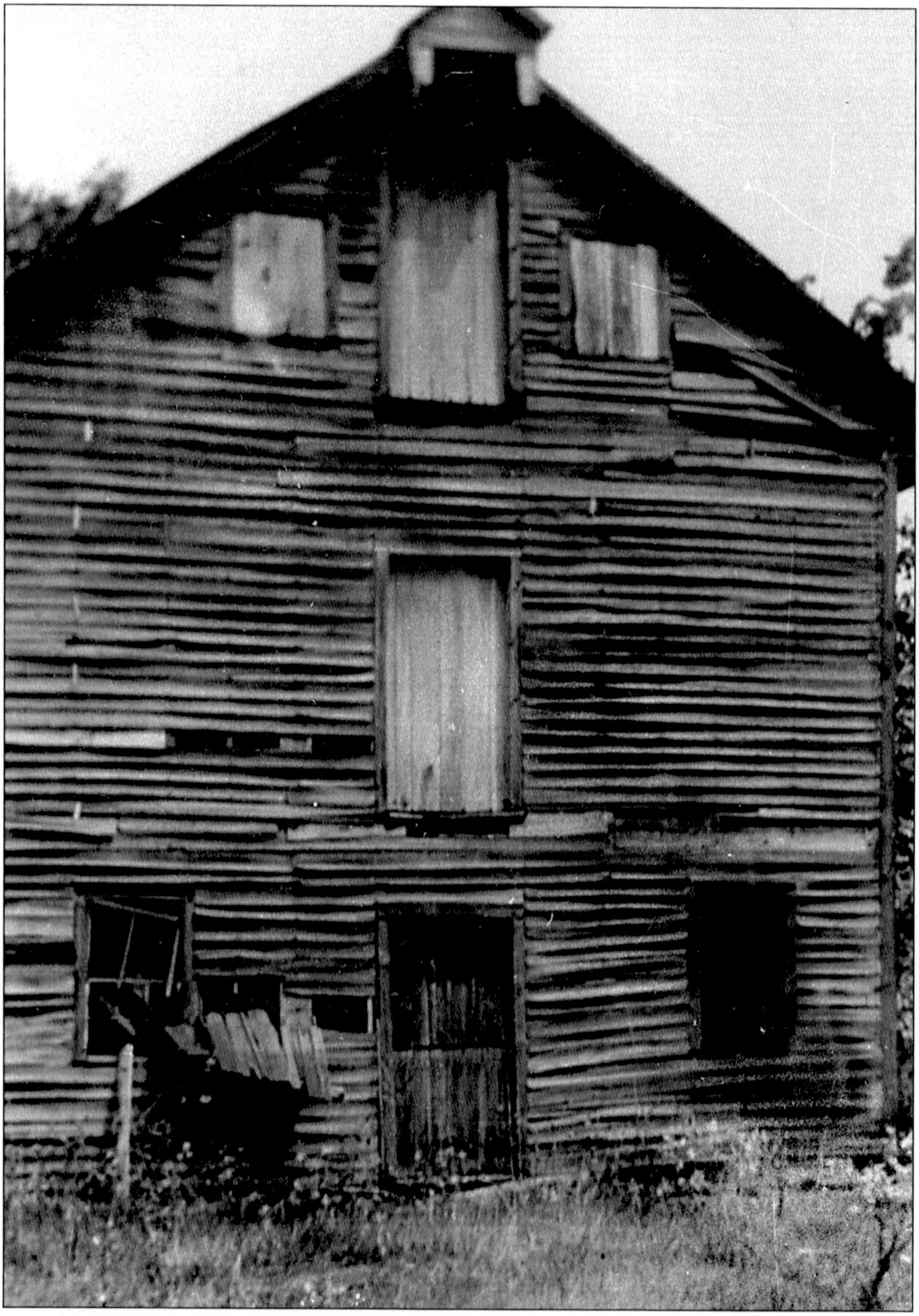

**Mill in Disrepair.** The location of this mill is not known, but it is indicative of buildings in Knox County that existed several years without being used or maintained. Old mills are getting scarce, but many unused barns and some old houses remain. (Photograph courtesy of the Knox County Agricultural Museum.)

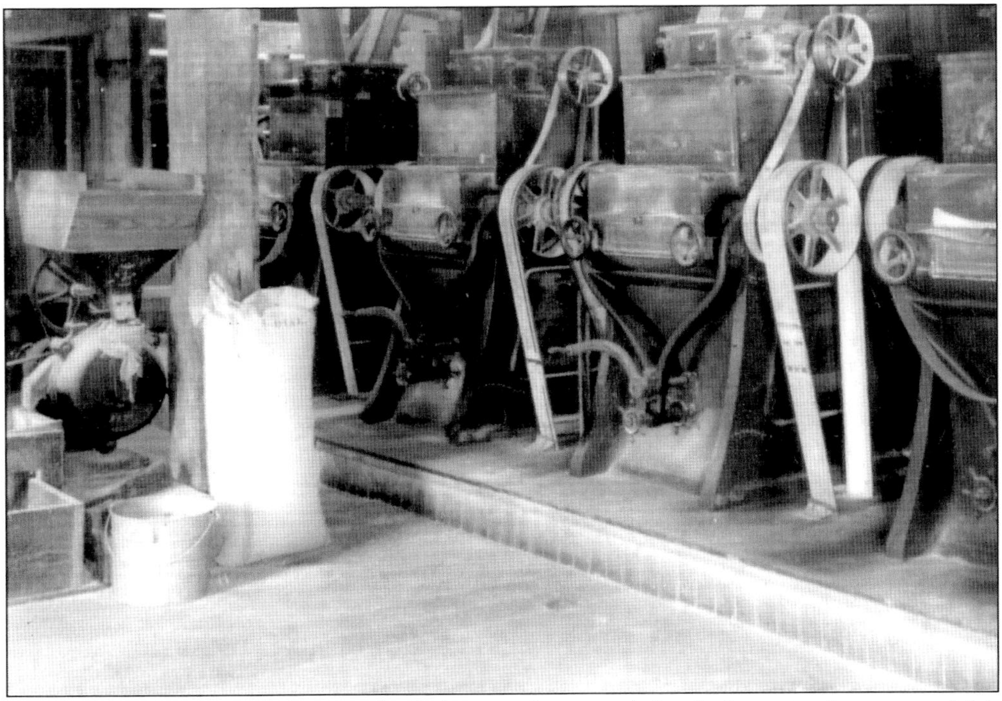

**INTERIOR MACHINERY.** A large sack of wheat or flour stands by the beam in the center of this mill's interior. (Photograph courtesy of the Knox County Agricultural Museum.)

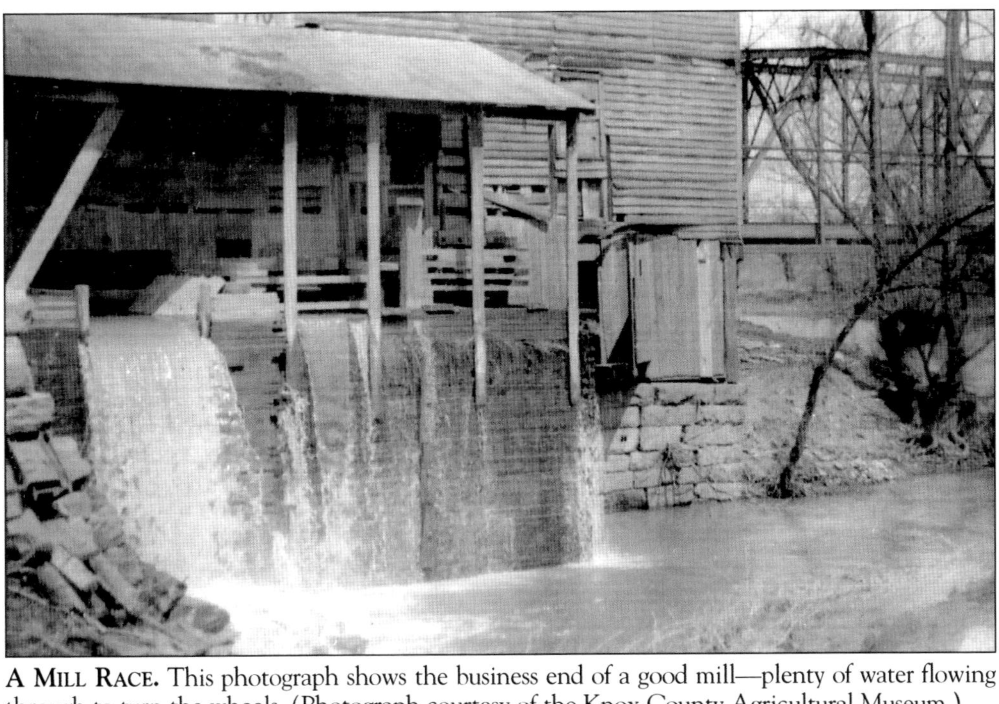

**A MILL RACE.** This photograph shows the business end of a good mill—plenty of water flowing through to turn the wheels. (Photograph courtesy of the Knox County Agricultural Museum.)

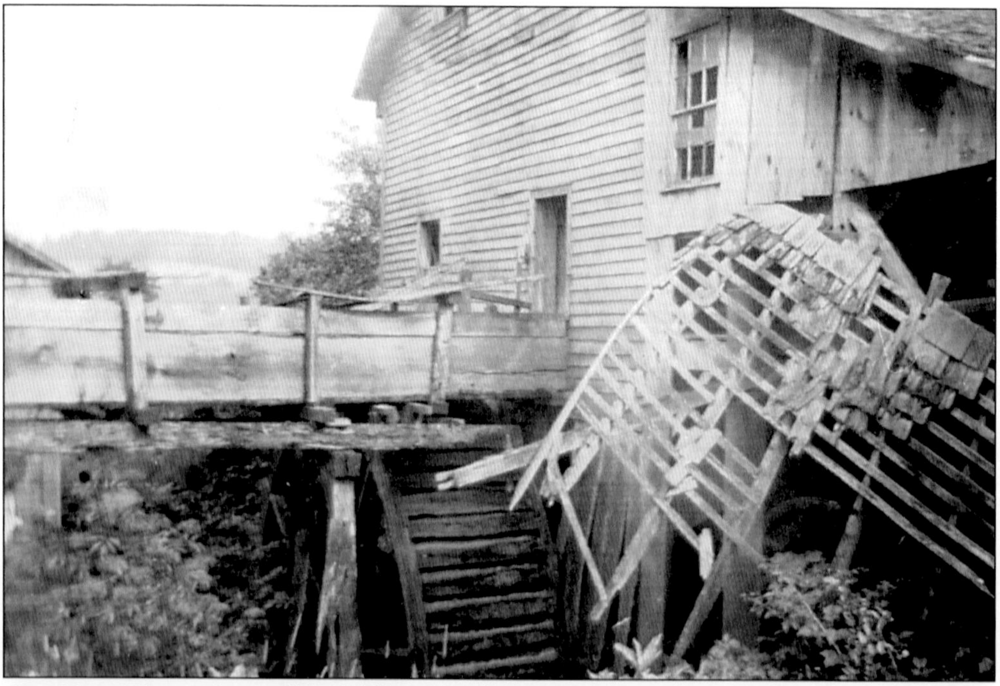

**OLD MILL.** This earlier mill had fallen into disrepair by the time this photograph was taken. (Photograph courtesy of the Knox County Agricultural Museum.)

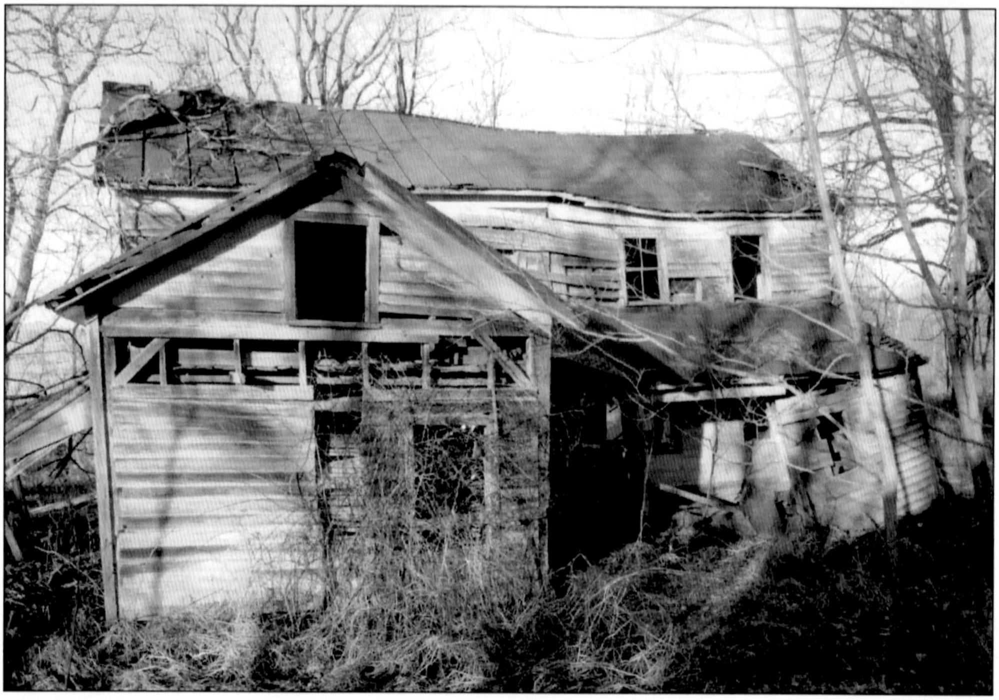

**NO SLUMS IN MOUNT VERNON.** This photograph shows an old farm house and barn in Knox County. When a farmer prospered, he or she often built a new house and let the old one go. (Photograph courtesy of the Knox County Agricultural Museum.)

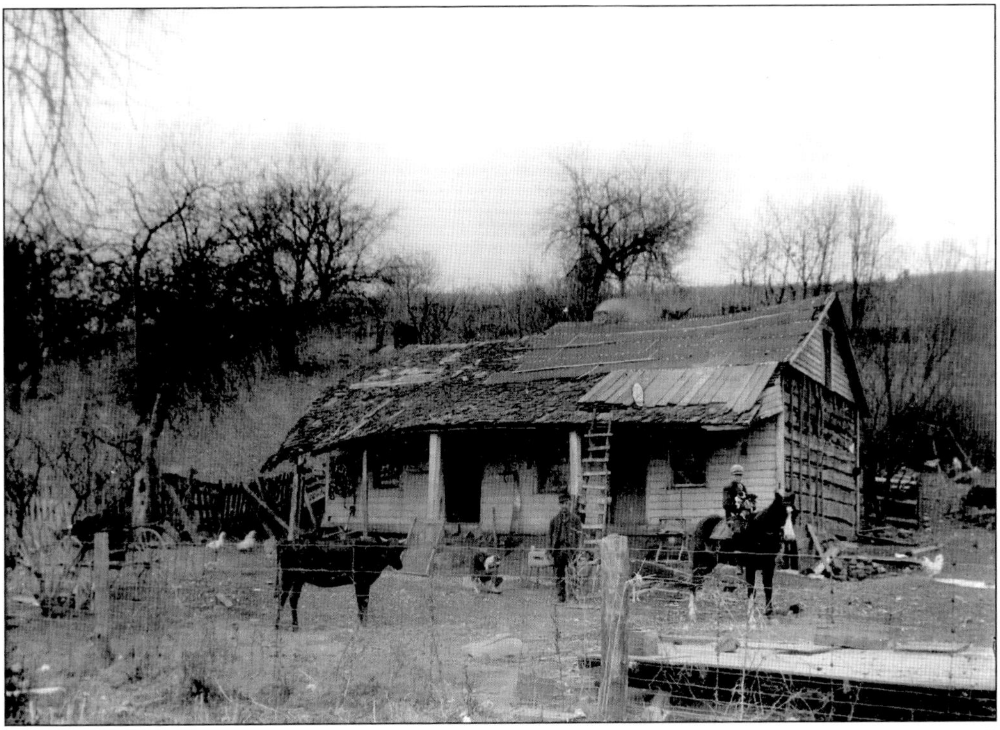

**STILL USEABLE.** This cabin near Howard, Ohio, somewhere near the turn of the century, is still very much inhabited. (Photograph courtesy of the Knox County Agricultural Museum.)

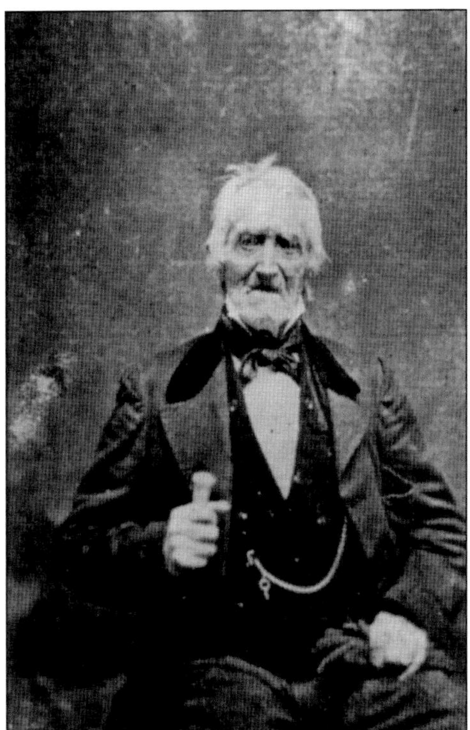

**FIRST MERCHANT.** John Garrison operated a trading post in Sandusky, but traveled three days through dense forests to get to Fredericktown with his family in 1812. He is the great-great grandfather of Harry Cassell. (Photograph courtesy of Fredericktown Historical Society.)

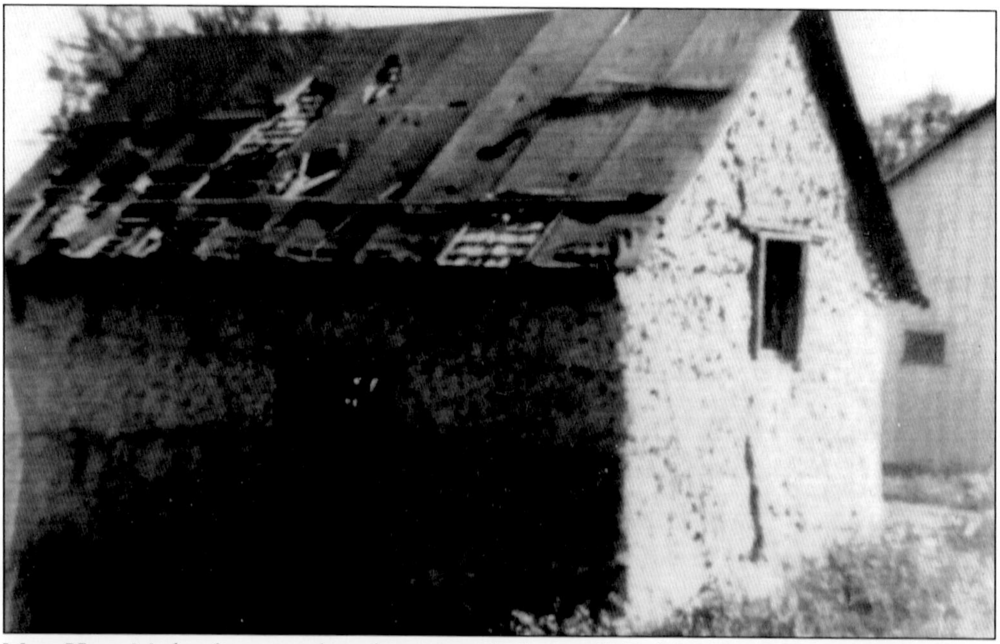

**MUD HUT.** Made of straw and mud over wood, this small building stood for over 100 years at the corner of Wooster Road and North Gay Street in the northeast section of Mount Vernon. (Photograph courtesy of the Knox County Agricultural Museum.)

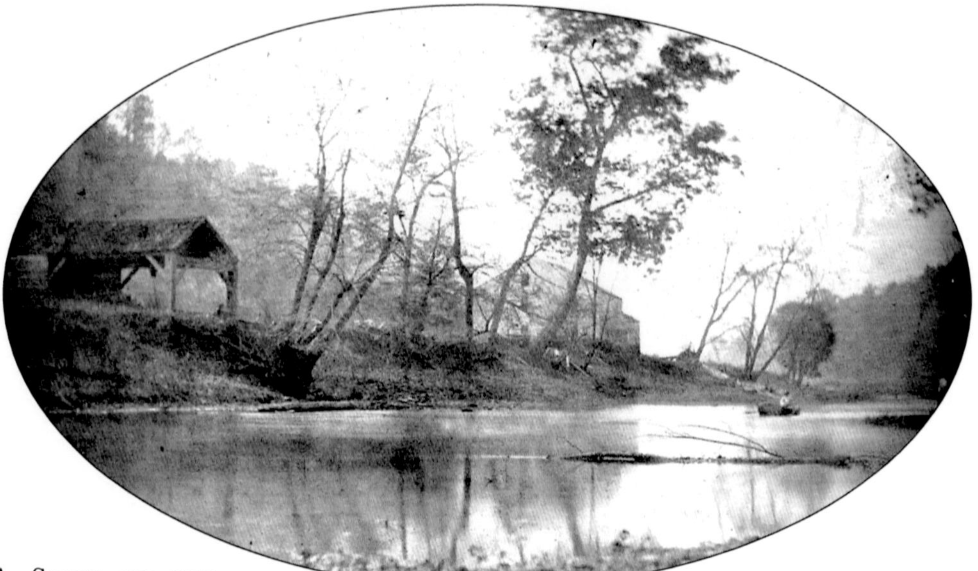

**A SCENE ON THE KOKOSING BY HAMILTON SMITH.** This is a photograph by Professor Smith, *c.* 1850s, and it shows an idyllic landscape of the Kokosing River, which runs very close to the south side of the hill where the campus is located in Gambier, Ohio. (Photograph courtesy of the Greenslade Special Collections and Archives, Olin Library, Kenyon College, Gambier, Ohio. Donated by Mr. and Mrs. William V. Bowen Jr. in memory of Jessie Vaughn Bowen.)

# *Two*

# PROGRESS

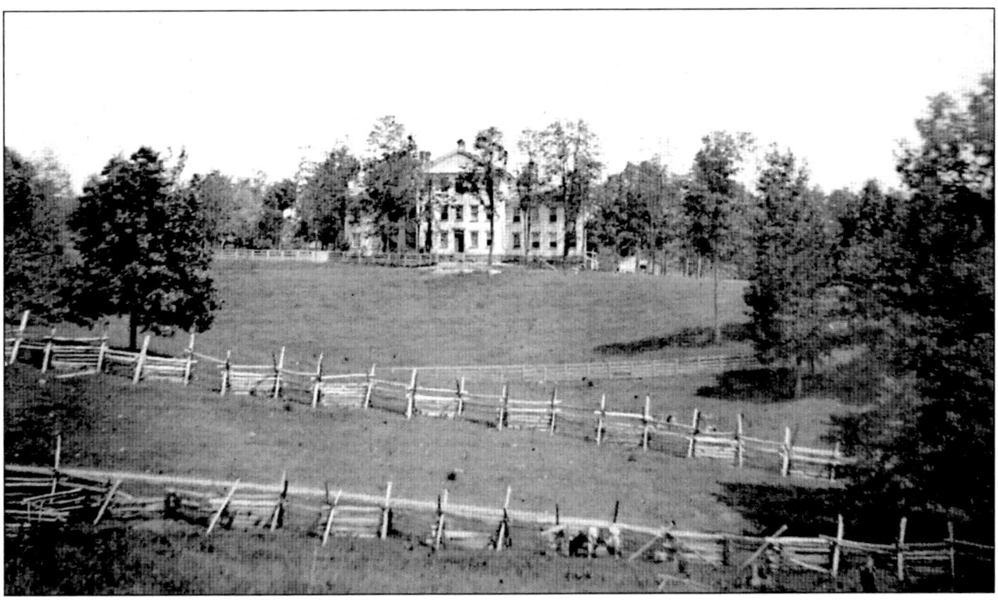

**THE MILITARY ACADEMY IN GAMBIER, OHIO.** This photograph, also believed to be by Hamilton Smith c. 1853, shows Milnor Hall, the prepatory school for Kenyon College. It became a military-oriented school around the time of the Civil War. The building later burned, and the school was became defunct. (Photograph courtesy of the Greenslade Special Collections and Archives, Olin Library, Kenyon College, Gambier, Ohio. Donated by Mr. and Mrs. William V. Bowen Jr. in memory of Jesse Vaughn Bowen.)

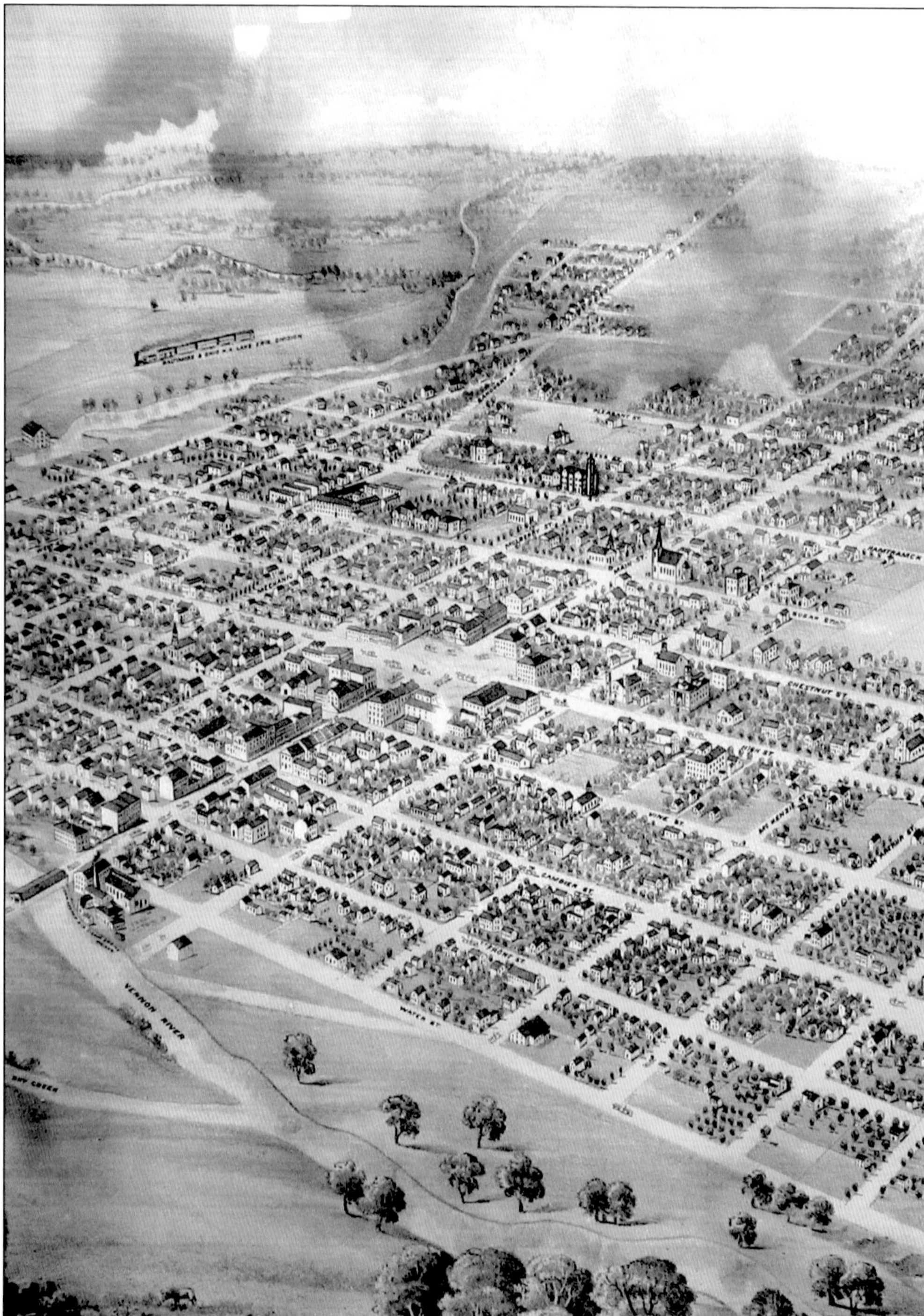


**BIRDS-EYE VIEW.** This three-dimensional version of an 1870s map of the City of Mount Vernon looks northwest. The river shown as the Vernon is known today as the Kokosing. Note the Square at this time was "unimproved." (Map courtesy of the Knox County Agricultural Museum, photograph by Andrew Lane.)

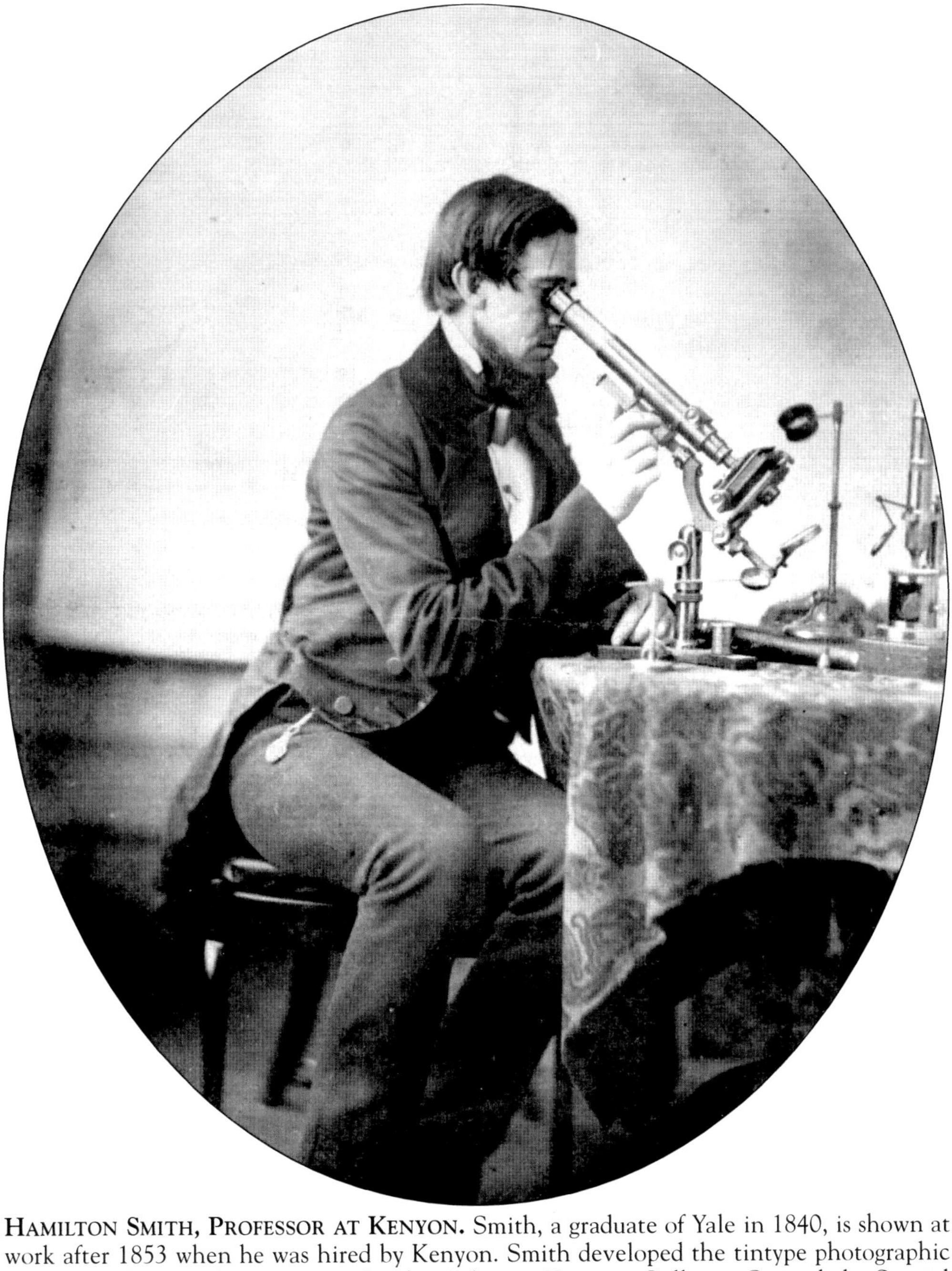

**Hamilton Smith, Professor at Kenyon.** Smith, a graduate of Yale in 1840, is shown at work after 1853 when he was hired by Kenyon. Smith developed the tintype photographic process. (Photograph courtesy of Olin Library, Kenyon College, Greenslade Special Collections and Archives.)

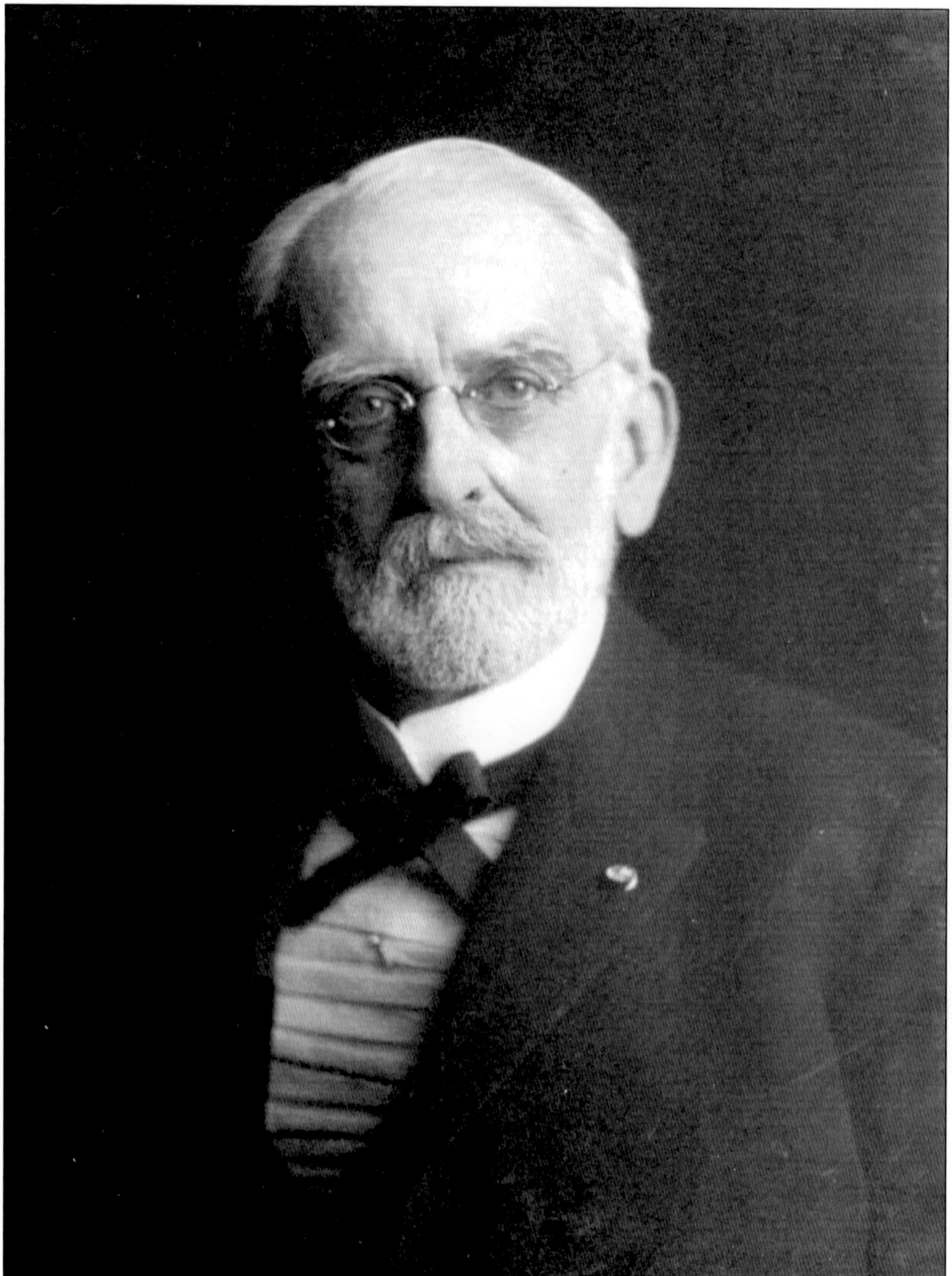

**PETER NEFF.** An 1849 graduate of Kenyon, Neff worked closely with Professor Smith. Neff and his father purchased the tintype patent from Smith c. 1854. (Photograph courtesy of Olin Library, Kenyon College, Greenslade Special Collections and Archives.)

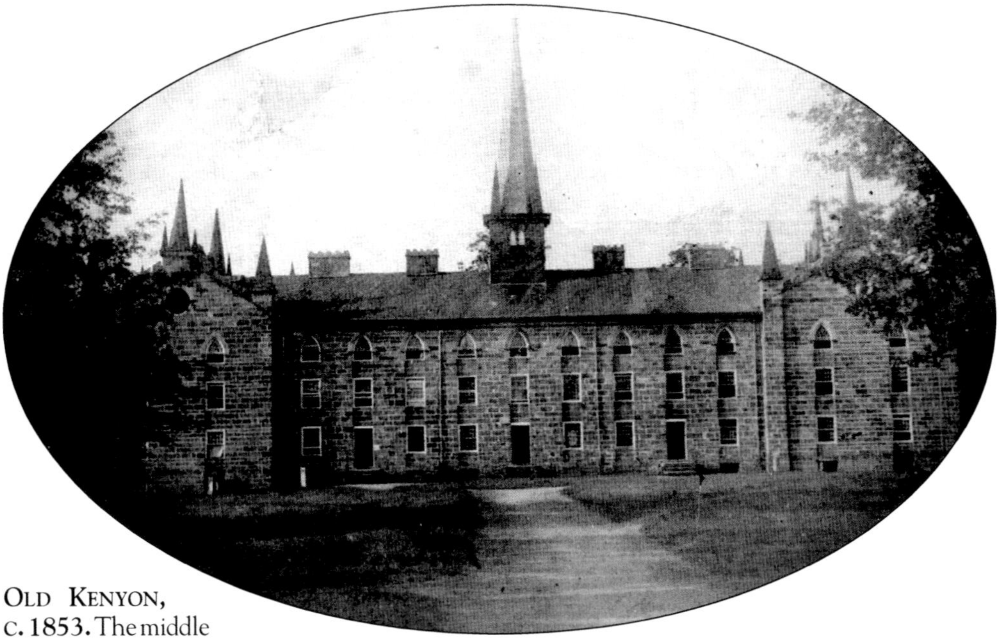

**OLD KENYON, C. 1853.** The middle section of this building is called Middle Hall. There were two pumps for water, and the word "Kenyon" is seen on the slate on the roof. This early photograph was probably taken by Hamilton Smith. (Photograph courtesy of Olin Library, Kenyon College, Greenslade Special Collections and Archives. Donated by Mr. and Mrs. William V. Bowen Jr. in memory of Jessie Vaughn Bowen.)

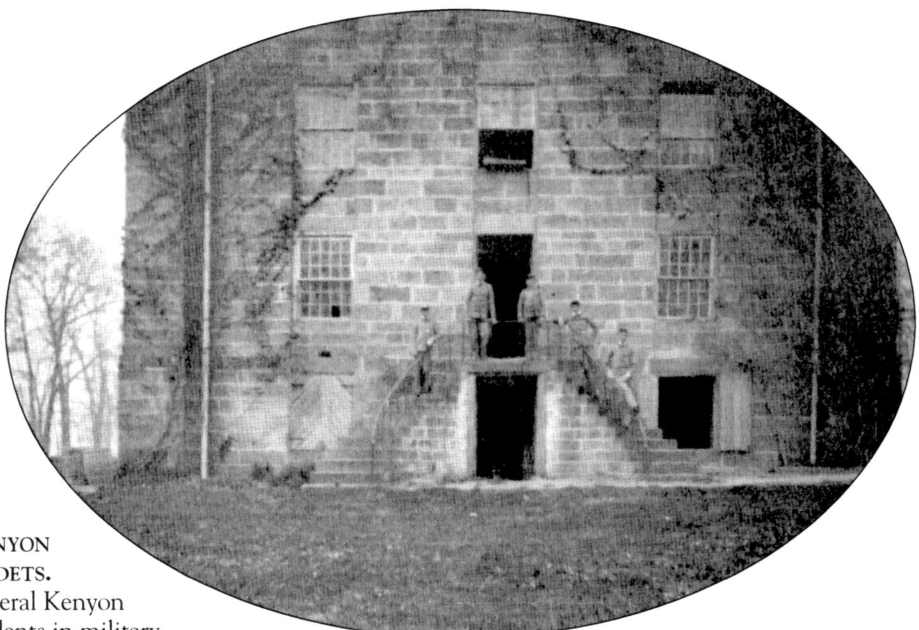

**KENYON CADETS.** Several Kenyon students in military-type uniforms stand on the stairs at the end of old Kenyon. This photograph was probably taken by Peter Neff. (Photograph courtesy of Olin Library, Kenyon College, Greenslade Special Collections and Archives.)

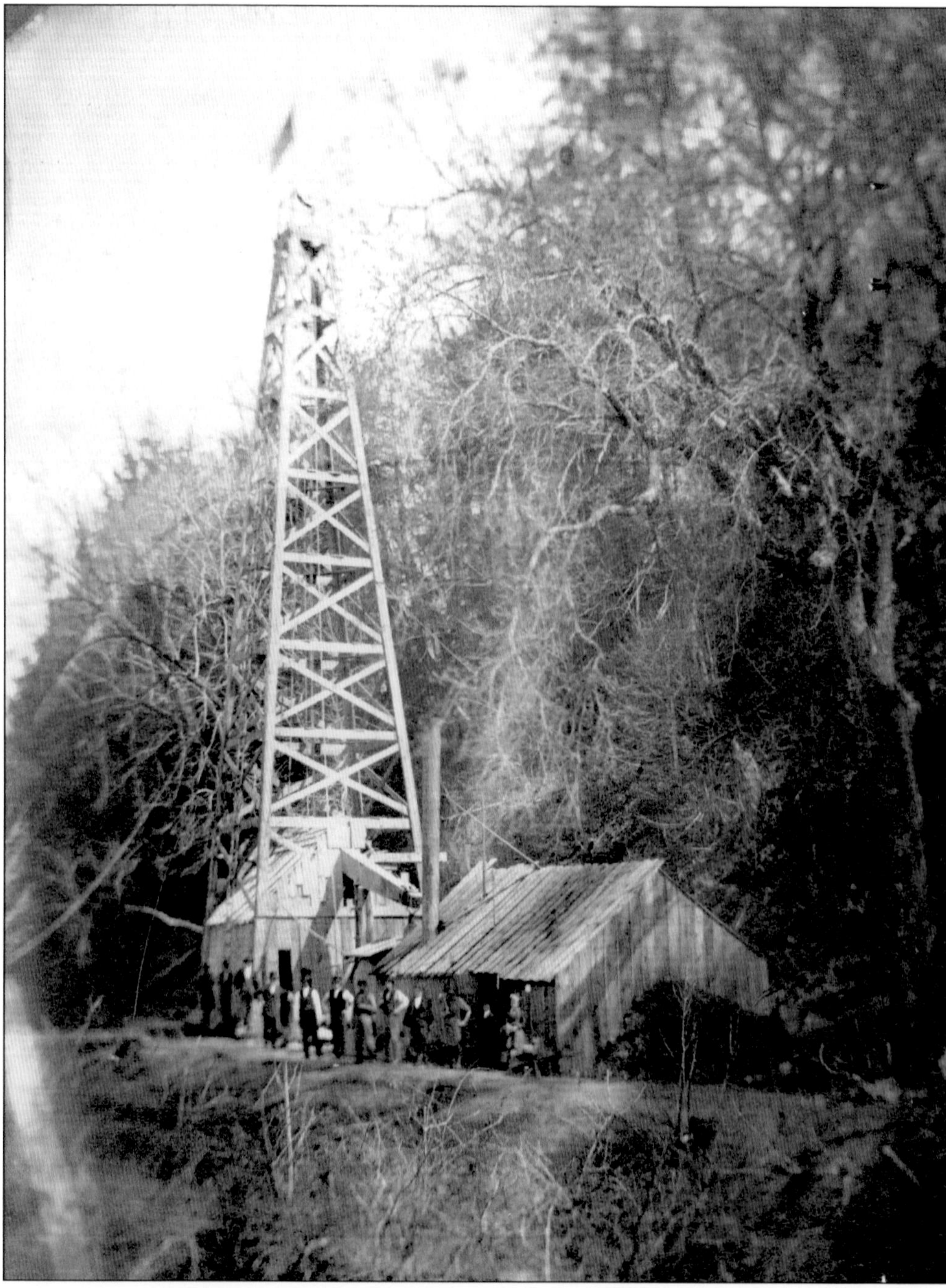

**Neff's Well.** In 1873, Peter Neff took this photograph of a well he purchased near Brinkhaven, Ohio, which is about 19 miles northeast of Gambier, Ohio. (Photograph courtesy of Olin Library, Kenyon College, Greenslade Special Collections and Archives.)

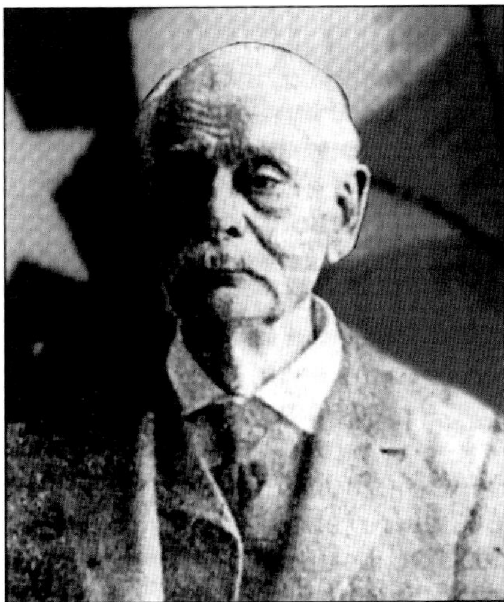

**UNCLE DAN EMMETT.** Mount Vernon's "favorite son" was born October 29, 1815, at the corner of Front and Mulberry Streets. A traveling show had lost their violinist, and the manager inquired around for a substitute. The consensus was "the blacksmith's son." At first, Dan was shy and declined the position, but he was finally convinced to play, and the manager exclaimed, "You'll do, all right!" When Dan appeared in black face and played "Old Dan Tucker," he stole the show. Dan was only 15. (Photograph art by Andrew Lane.)

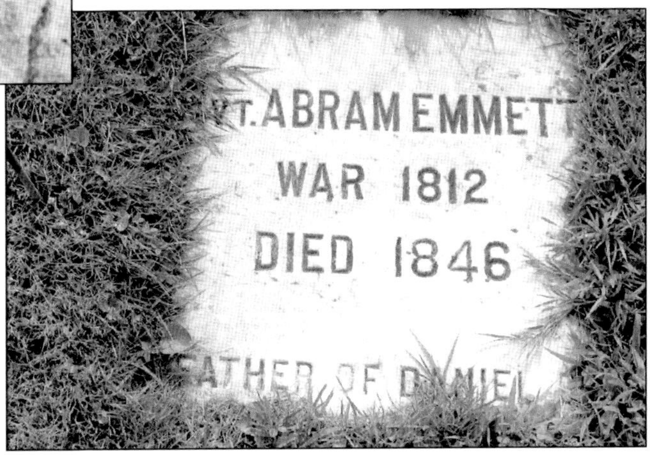


**DAN EMMETT'S FATHER.** Private Abram Emmett fought in the War of 1812 and died in 1846. His grave is marked with this small marble stone and a metal veteran's marker. (Photograph by D.E. Boyd.)

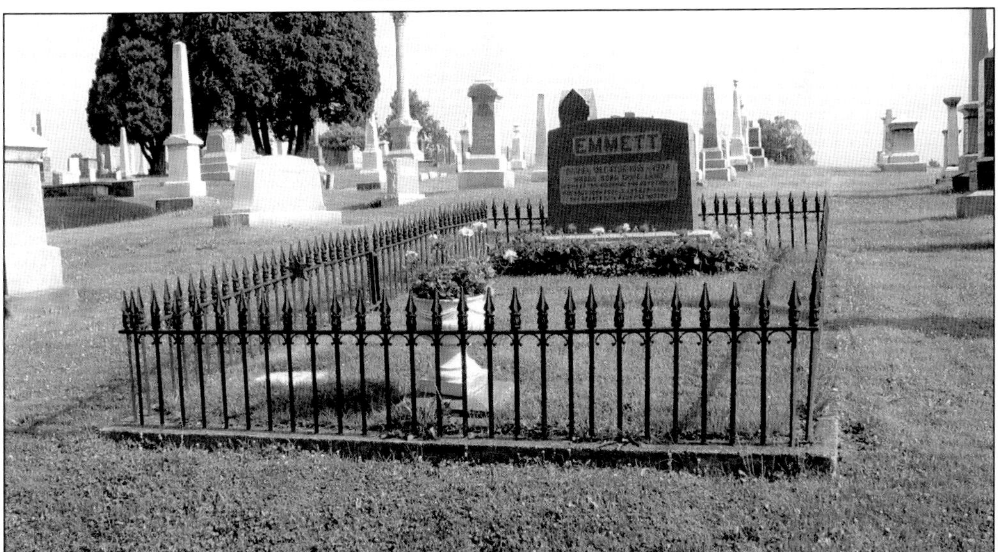


**THE EMMETT FAMILY PLOT.** Dan's stone is the largest stone in the fenced-in site. Each year, a ceremony is held at the grave during the Dan Emmett Music and Arts Festival in August in Mount Vernon. Dan died June 28, 1904. (Photograph by D.E. Boyd.)

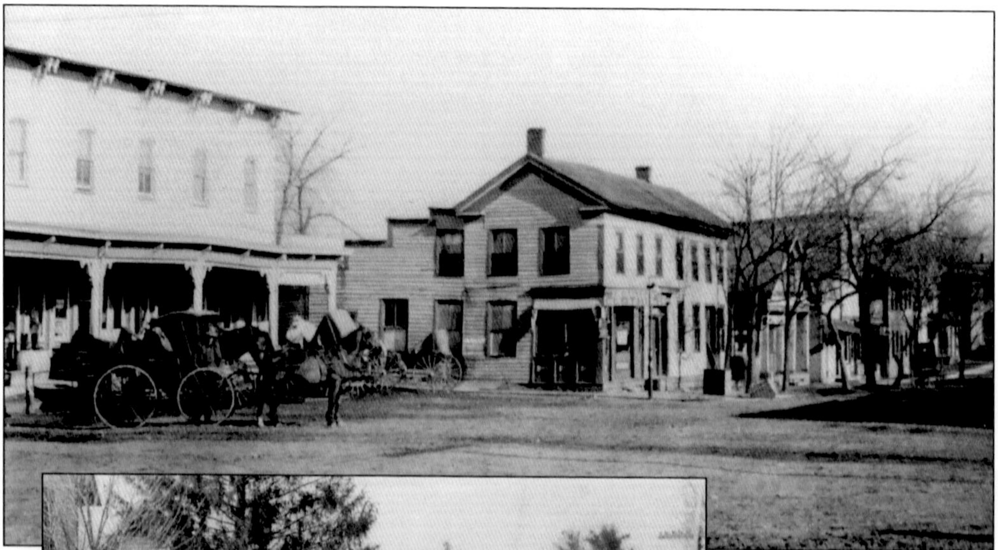

(*above*) **MAIN DRAG.** Most streets and roads were still dirt when this photograph was taken in Danville. (Photograph courtesy of the Knox County Agricultural Museum.)

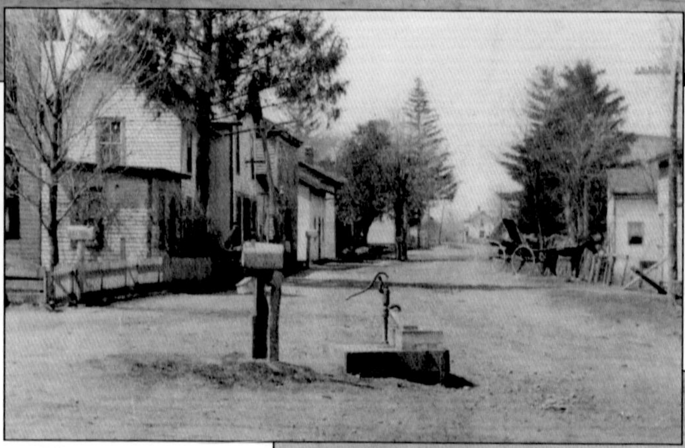

**TIMES WERE SLOW.** There were often roadside watering troughs in Knox County, even until the 1950s, but this pump and mailbox are right in the street in Waterford. (Photograph courtesy of the Knox County Agricultural Museum.)

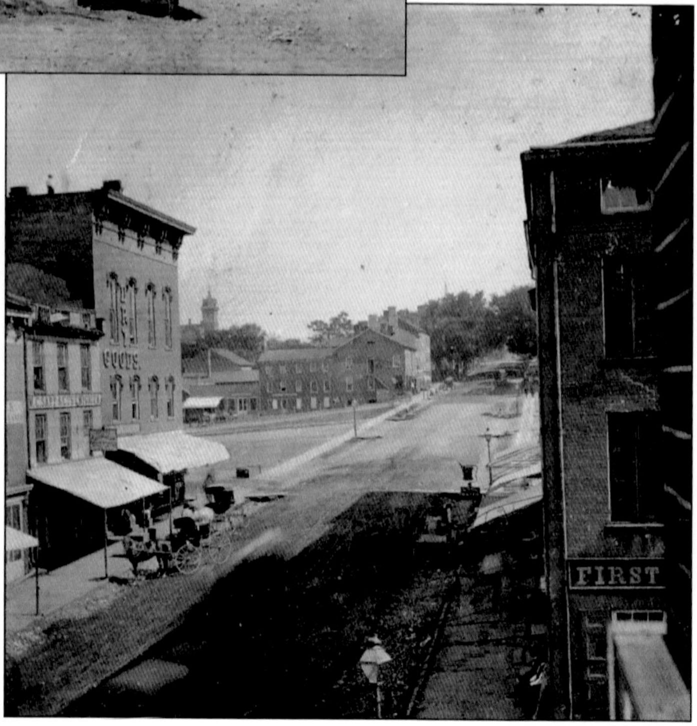


**UNUSUAL VIEW.** This view, from just below the empty Square, looks north. This photograph was taken before the Soldier's Monument was put up in 1877. (Photograph courtesy of the Knox County Agricultural Museum.)

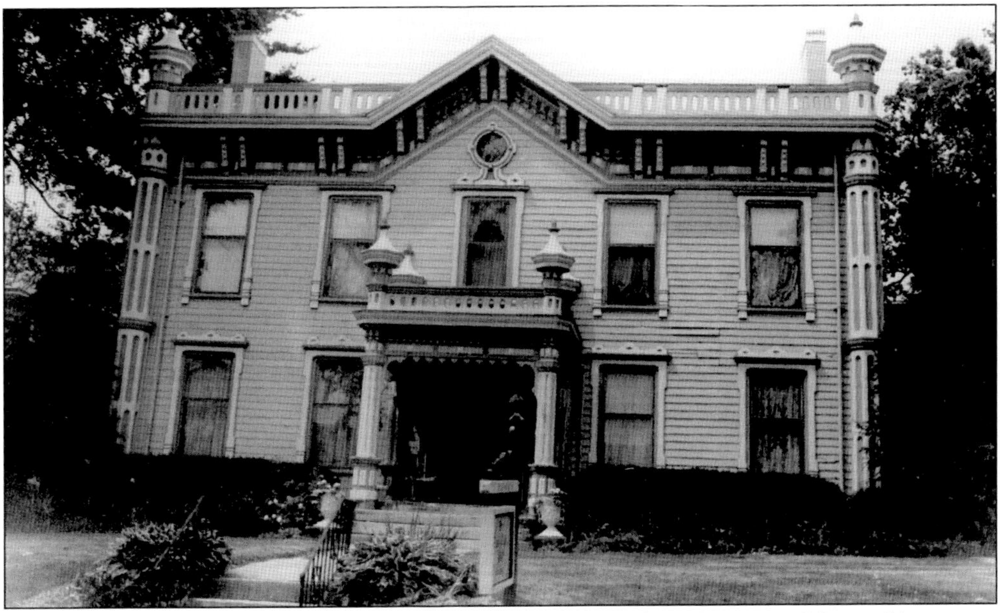

**The Russell Cooper House.** Located at 115 East Gambier Street in Mount Vernon, c. 1830, this house is one of the oldest and most elaborate of numerous historic homes in Mount Vernon. (Photograph by D.E. Boyd.)

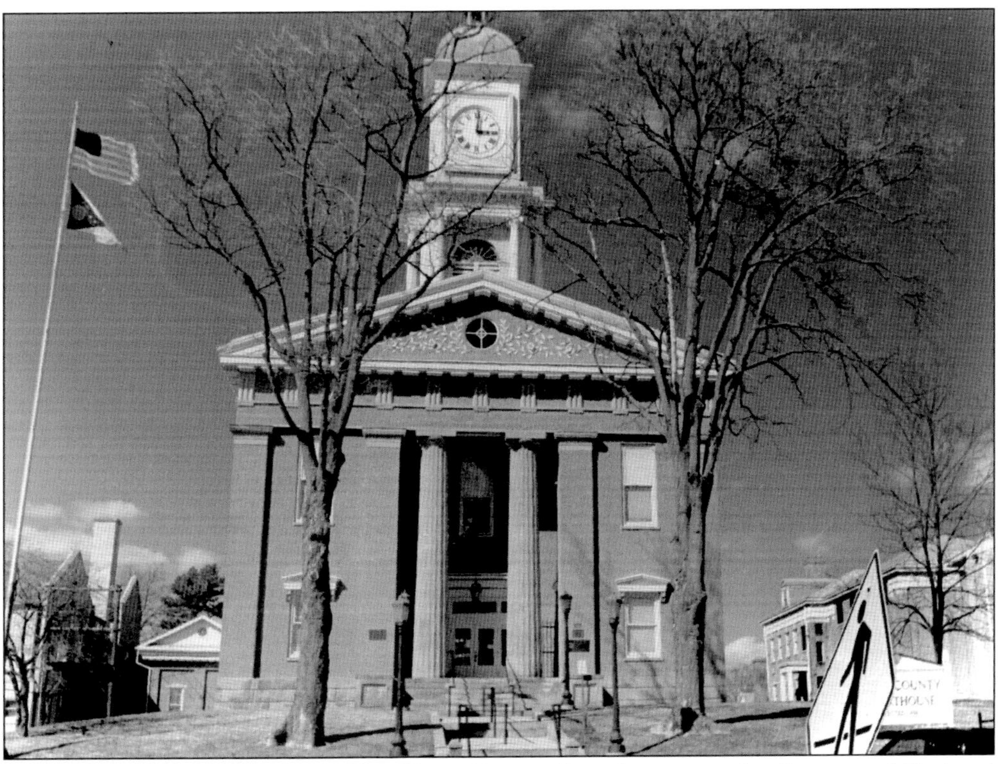

**Knox County Courthouse.** The Knox County Courthouse, on the Register of National Historic places, was built in 1854. (Photograph by D.E. Boyd.)

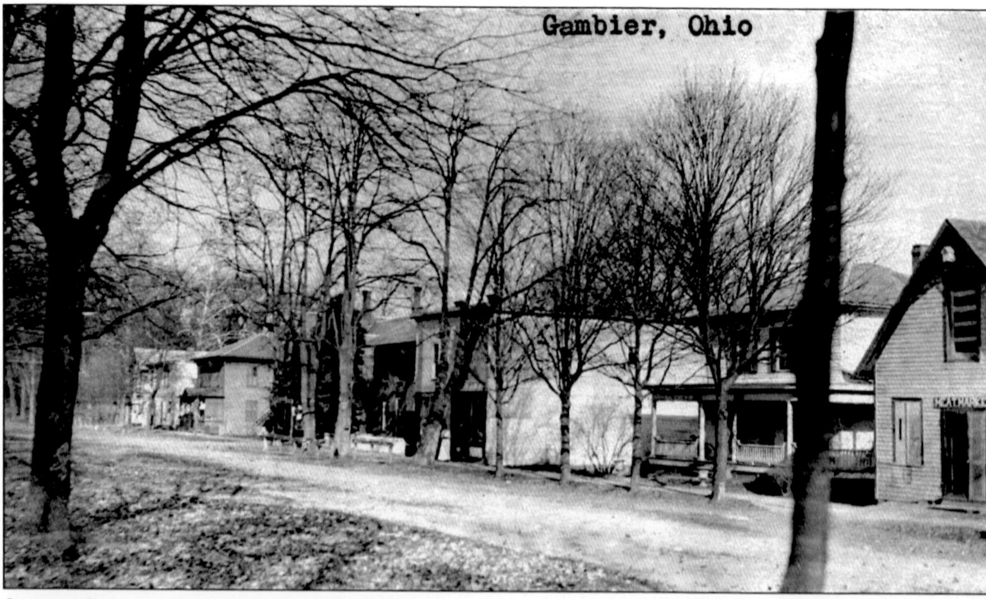


**SOUTH END OF CHASE AVENUE.** This is the extension north of Middle Path that ran from Old Kenyon to the Divinity School, Bexley Hall. In later years, it became a boulevard with Chase on the west and Gaskin on the east. (Photograph courtesy of Olin Library, Kenyon College, Greenslade Special Collections and Archives.)

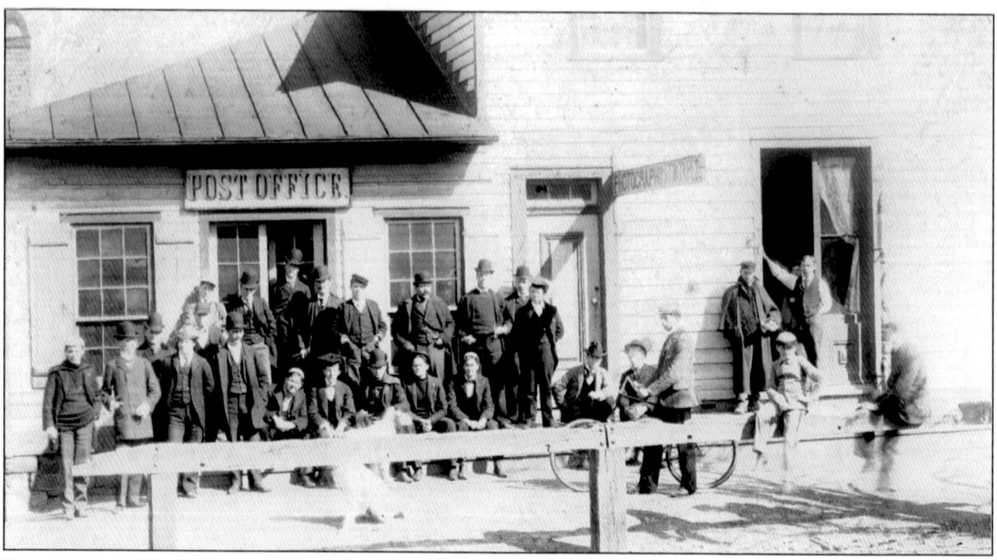


**PLENTY OF KENYON STUDENTS AND TOWNSPEOPLE.** This photograph was taken at the Gambier Post Office on the corner of Brooklyn and Gaskin Streets. (Photograph courtesy of the Olin Library, Kenyon College, Greenslade Special Collections and Archives.)

# *Three*

# BUILDINGS, BUSINESSES, AND STREET SCENES

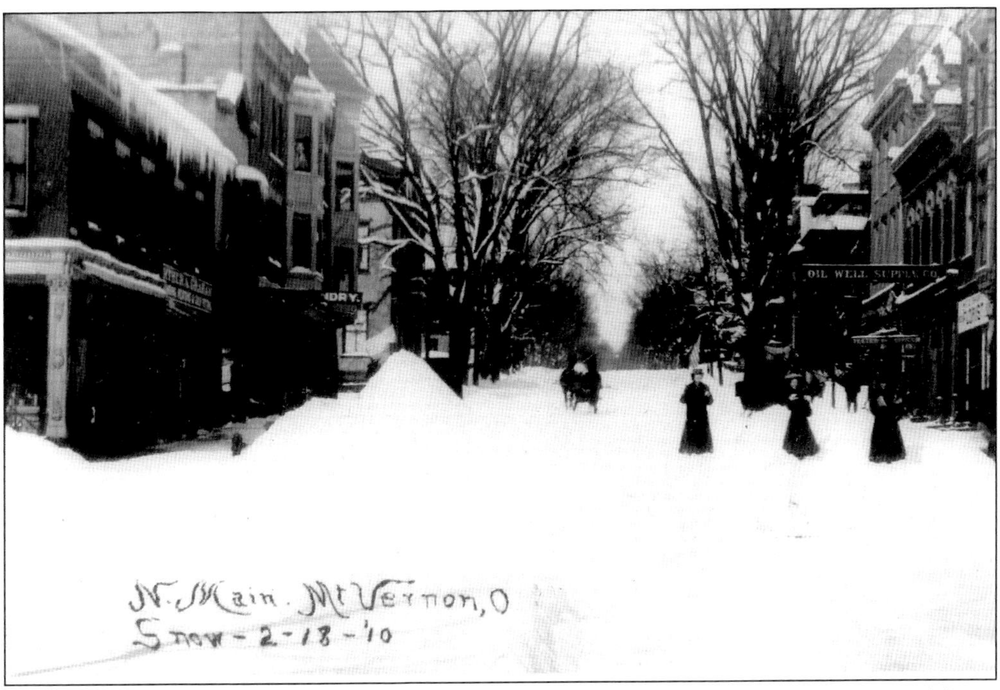


**A SNOW SCENE.** This photograph was taken on the first block of North Main Street in Mount Vernon on February 18, 1910. (Photograph courtesy of the Knox County Agricultural Museum.)

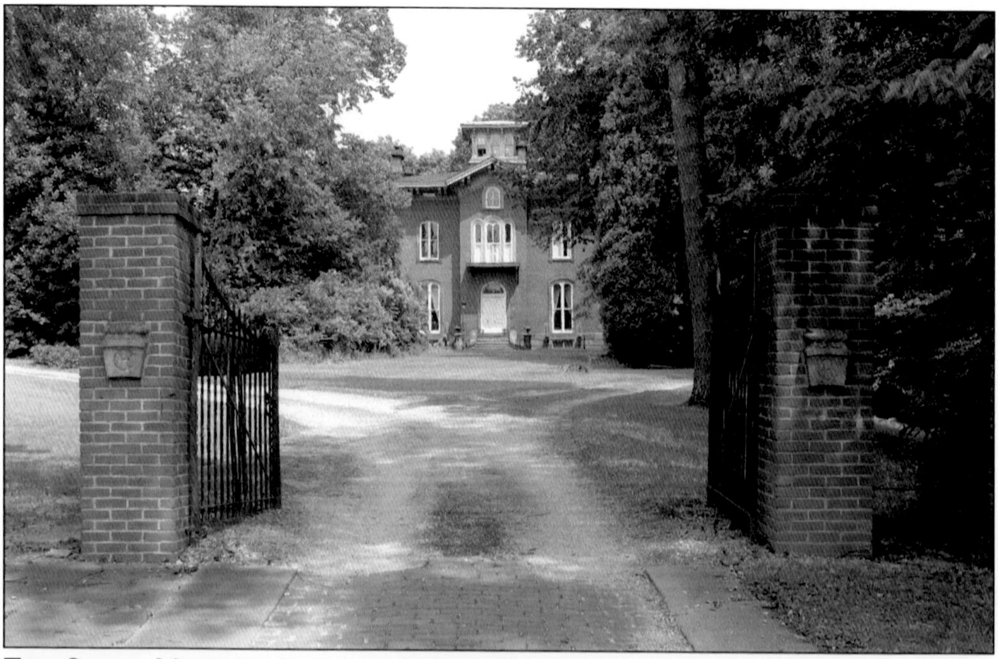

**THE CURTIS MANSION.** Just east of North Gay Street and south of Route 3 in Mount Vernon is the Curtis farm. "Round Hill" described as "perhaps the oldest and most significant Italian (style) villa ever built west of the Appalachians," by Roger Kennedy, director of the Smithsonian's American History Museum. It was built between 1853 and 1857. (Photograph by D.E. Boyd.)

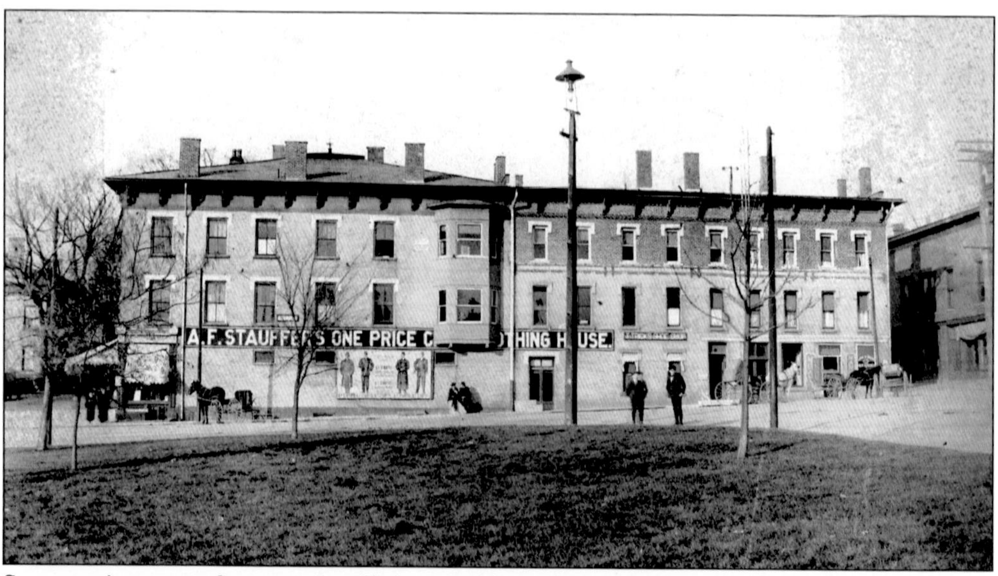


**STAUFFER'S ON THE SQUARE.** Stauffer's moved from the northwest corner of the Mount Vernon Public Square across North Main Street to a much larger building, shown in this photograph. The Stauffer Building and the old City Hall across Blackberry Alley were razed in 1962 to build the present City Hall. (Photograph courtesy of John and Vivian Lahmon.)

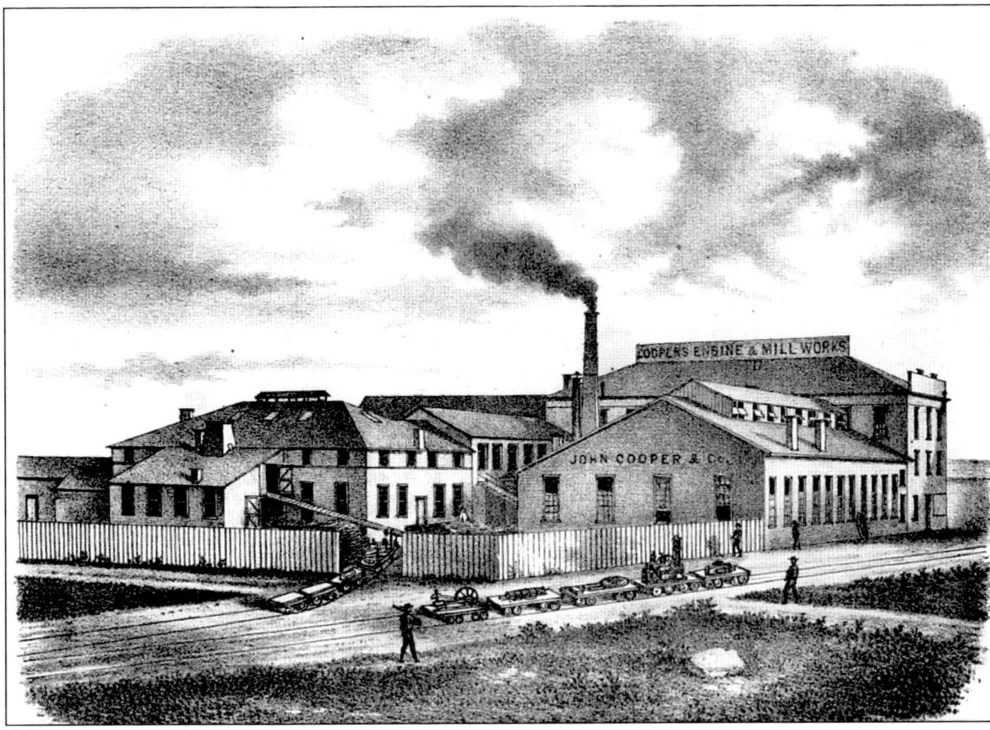


**COOPERS MANUFACTURING COMPANY.** This engraving shows the Cooper factory in 1870. (Image courtesy of Olin Library, Kenyon College, Greenslade Special Collections and Archives.)

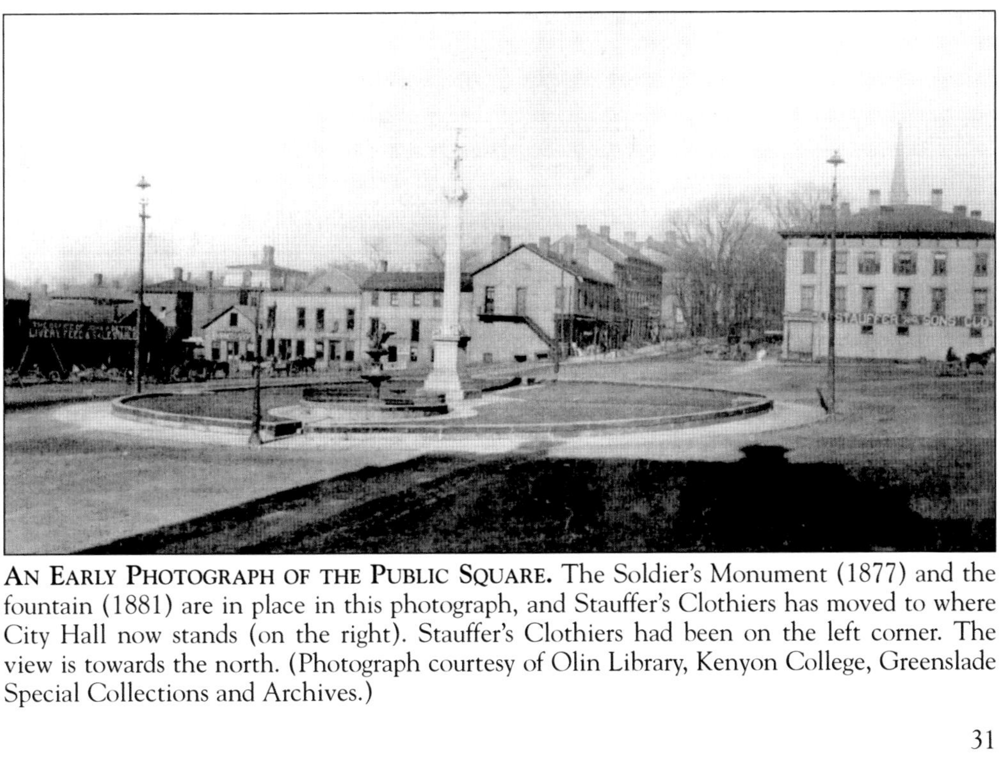

**AN EARLY PHOTOGRAPH OF THE PUBLIC SQUARE.** The Soldier's Monument (1877) and the fountain (1881) are in place in this photograph, and Stauffer's Clothiers has moved to where City Hall now stands (on the right). Stauffer's Clothiers had been on the left corner. The view is towards the north. (Photograph courtesy of Olin Library, Kenyon College, Greenslade Special Collections and Archives.)

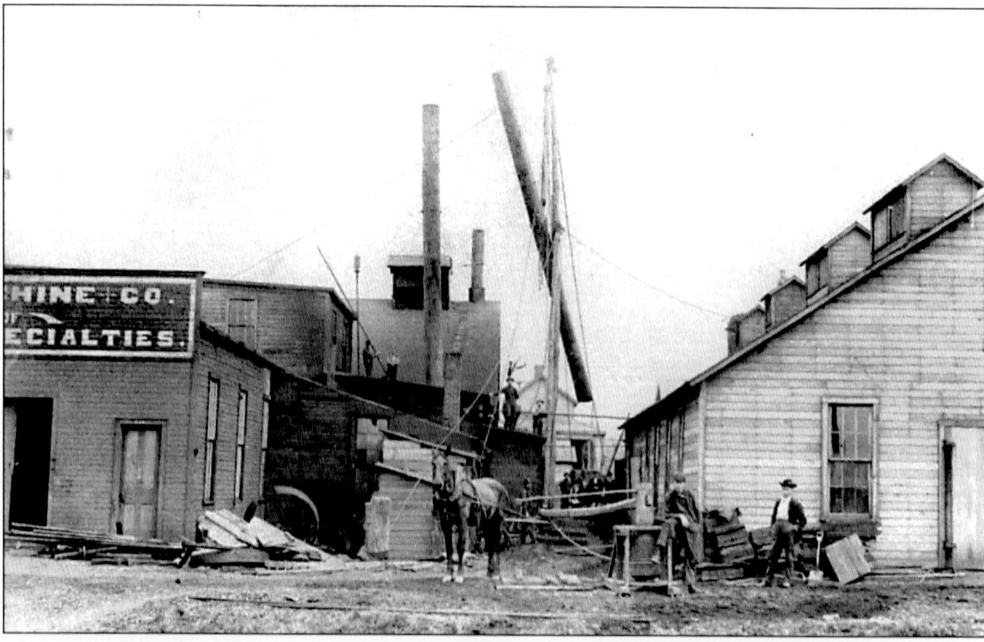


**MACHINE COMPANY.** The long poles and pulleys near the center of this photograph are "ginn" poles, using a single horse to lift great weights. (Photograph courtesy of the Knox County Agricultural Museum.)

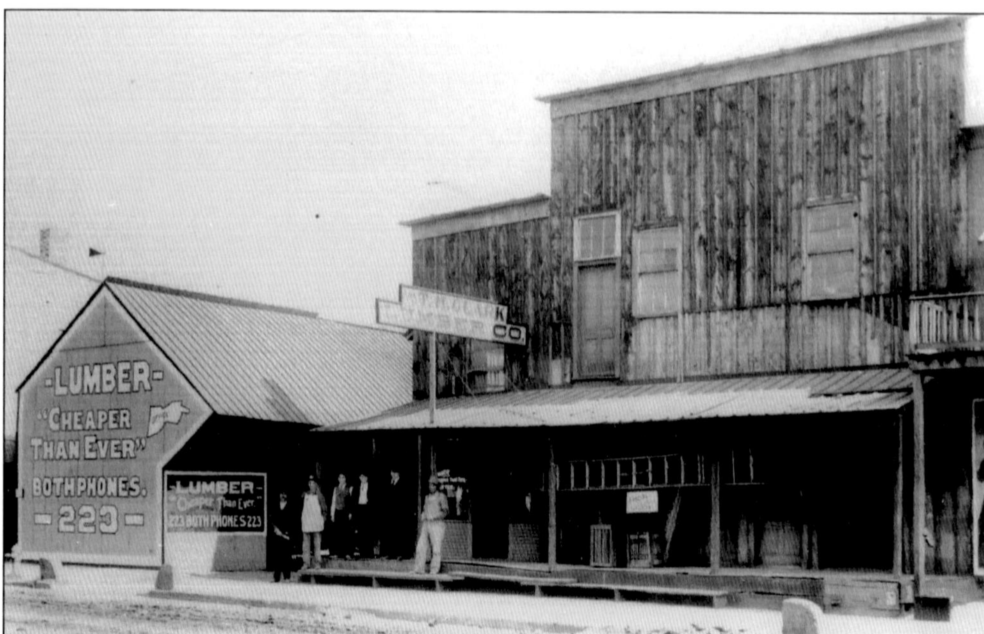


**LUMBER "CHEAPER THAN EVER."** T.H. Clark operated this early lumber store in Knox County. (Photograph courtesy of the Knox County Agricultural Museum.)

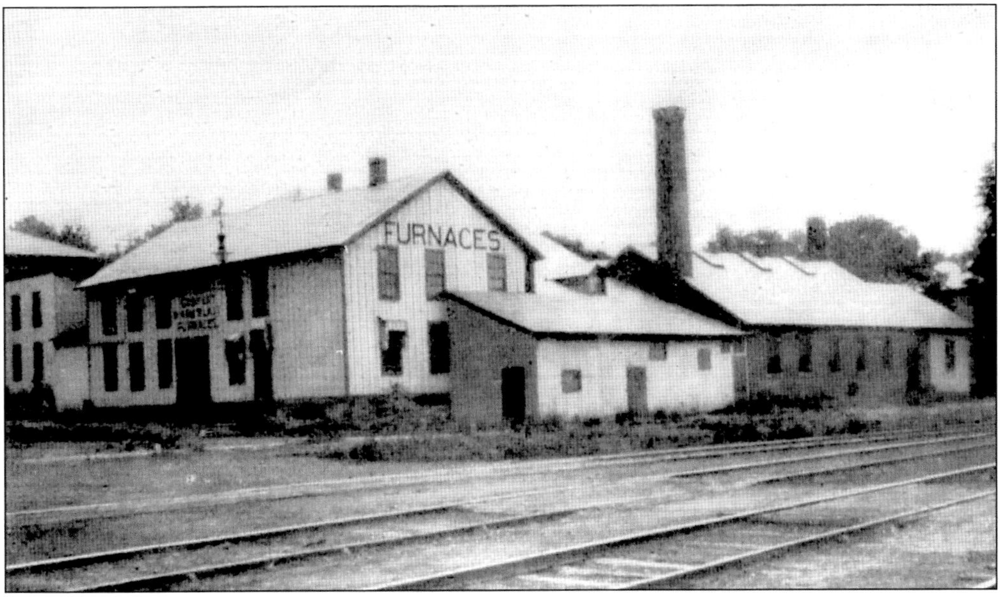


**FURNACE FACTORY.** Mount Vernon has been the home to numerous foundries through the years. This one produced "furnaces," which is what most of the larger stoves were called at the time. (Photograph courtesy of the Knox County Agricultural Museum.)

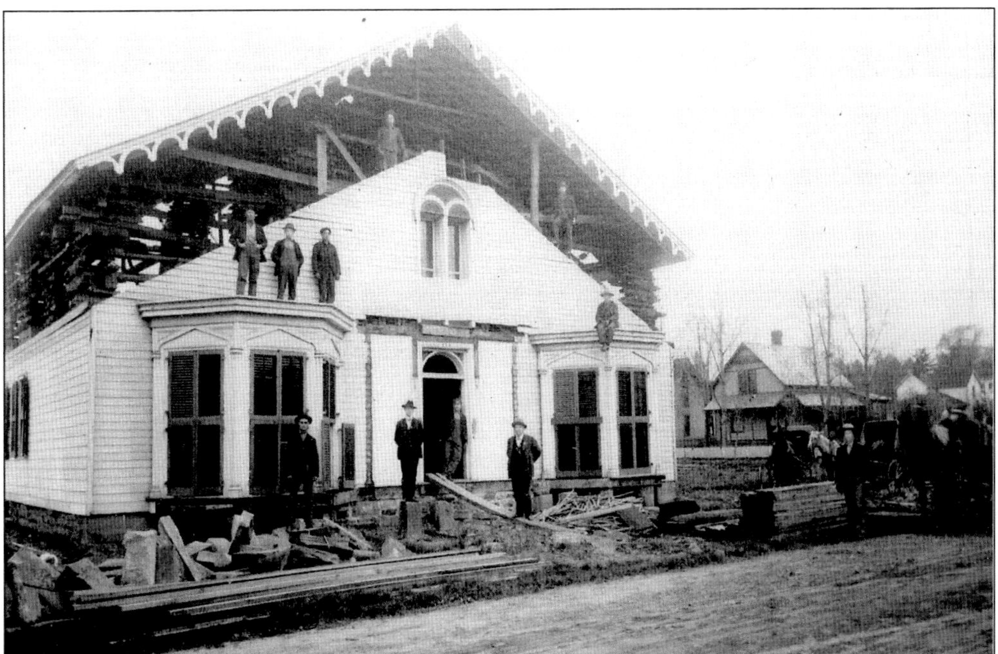

**RAISING THE ROOF.** This enterprising crew of the late 19th century pauses from working on a house in Mount Vernon. The older cameras were large and time-consuming to operate, so people were recruited to pose. (Photograph courtesy of the Knox County Agricultural Museum.)

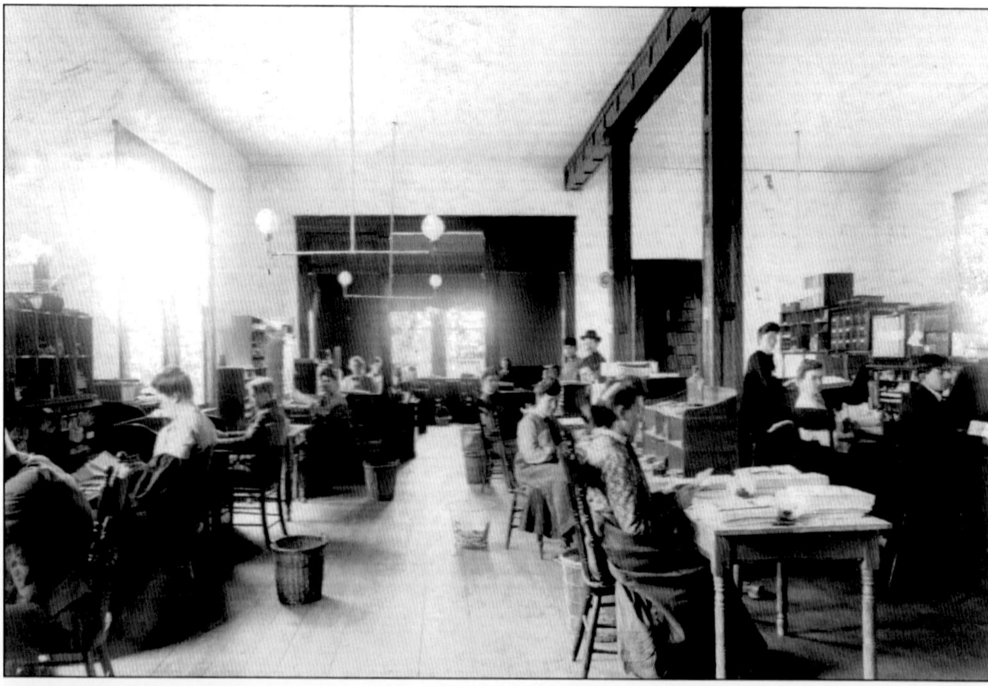

**Foote Foundry Office Scene.** This photograph shows the interior of the J.B. Foote Bell Foundry, *c.* 1900. (Photograph courtesy of the Fredericktown Historical Society.)

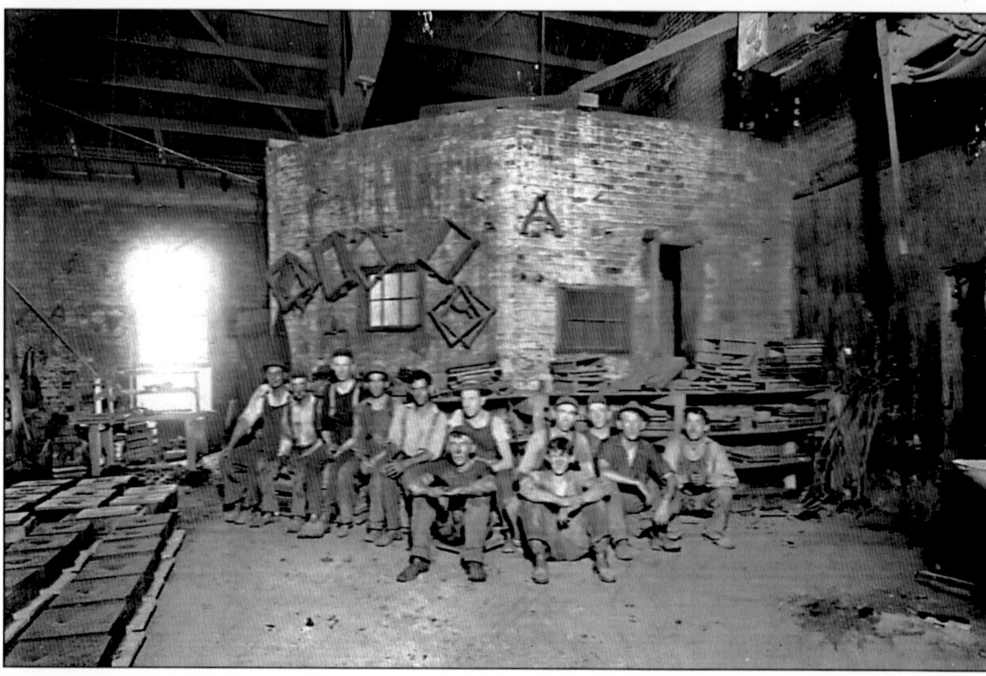

**Foote Foundry Workers.** These men take a break for the photographer, *c.* 1900s. The Foote Foundry was established in 1856, and the foundry operation did not change until much later. The sand molds on the left stand ready to receive the molten iron. (Photograph courtesy of the Fredericktown Historical Society.)

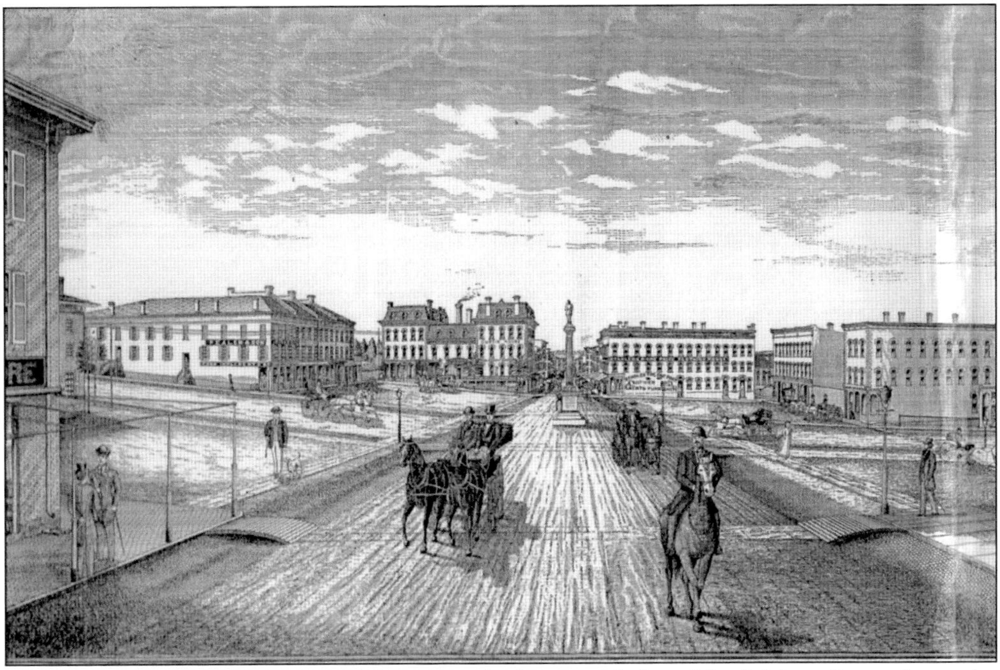

**ENGRAVED SQUARE.** This view of the Square looking south from North Main Street shows the Soldiers Monument in the center. The large store on the right, near the monument, is "Stabler's one price clothier, gents furnishings." It later became Ringwalts. (Photograph courtesy of the Knox County Agricultural Museum.)

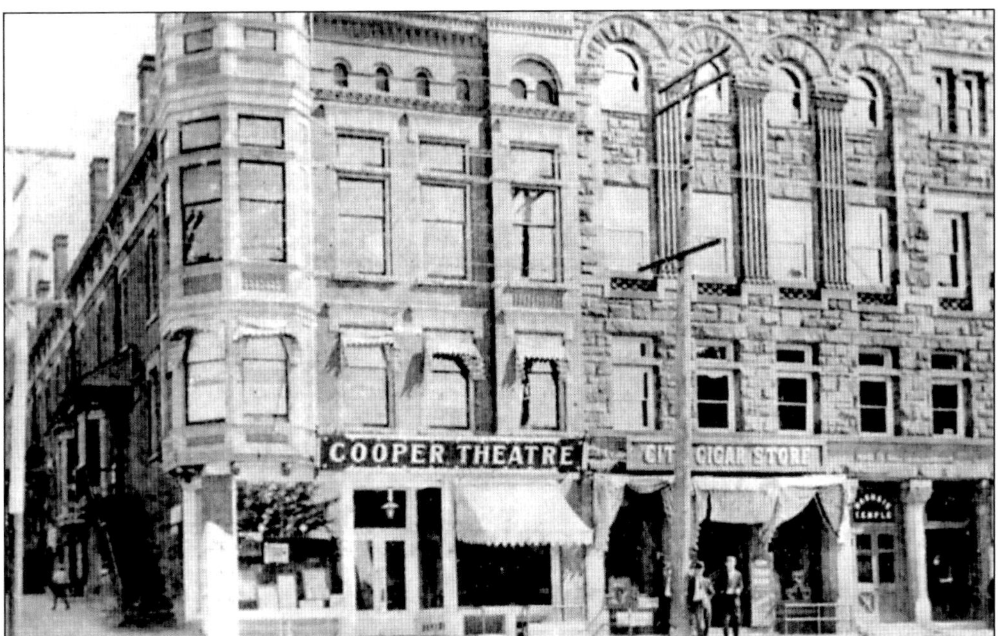


**COOPER THEATRE.** The theater is a new tenant in the Mason's Building in this photograph of the southeast corner of the Square. The building is on the East High Street corner. (Photograph courtesy of the Knox County Agricultural Museum.)

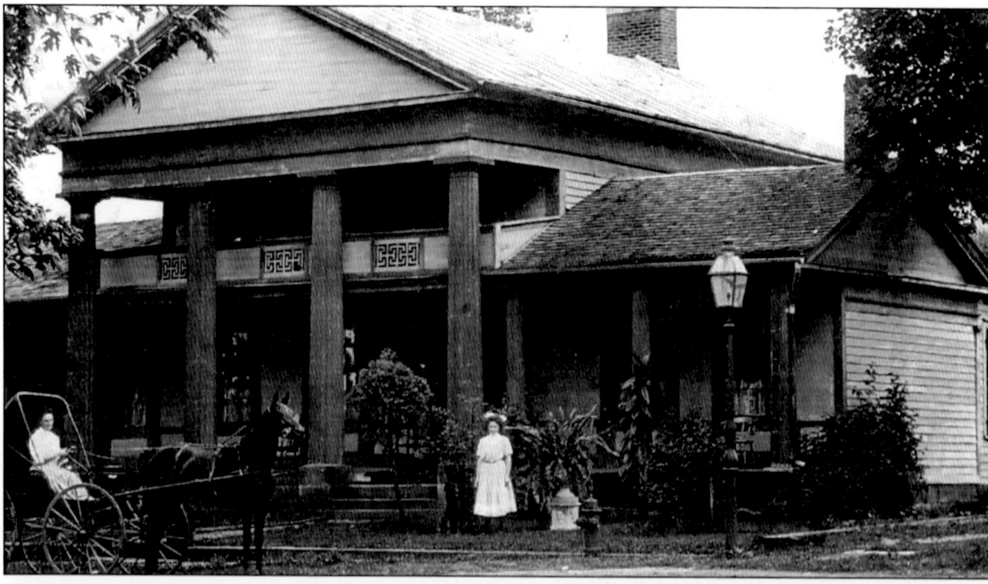

**HILDRETH RESIDENCE.** C.M. Hildreth was born in Mount Vernon *c.* 1850 and married Samuel S. Tuttle's daughter, Marie, in 1877. The couple then moved to Fredericktown in 1879 where Mr. Hildreth prospered as a wool and grain dealer. He served on the town council several years and is credited with helping to improve the water and street systems and the public square. (Photograph courtesy of the Fredericktown Historical Society.)

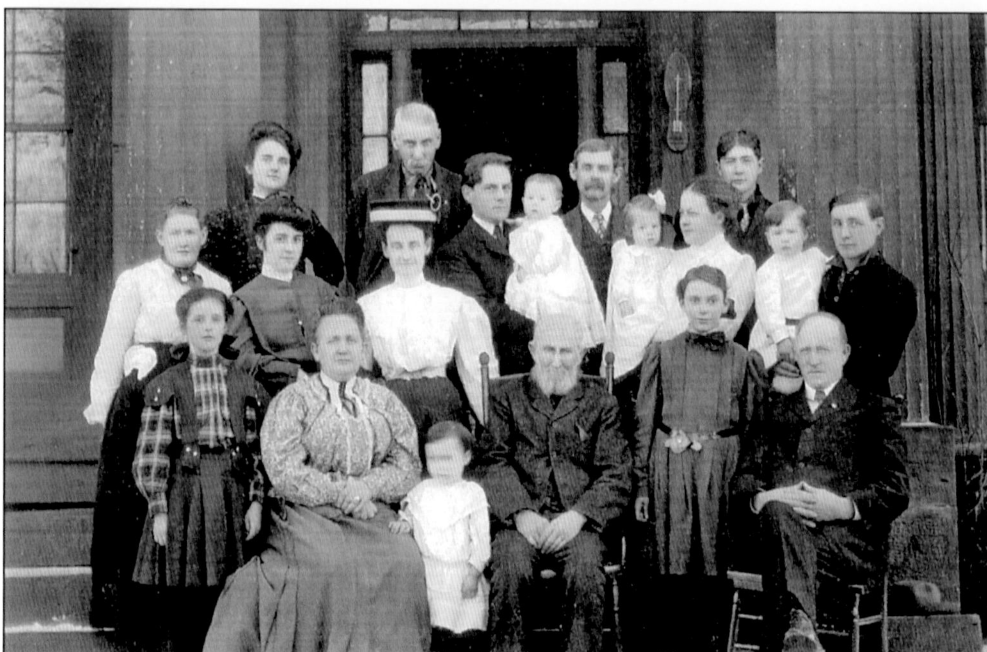

**THE TUTTLE AND HILDRETH FAMILIES.** Samuel S. Tuttle is shown in the front row center of this photograph. His daughter Marie is second from the left in the front row, and her husband, C.M. Hildreth, is most likely the man on the far right in the front row. (Photograph courtesy of the Fredericktown Historical Society.)

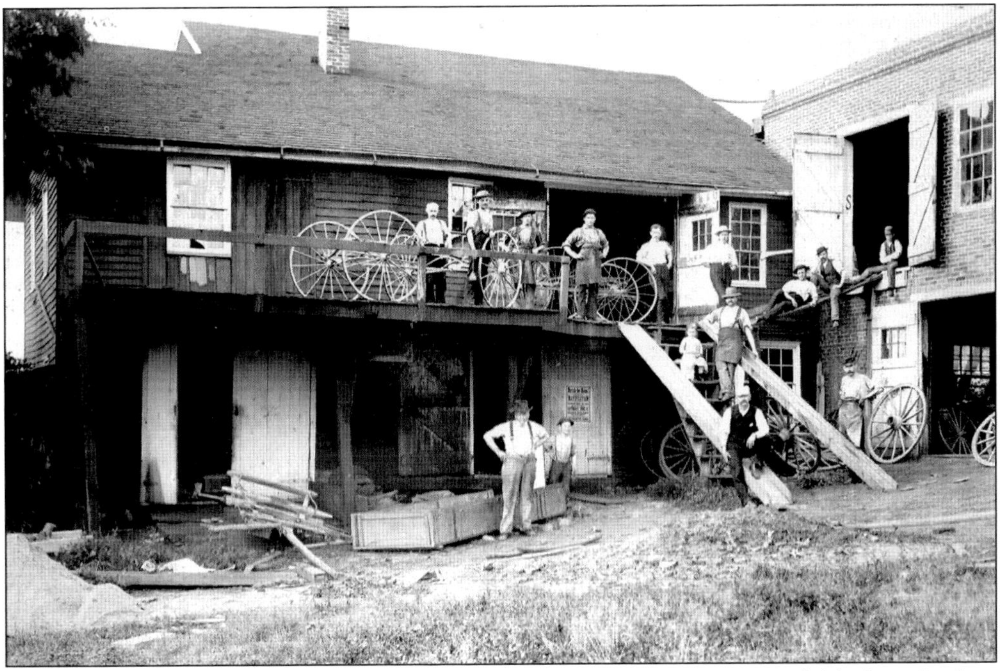

**Buggy Works.** White, Stephen, and Lindley operated a carriage and blacksmith shop in Fredericktown in the late 19th century. The upper floor was where the tops, trim, and upholstering were done. Many Amish in the area still have their own buggy shops. (Photograph courtesy of the Fredericktown Historical Society.)

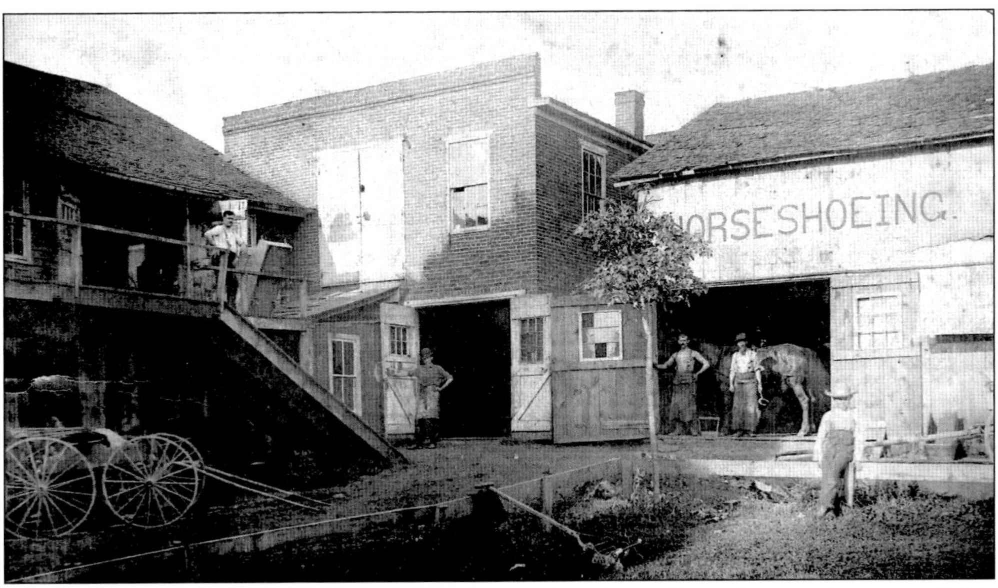

**Horseshoeing.** This is the carriage shop somewhat later. Note that at the time of this photograph the "horseshoeing" was done in the shed at the right. (Photograph courtesy of the Fredericktown Historical Society.)

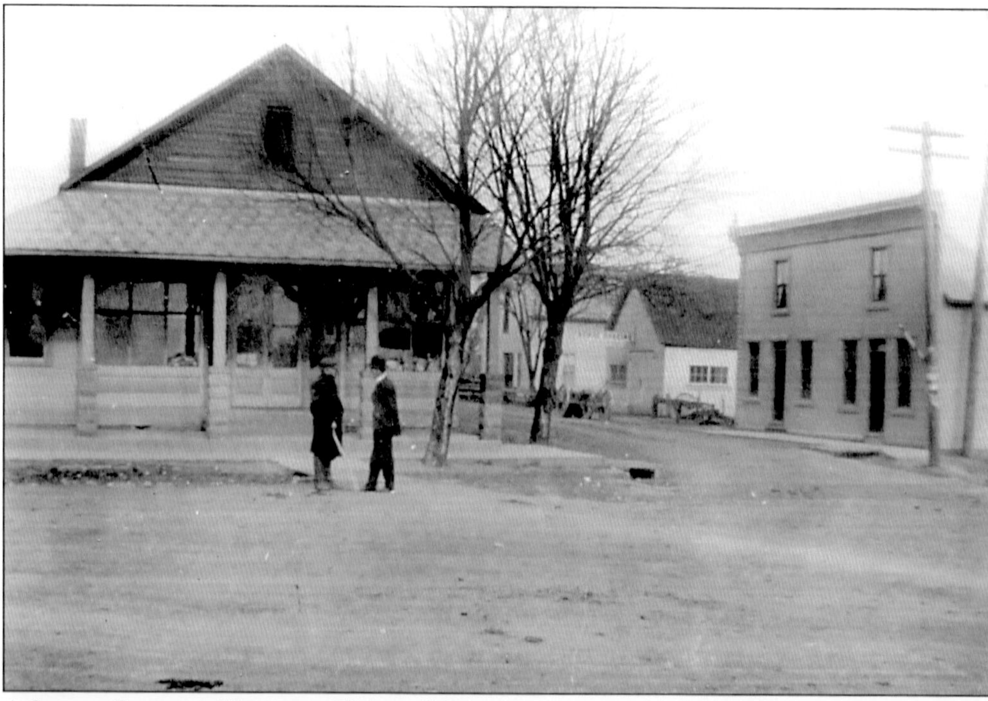

**A Street Scene in Howard.** This small Knox County town is 11 miles east of Mount Vernon on State Route 36. (Photograph courtesy of the Knox County Agricultural Museum.)

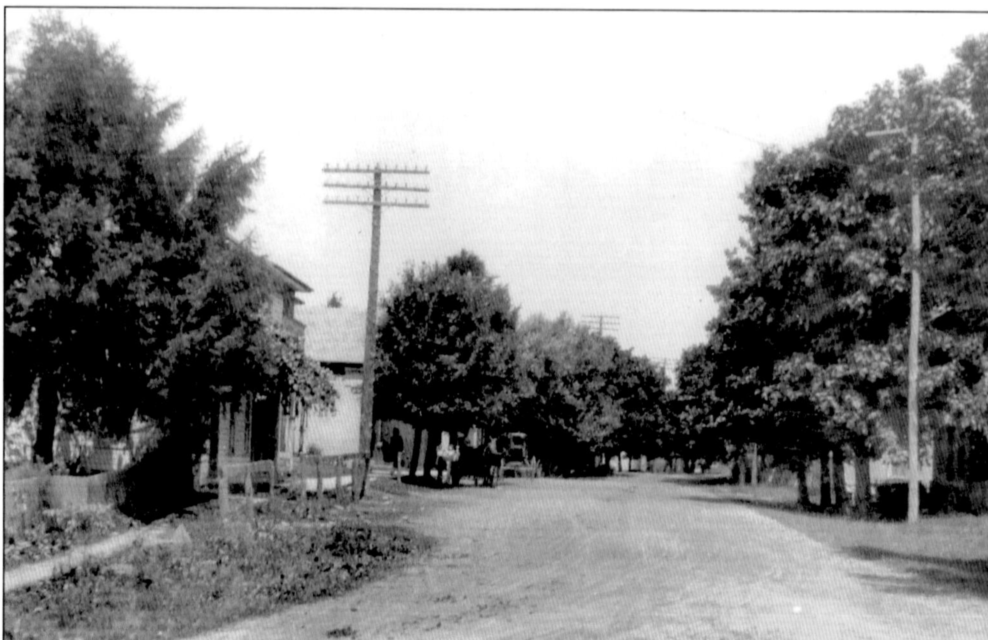

**Jelloway on State Route 3.** Jelloway is in the northeast corner of Knox County on State Route 3, often called "the 3-C Highway" because it connects Cleveland, Columbus, and Cincinnati. (Photograph courtesy of the Knox County Agricultural Museum.)

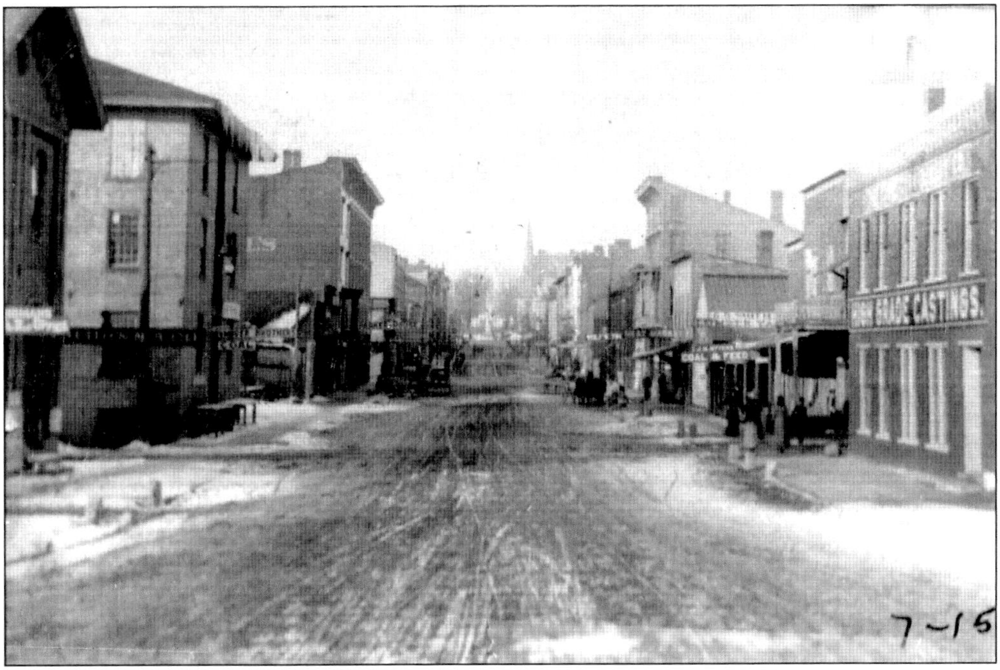

**SOUTH MAIN.** In this photograph, you can see two coal company signs, plus a meat market and a "High Grade Castings" sign on the building to the right. In 1854, Amelia Bloomer, a native of Mount Vernon, published *The Lily*, a women's rights magazine, in a building on this corner. She urged women to discard their corsets and wear loose-fitting garments, which later became known as "bloomers." (Photograph courtesy of the Knox County Agricultural Museum.)

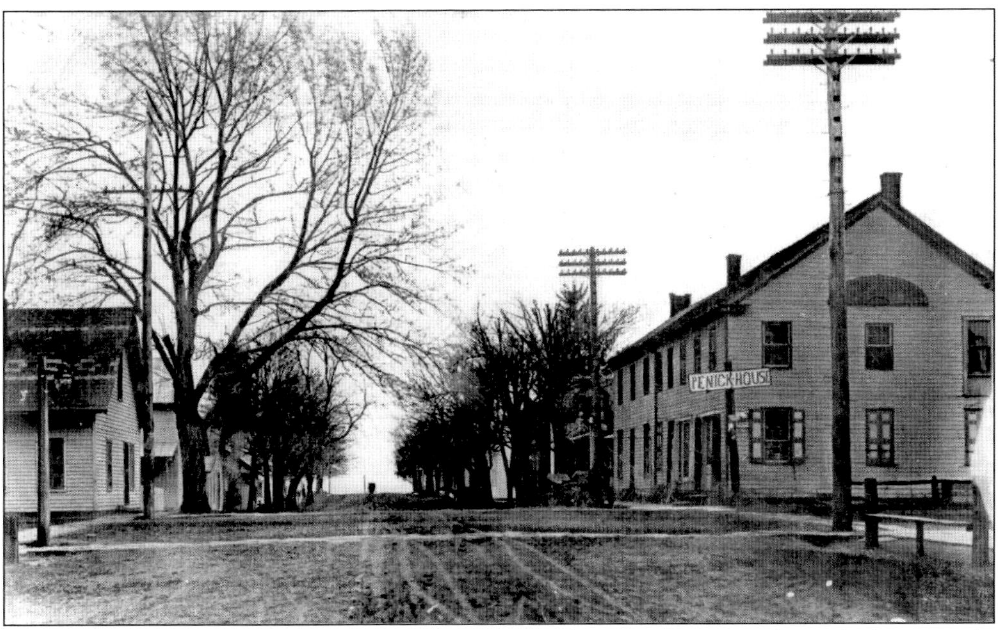

**PENICK HOUSE.** This hotel is near the center of town in Martinsburg, looking south. (Photograph courtesy of the Knox County Agricultural Museum.)

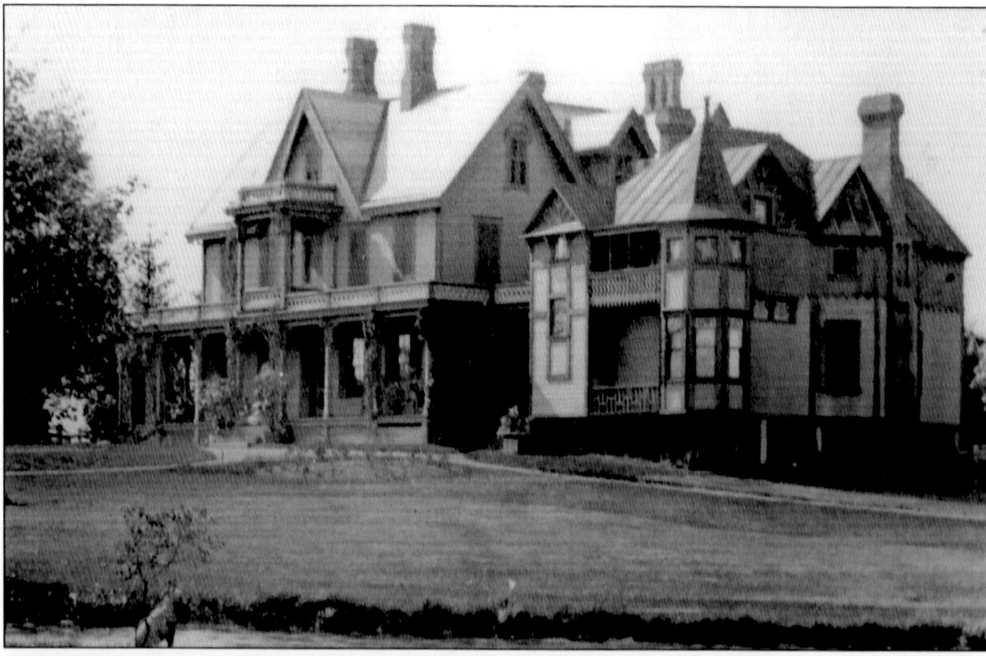

**LAKE HOME FARM.** This magnificent house was built by Columbus Delano south of Mount Vernon on Martinsburg Road in 1871. Delano was Secretary of the Interior under U.S. Grant and built the home while serving his term from 1870 to 1875. In 1966, 209 acres of the farm were acquired for the Mount Vernon Nazarene College, in what Paul Mayle, history professor of the College termed, "The Miracle on the Kokosing." The college became a university in 2002. The farm's name was shortened to "Lakeholm" some time previous to 2002. (Photograph courtesy of the Knox County Agricultural Museum.)

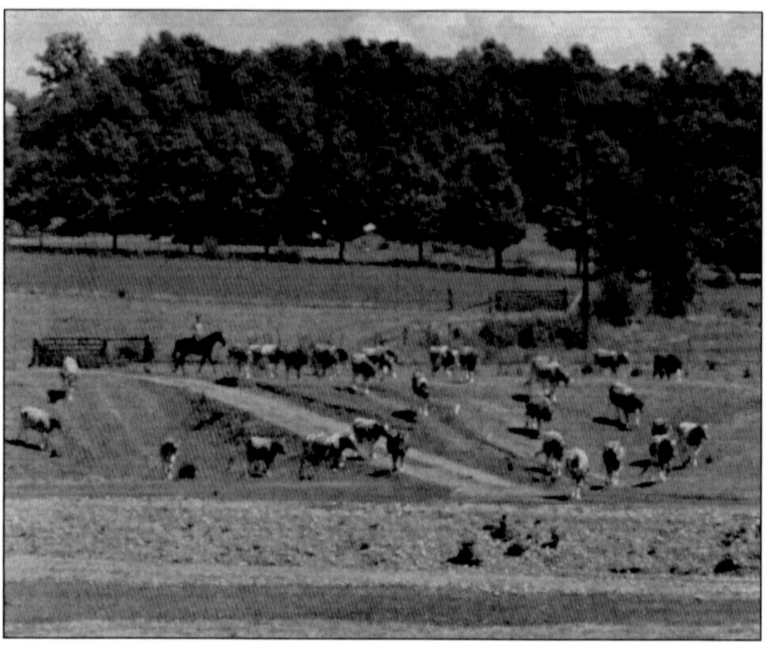

**COWS IN MOUNT VERNON.** These cows were grazing on the Bert Martin farm, formerly the Columbus Delano farm, just on the south edge of Mount Vernon. In 1883, Jersey Lily, a cow from a herd being driven through town, wandered into the Young & Allen's shoe store. (Photograph courtesy of Anita V. Lahmon.)

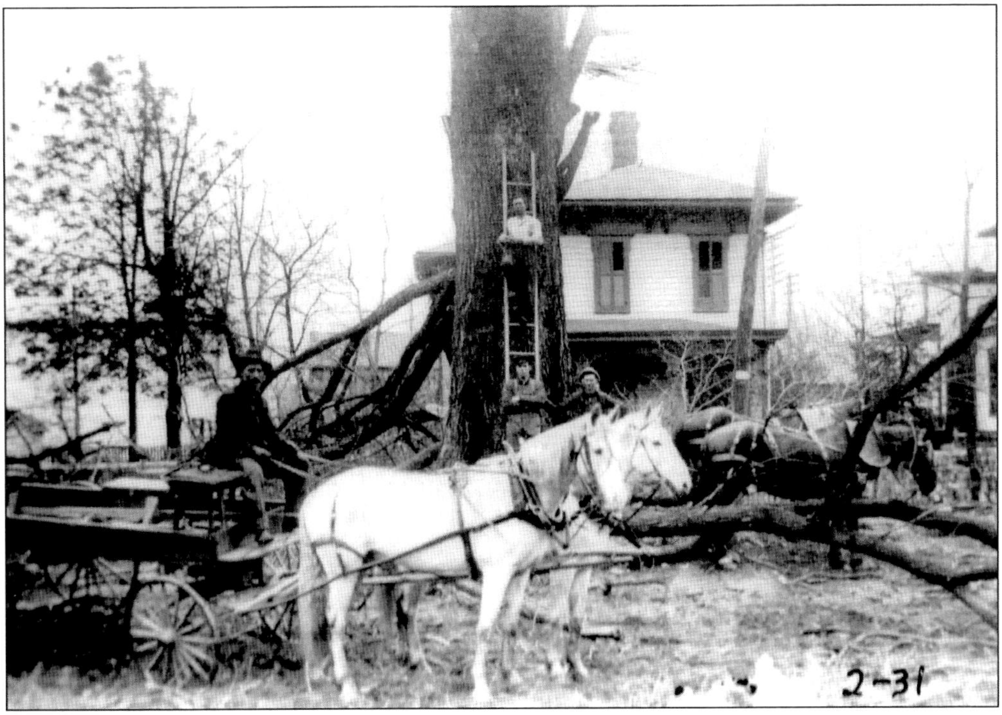


**CLEARING STORM DAMAGE.** There were no chainsaws to help clean up fallen trees at the time this picture was taken on what seems to be East Vine Street in Mount Vernon. (Photograph courtesy of the Knox County Agricultural Museum.)

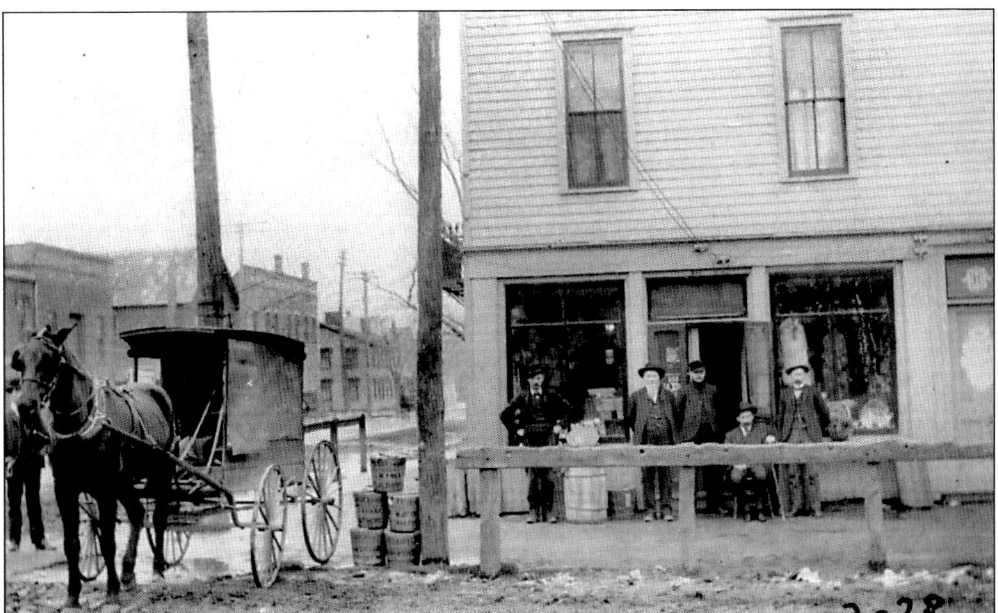


**GROCERY LINE.** Men pose outside a grocery in Mount Vernon, *c.* 1900. Another man holds the reins to his horse as he waits to load his buggy until after the photograph is taken. (Photograph courtesy of the Knox County Agricultural Museum.)

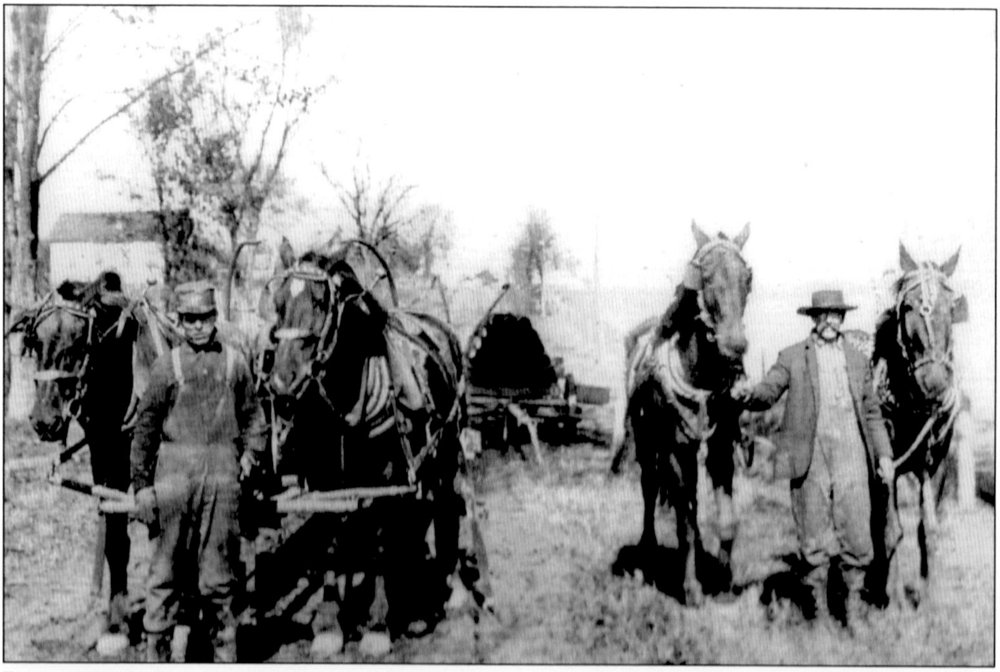

**ROAD WORK.** Two men work two teams on Knox County roads *c.* 1890s. There are pipes on the wagon behind them. (Photograph courtesy of the Knox County Agricultural Museum.)

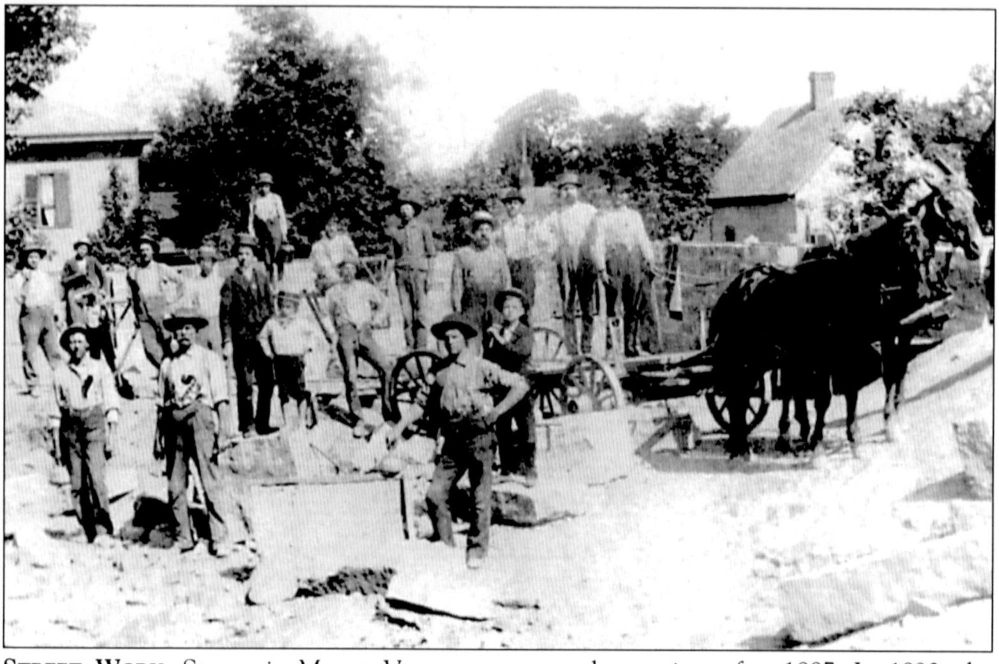

**STREET WORK.** Streets in Mount Vernon were paved sometime after 1887. In 1890, the city passed an ordinance requiring all businesses and residences to be numbered. There were sprinklers on some main streets to keep the dust down. (Photograph courtesy of the Knox County Agricultural Museum.)

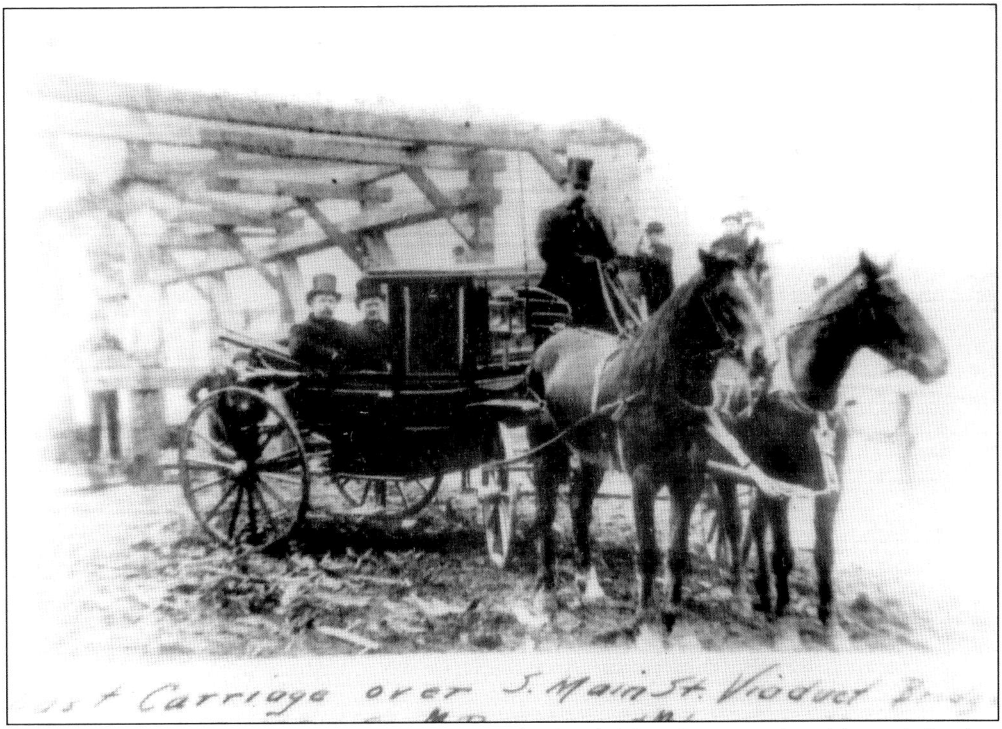


**LAST CARRIAGE.** Watching the last carriage cross the South Main Street viaduct (shown below) in 1890 was thought to be an auspicious event. Mr. Ramey and Mr. Leroy Hunt were in the carriage with J. George driving. (Photograph courtesy of the Knox County Agricultural Museum.)

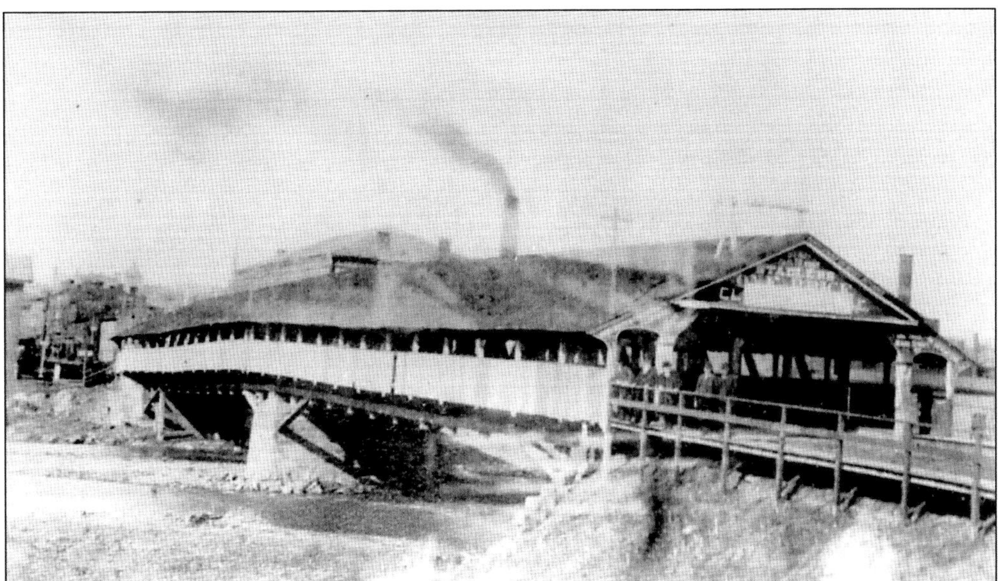

**WAVY BRIDGE.** This is one of the various bridges that has spanned the Kokosing at the south entrance to Mount Vernon. This photograph was taken before 1890. Notice the advertising on the bridge end for Stabler's Department Store. The view is looking north, up Main Street. (Photograph courtesy of the Knox County Agricultural Museum.)

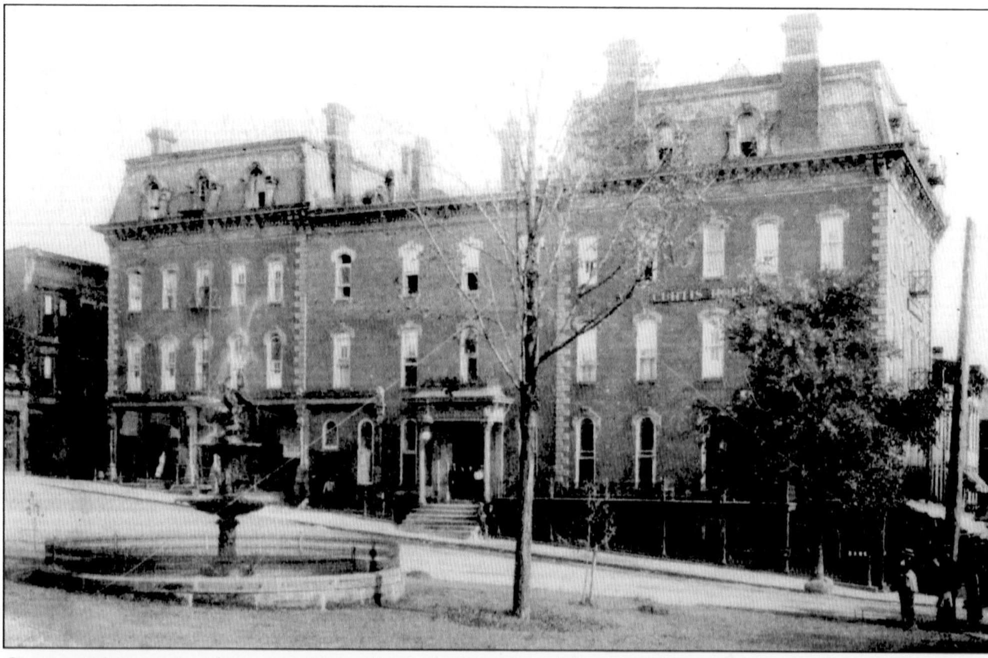

**CURTIS HOUSE.** Looking southeast from the center of the Square, you can see the new fountain that was cast at Coopers and donated to the city. Wires support the newly planted trees, *c.* 1881. (Photograph courtesy of the Knox County Agricultural Museum.)

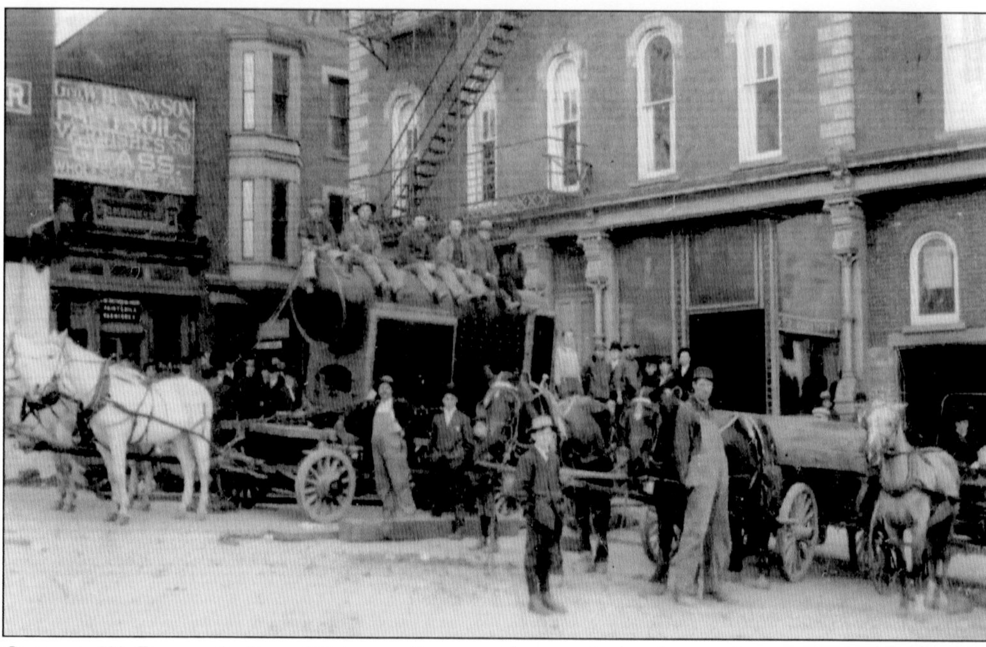


**GEORGE W. BUNN & SON.** "Paints, oils, varnishes, and glass" are advertised on this sign for George W. Bunn & Son. Bunn was listed in the 1879 Mount Vernon Directory and had a home on East Chestnut Street. According to Charles Whitney, Mount Vernon historian and barn expert, the large contraption on the wagon may be a furnace for the Curtis House, later the Curtis Hotel. (Photograph courtesy of the Knox County Agricultural Museum.)

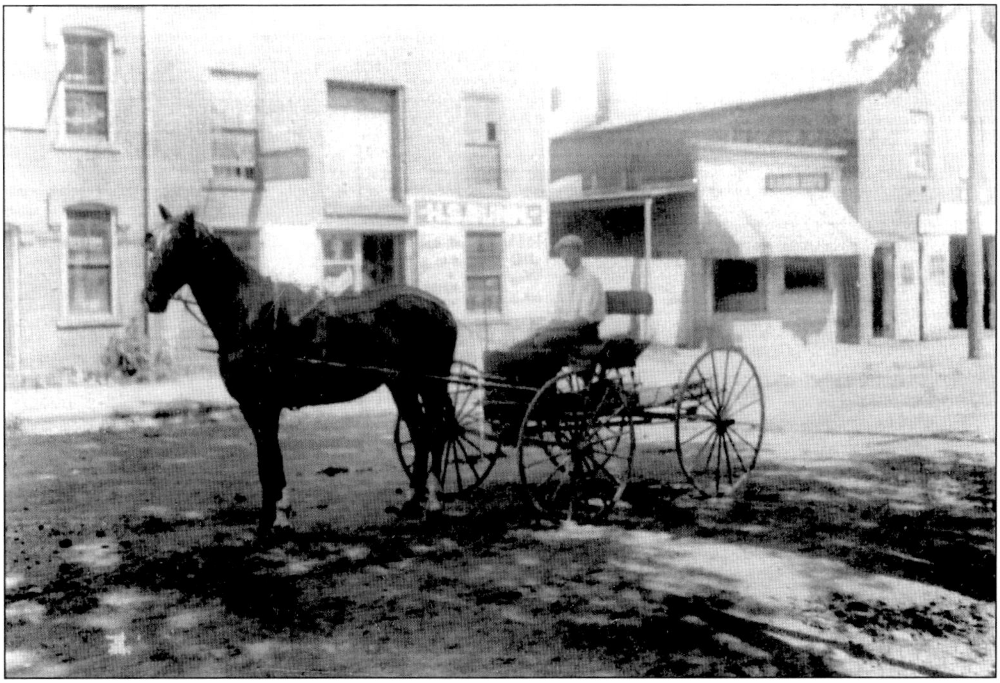

**RESTING IN THE SHADE.** A man rests his horse in the shade in Mount Vernon in front of Bunn's paints and varnish store. This is the second location for Bunn's paints and varnishes and probably is later than the previous view of the store. (Photograph courtesy of the Knox County Agricultural Museum.)

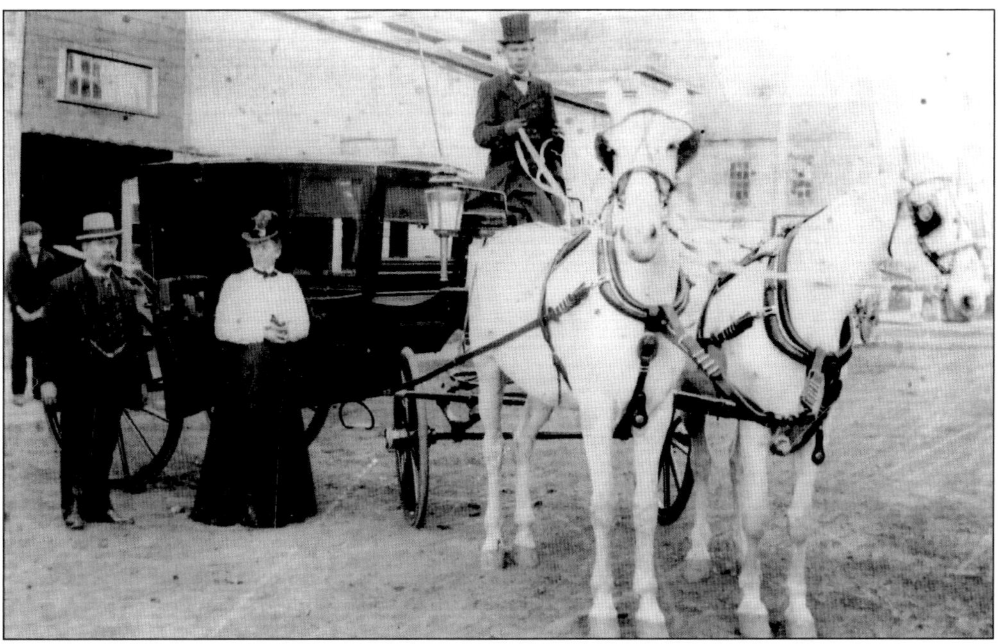

**GREAT RIG.** This elaborate couple, along with their driver, coach, and team of horses, were photographed in Mount Vernon in the late 19th century. (Photograph courtesy of the Knox County Agricultural Museum.)

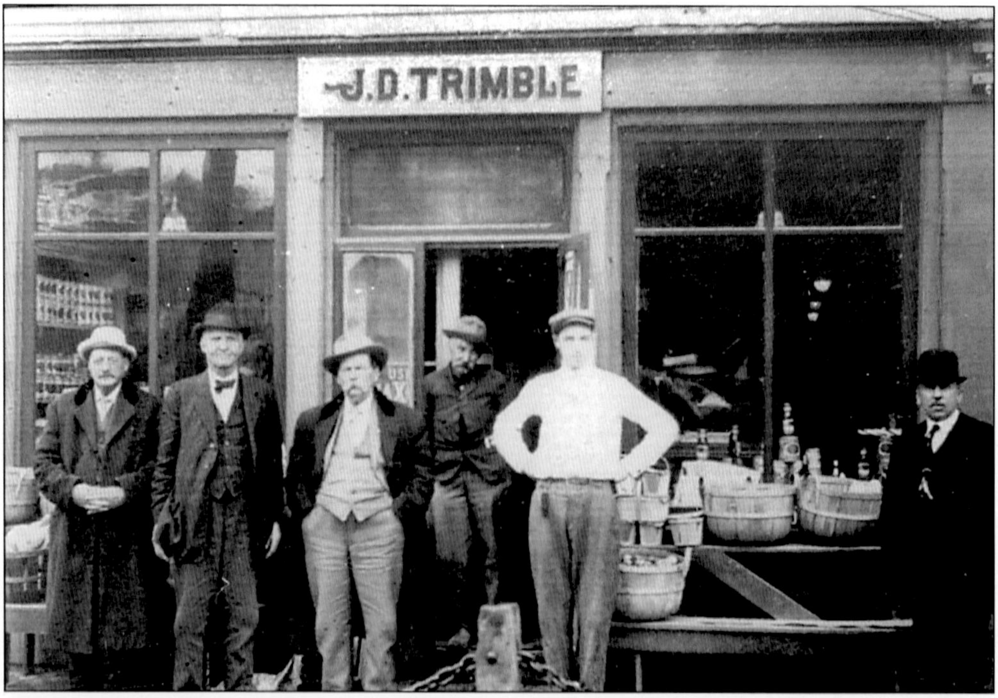


**GROCER J.D. TRIMBLE.** Mr. Trimble is believed to be the man second from the left in this group of men. Grocery stores often attracted men who didn't have much to do, along with those who worked hard in the business. (Photograph courtesy of the Knox County Agricultural Museum.)

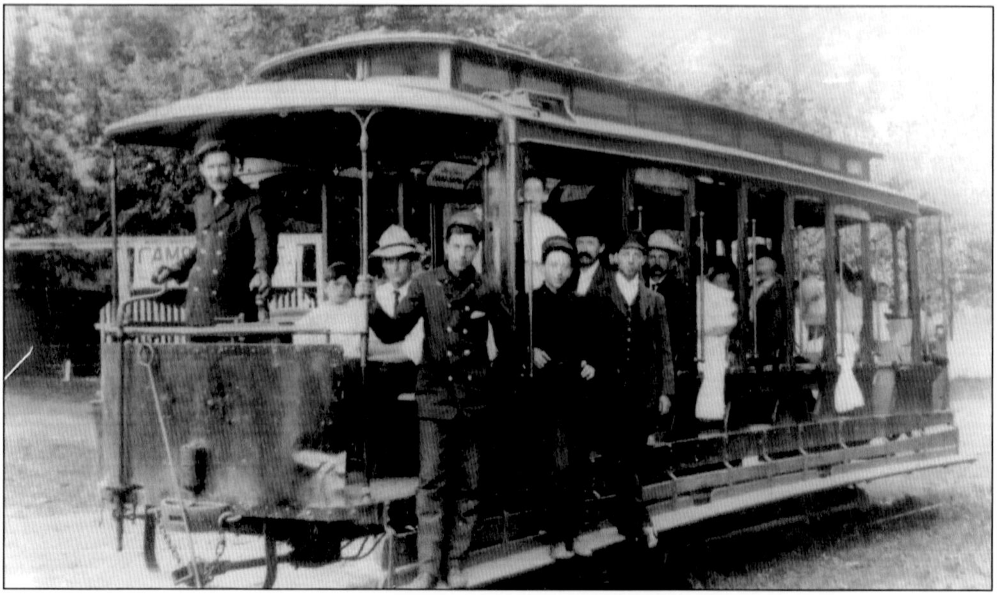

**MOUNT VERNON CABLE CAR.** Streetcars or trolleys ran from Mount Vernon to Hiawatha Park c. 1895. Hiawatha Park was developed by P.B. Chase to promote the use of electricity. It is now the Knox County Fairgrounds. (Photograph courtesy of the Knox County Agricultural Museum.)

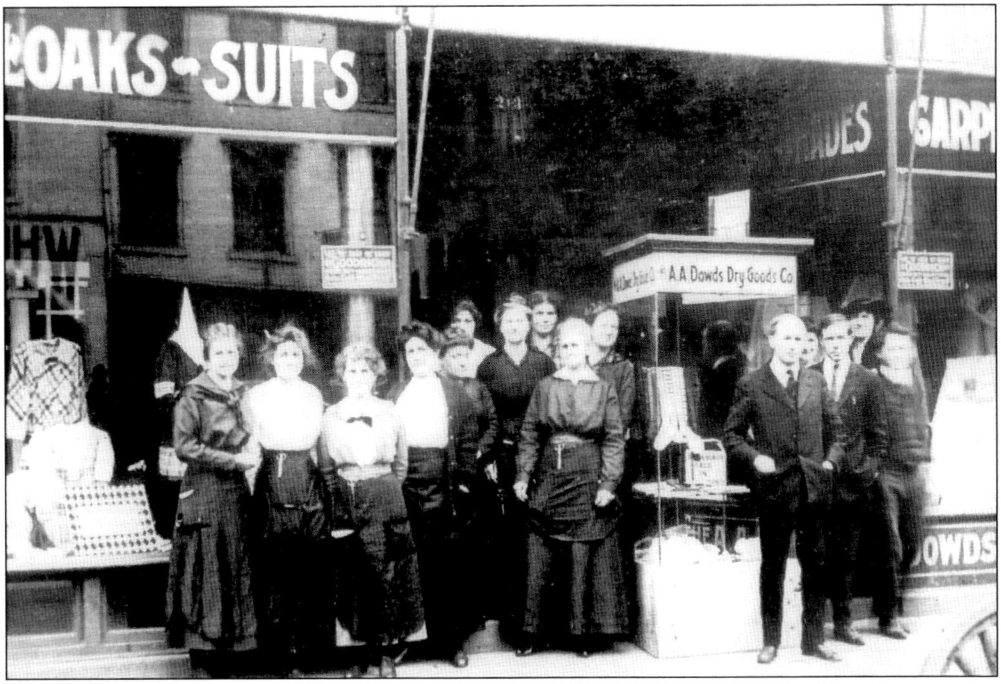


**BEFORE MOTORCARS.** Here are the Dowds sales staff and managers, *c.* 1900. There are 12 women and three men. (Photograph courtesy of the Knox County Agricultural Museum.)

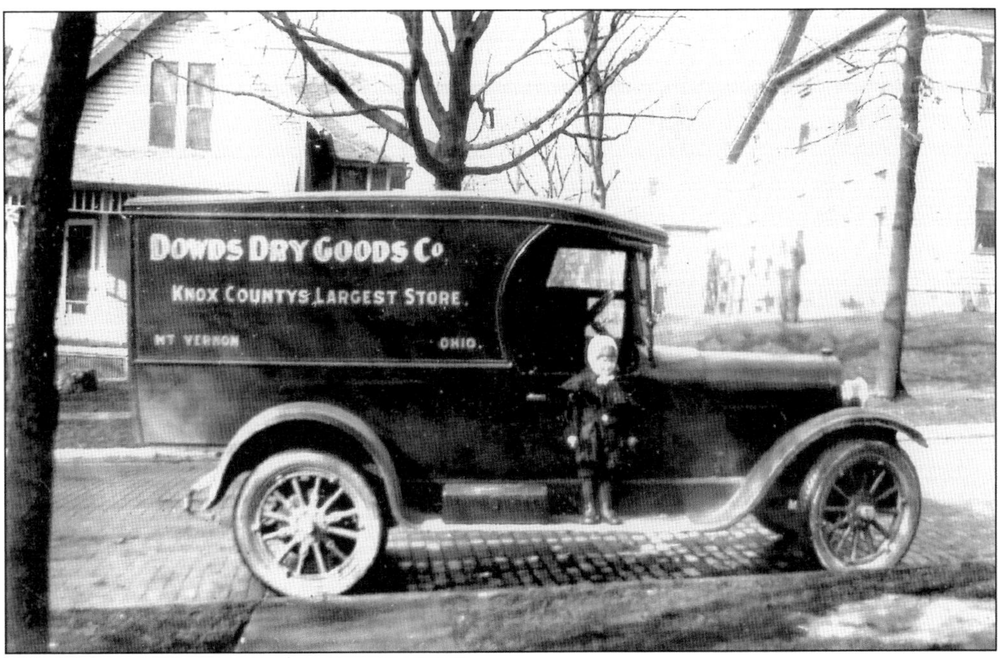


**DOWDS TRUCK.** Dowds prospered in the early 20th century. A local young man, J.W. Rudin (not shown in this photograph), started as a clerk in the store and later purchased the business. Dowds-Rudin operated until the mid-20th century. (Photograph courtesy of Jeff Boucher, Flapper's Bar & Grille.)

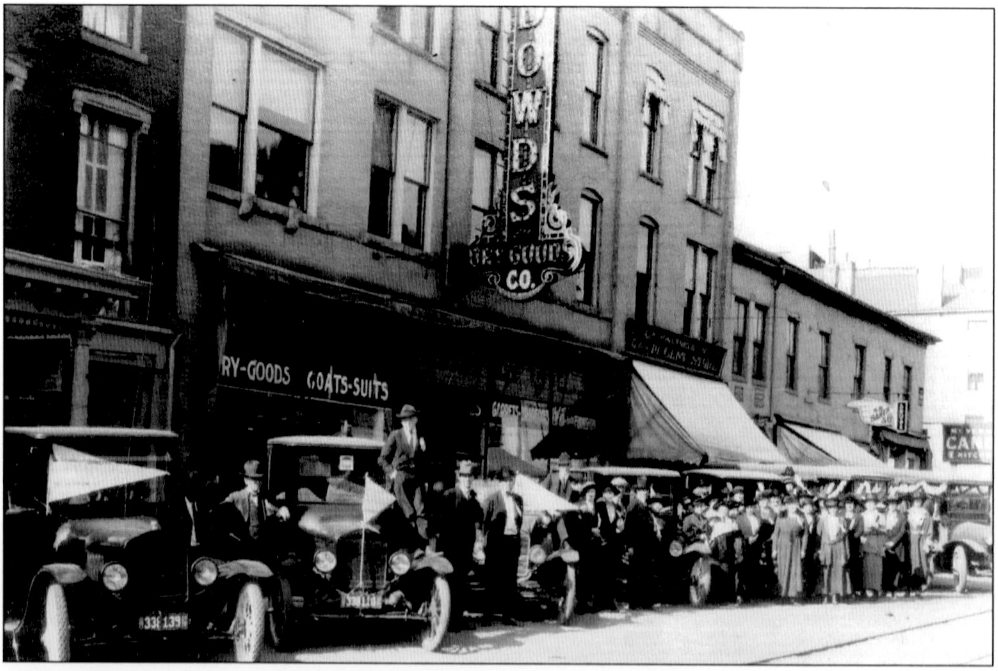


**AFTER MOTORCARS.** Automobiles lined the street in front of Dowds a few years later. The staff has also grown. (Photograph courtesy of the Knox County Agricultural Museum.)

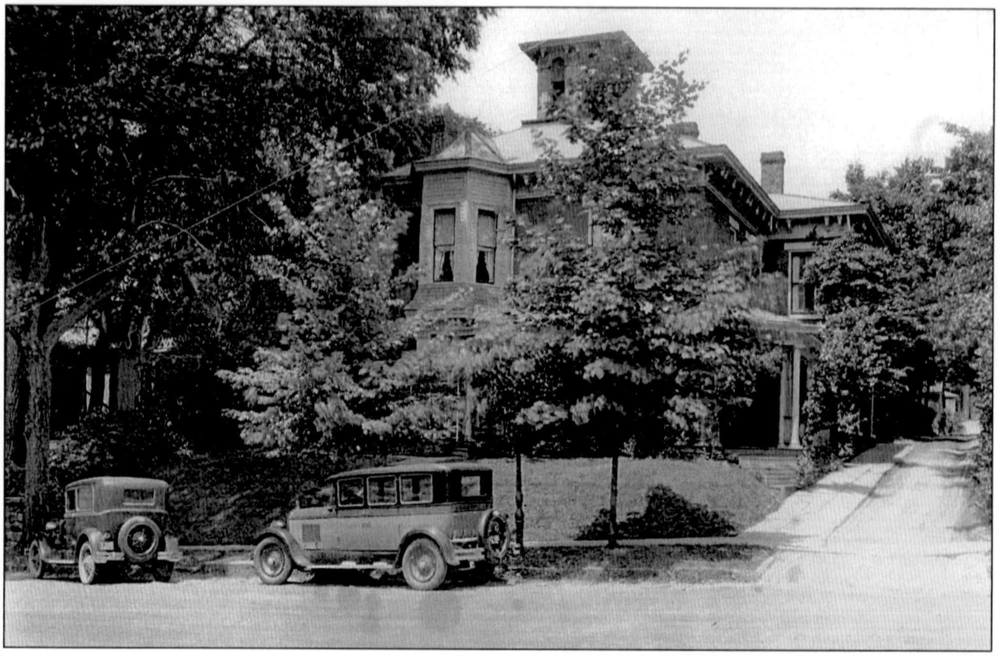

**E.A. SCHLAIRET'S HOME.** The Schlairet family lived at this impressive home at 101 West Sugar Street in Mount Vernon. Mr. Schlairet was in the trucking business in Mount Vernon for 40 years. (Photograph courtesy of Ken Blubaugh.)

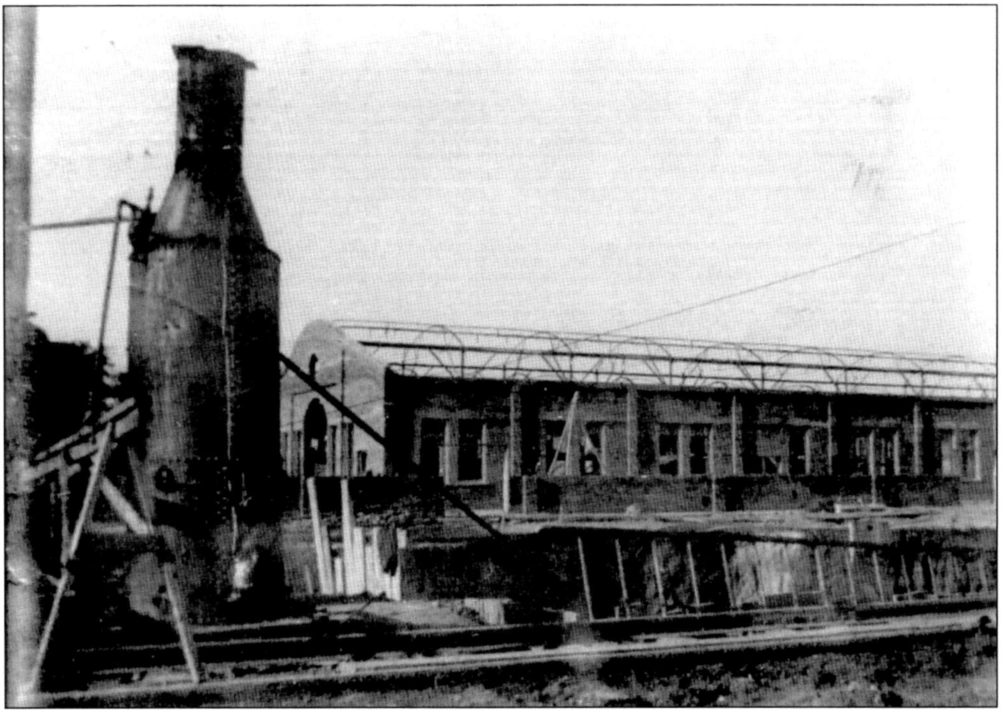

GLASS FACTORY STARTED. This photograph is thought to be of Essex Glass, which was started in Mount Vernon in 1906 and lasted until 1920. Rex Lamb took over the operations in 1921, and it became Lamb Glass. (Photograph courtesy of the Knox County Agricultural Museum.)

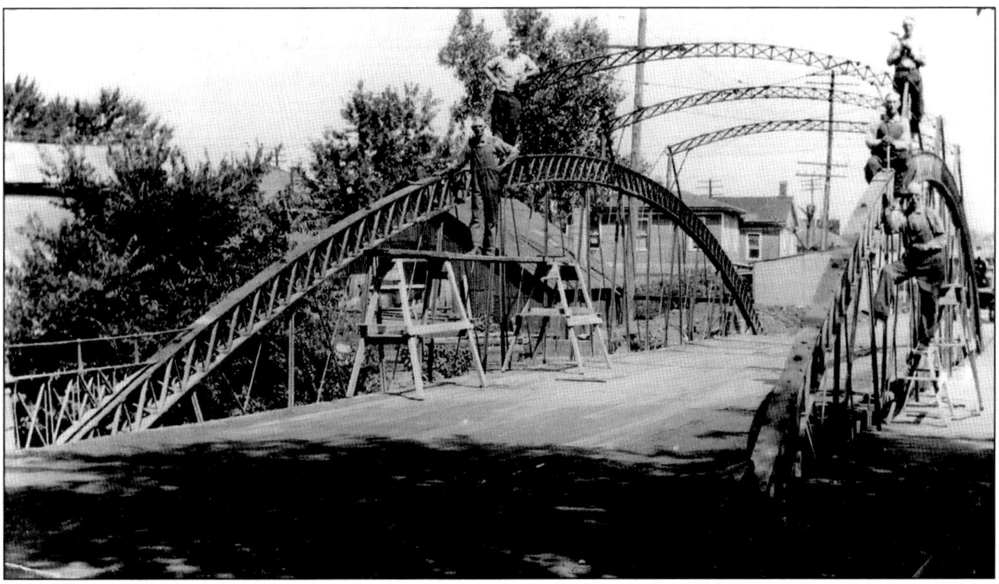

THE MOUNT VERNON BRIDGE WORKS. In 1924, a newsreel at the Vine Theater featured Mount Vernon Bridge Company work on the Omaha and Council Bluffs Bridge on the Missouri River between Iowa and Nebraska. The Mount Vernon Bridge Company also provided steel for the Ohio State University "Horseshoe Stadium" at about the same time. (Photograph courtesy of the Knox County Agricultural Museum.)

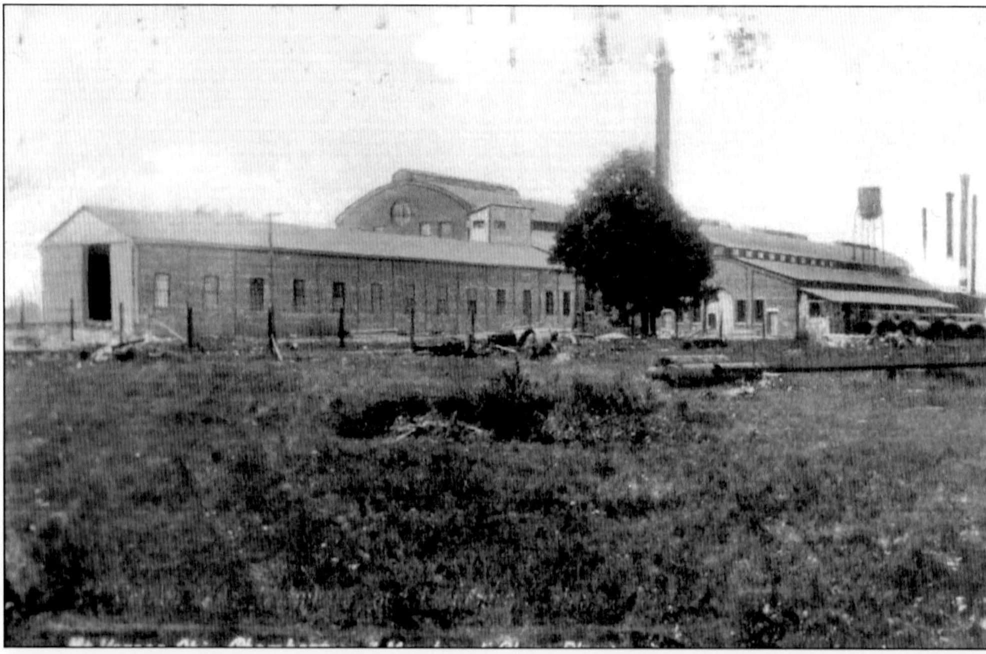

**GLASS FACTORY.** Chambers and Mamburg Glass Co. was built in the southwest part of Mount Vernon just north of Route 36, adjacent to the railroad. They employed hundreds of workers until the plant closed in the 1960s. This factory complex later became Pittsburgh Plate. (Photograph courtesy of the Knox County Agricultural Museum.)

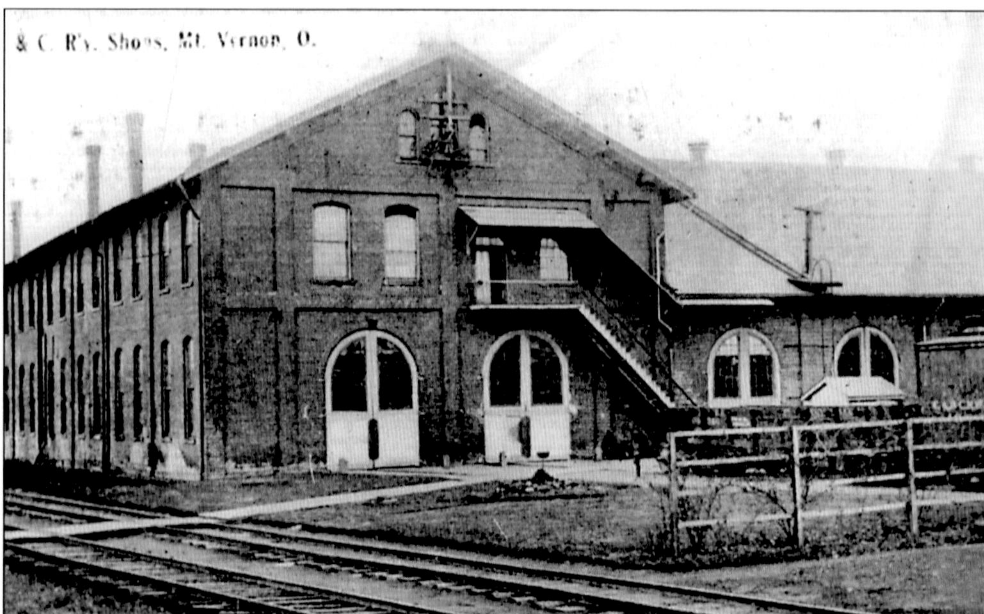


**SHOE FACTORY.** This photograph is of a shoe factory that operated in Mount Vernon at one time. (Photograph courtesy of the Knox County Agricultural Museum.)

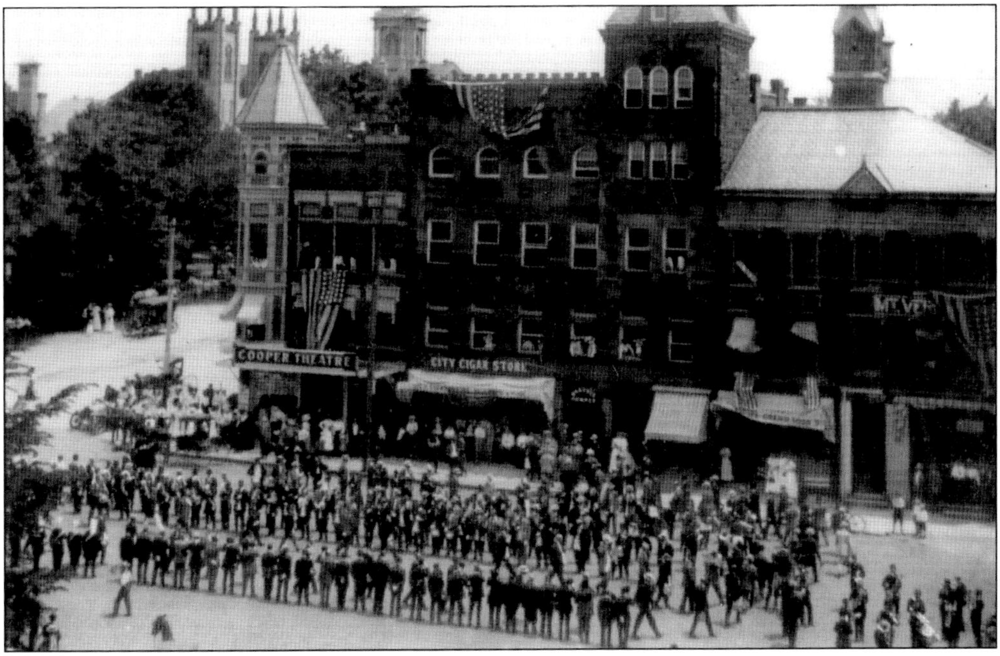


**THE MASON'S 100TH ANNIVERSARY.** Masons assembled in front of their headquarters on the southeast corner of the Mount Vernon Square in 1910. (Photograph courtesy of the Knox County Agricultural Museum.)

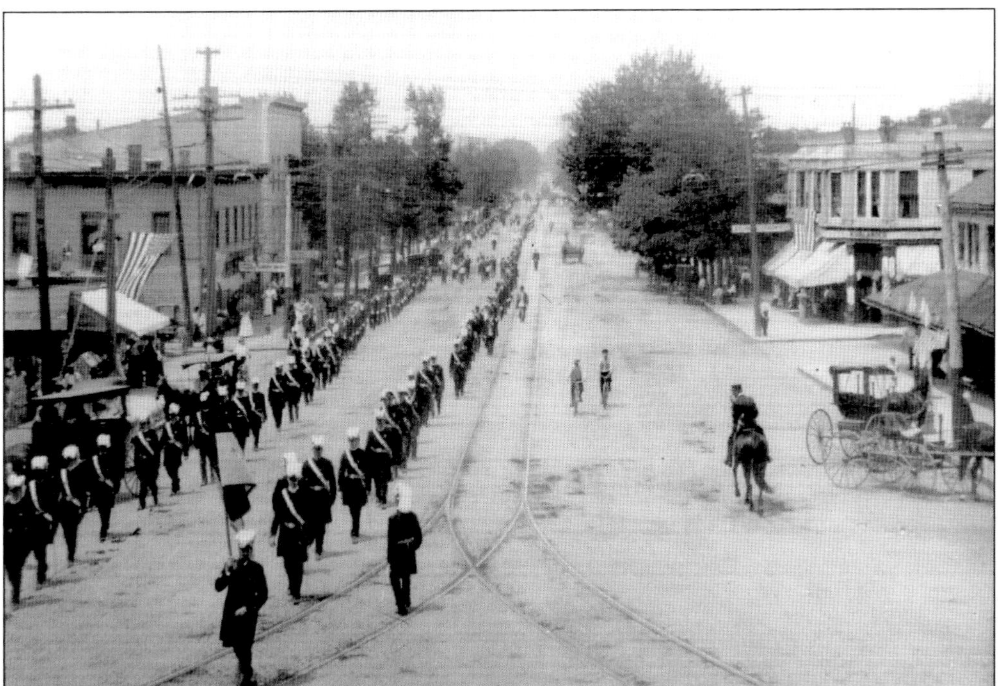

**MASONS' PARADE.** The 100th anniversary of the Masons in Mount Vernon was celebrated by this parade up West High Street in 1910. (Photograph courtesy of the Knox County Agricultural Museum.)

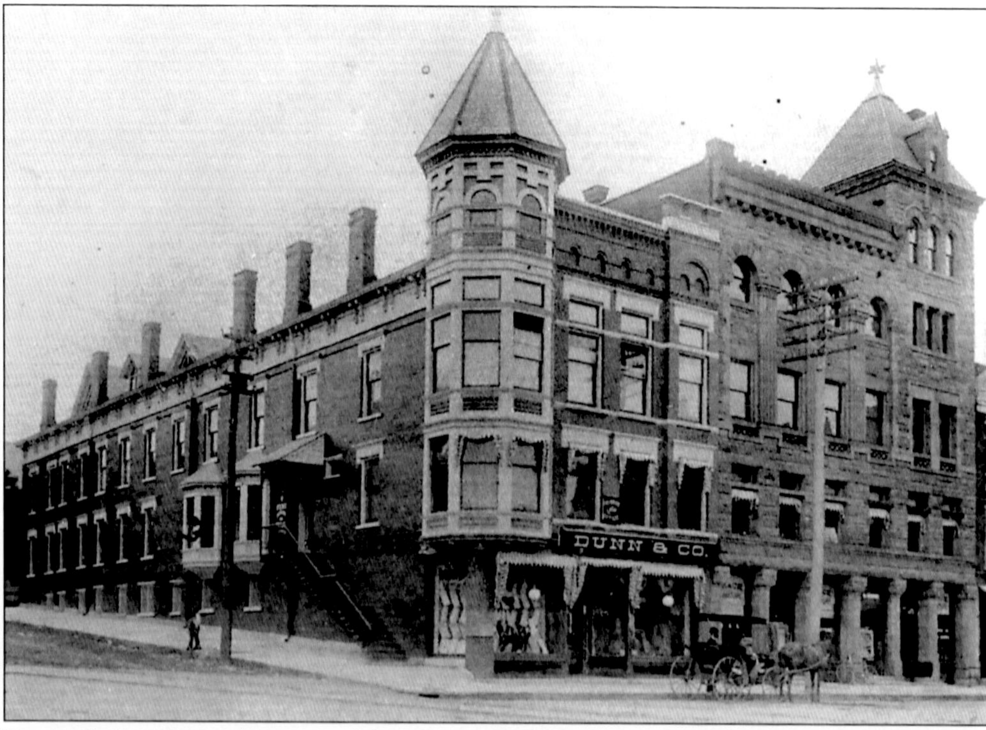


**Dunn & Co.** This earlier view of the Mason's Building shows Dunn & Co. occupying the first floor. The large stone columns along the ground floor were later removed. (Photograph courtesy of the Knox County Agricultural Museum.)

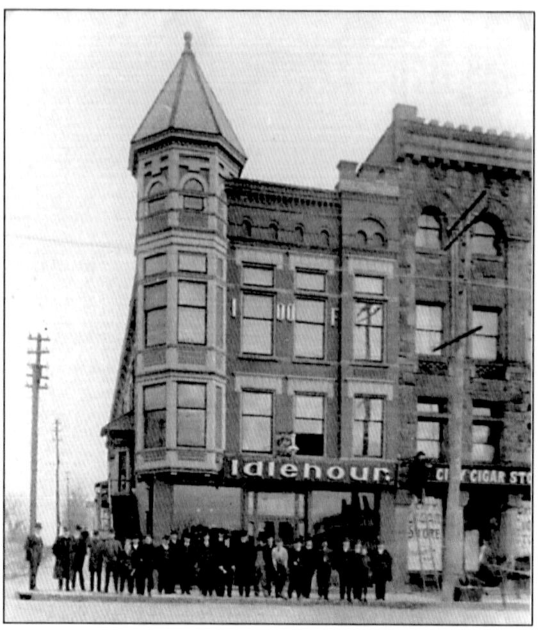


**Mason's Building.** This large stone building on the southeast corner of the Mount Vernon Square has housed numerous tenants on the first floor, but the Masons have met on the second floor for many years. (Photograph courtesy of the Knox County Agricultural Museum.)

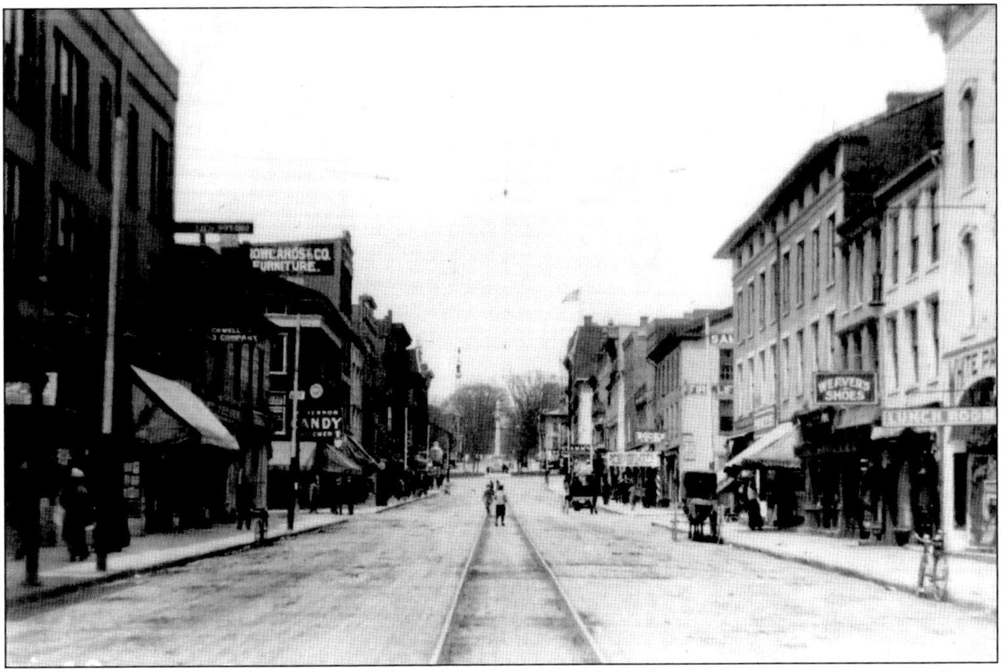


**GAMBIER AND MAIN.** The cable rails are in place, and children play in the street—a typical day in Mount Vernon. (Photograph courtesy of the Knox County Agricultural Museum.)

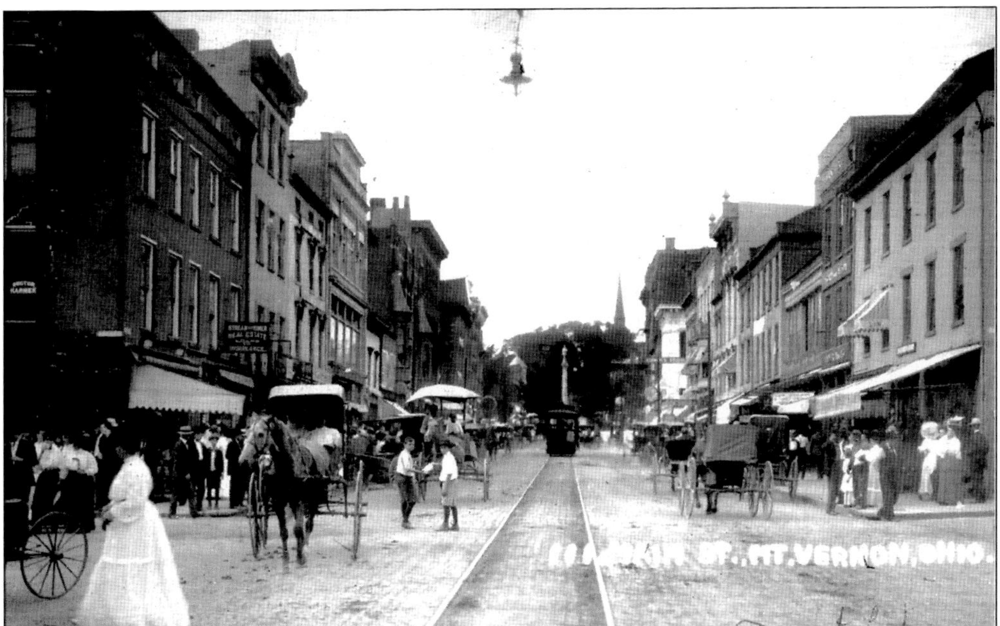


**HISTORIC CORNER.** South Main and Vine has seen numerous events. A gaslight can be seen hanging over the center of the photograph. (Photograph courtesy of the Knox County Agricultural Museum.)

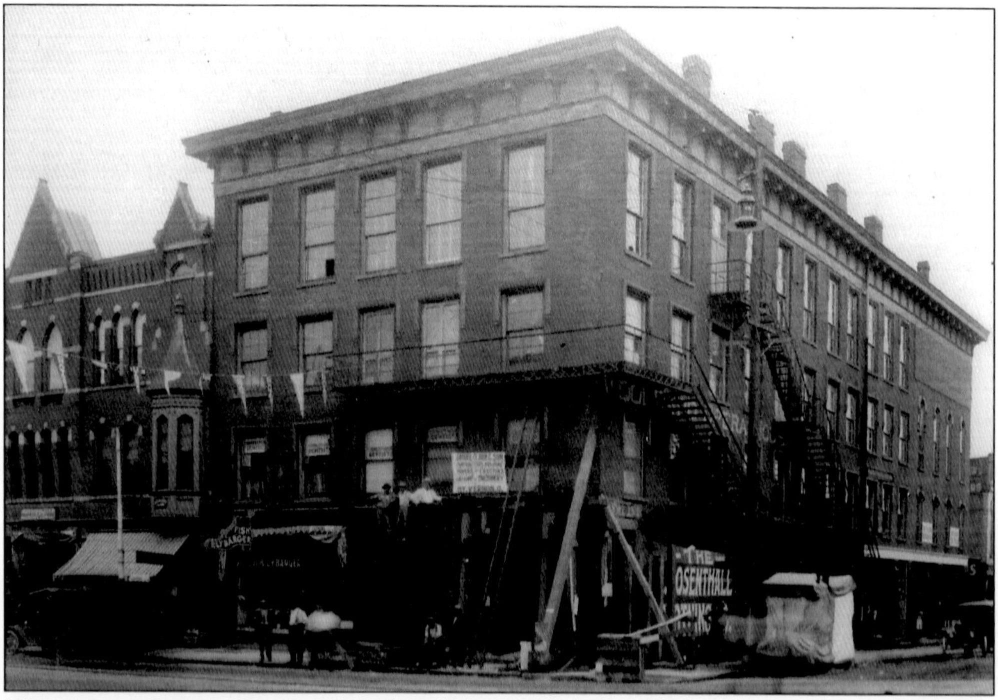

**WOODWARD OPERA HOUSE.** Now the oldest, "authentic 19th-century theater" in America, as researched by the Woodward Development Corporation, the Woodward Opera House dates from 1850. It hosted Victoria Woodhull, formerly of Homer, Ohio (10 miles south of Mount Vernon), who was the first female candidate for president of the United States. She spoke there on November 19, 1872. (Photograph courtesy of the Knox County Agricultural Museum.)

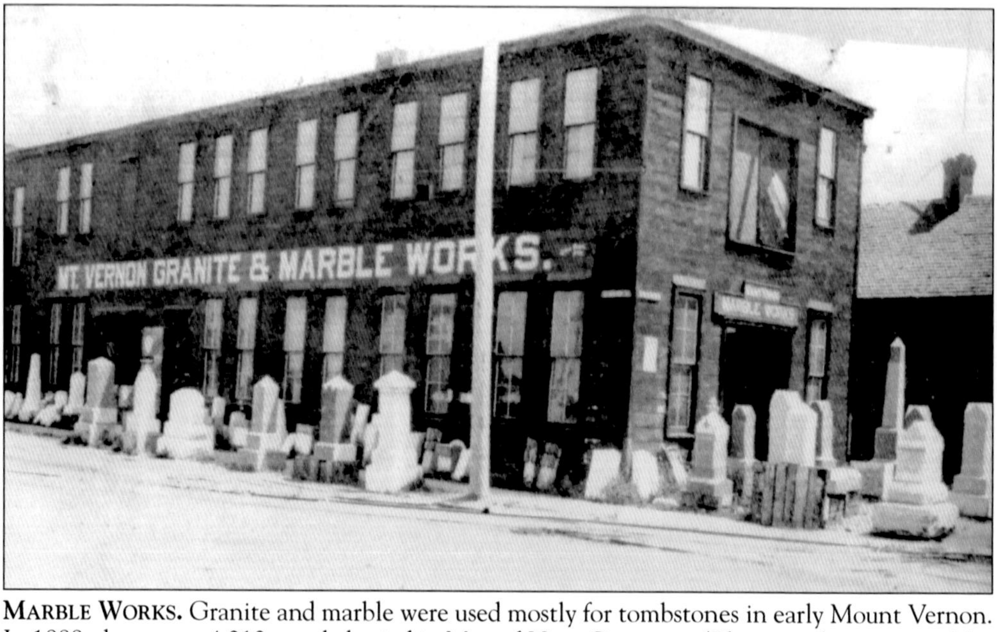


**MARBLE WORKS.** Granite and marble were used mostly for tombstones in early Mount Vernon. In 1888, there were 4,010 people buried in Mound View Cemetery. (Photograph courtesy of the Knox County Agricultural Museum.)

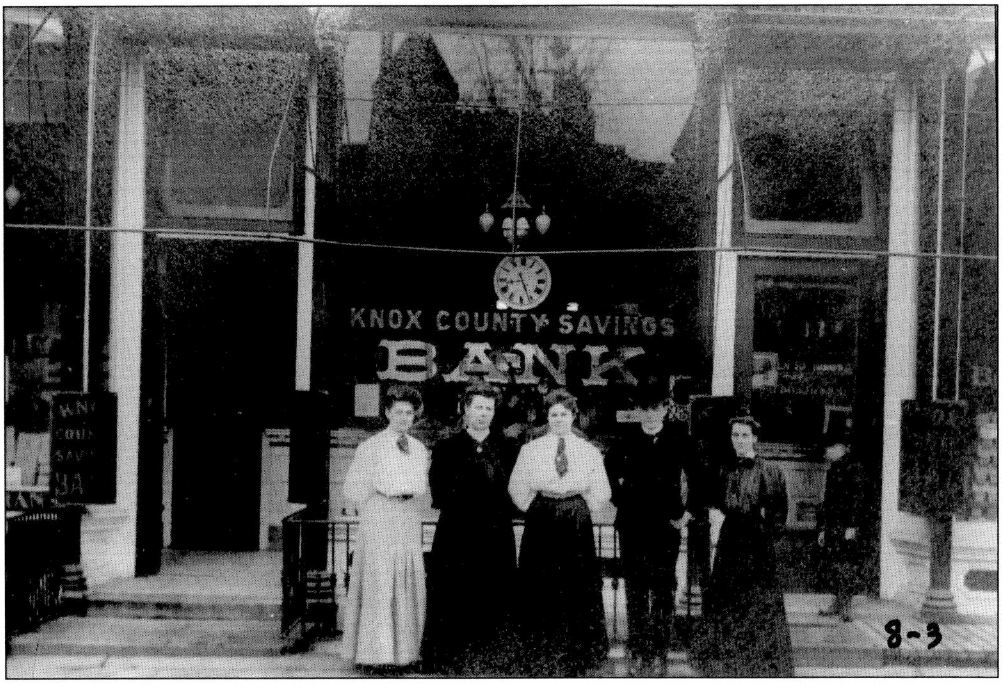


THE KNOX COUNTY SAVINGS BANK. The Knox County Savings Bank has had several locations in Mount Vernon and Knox County over the years. (Photograph courtesy of the Knox County Agricultural Museum.)

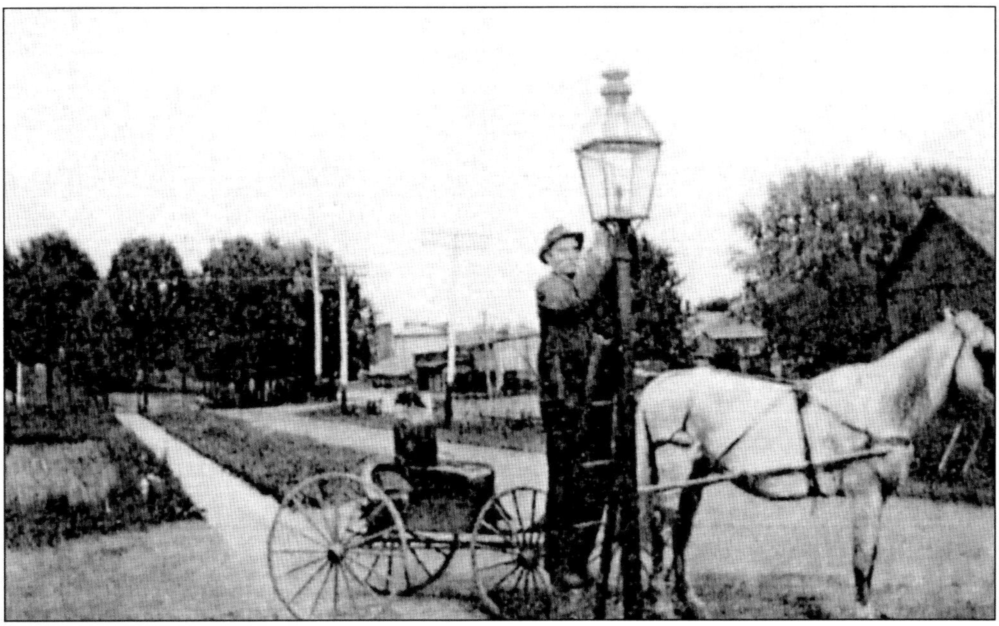

THE OLD LAMPLIGHTER. This photograph was taken in Fredericktown around the turn of the century. Tom Burke would sometimes haul neighborhood children on his rounds. His brother was an internationally known clown, and his daughter was Billie Burke, the famous comedienne. (Photograph courtesy of the Fredericktown Historical Society.)

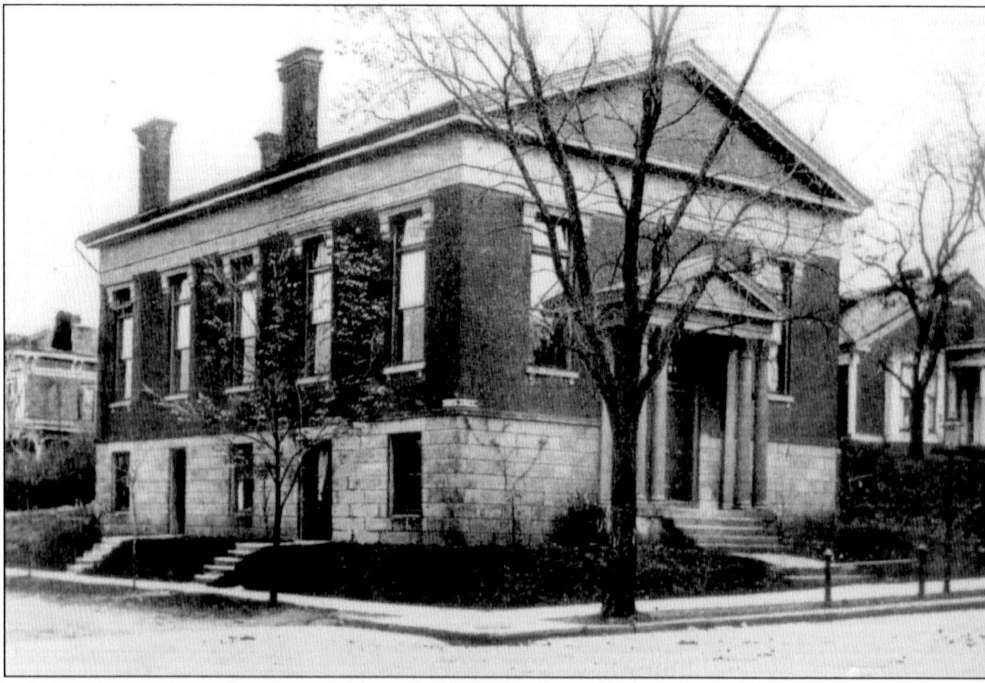

**AN EARLY LIBRARY.** Mount Vernon's first library was organized in 1816 with Hosmer Curtis as librarian. This building is a later incarnation. (Photograph courtesy of the Knox County Agricultural Museum.)

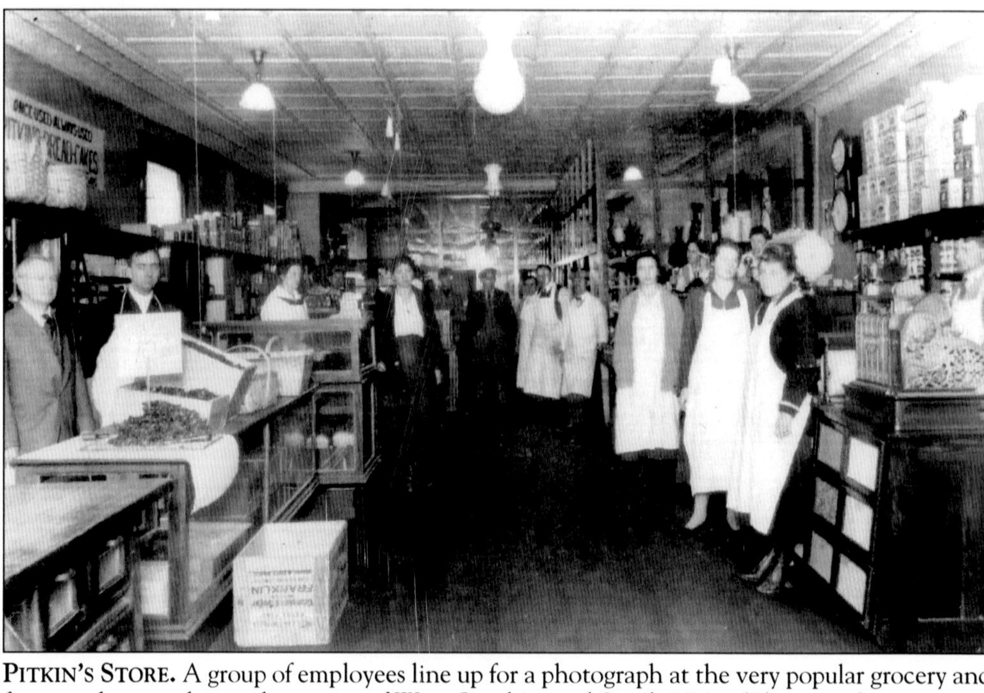

**PITKIN'S STORE.** A group of employees line up for a photograph at the very popular grocery and farm-produce market at the corner of West Gambier and South Main. (Photograph courtesy of the Knox County Agricultural Museum.)

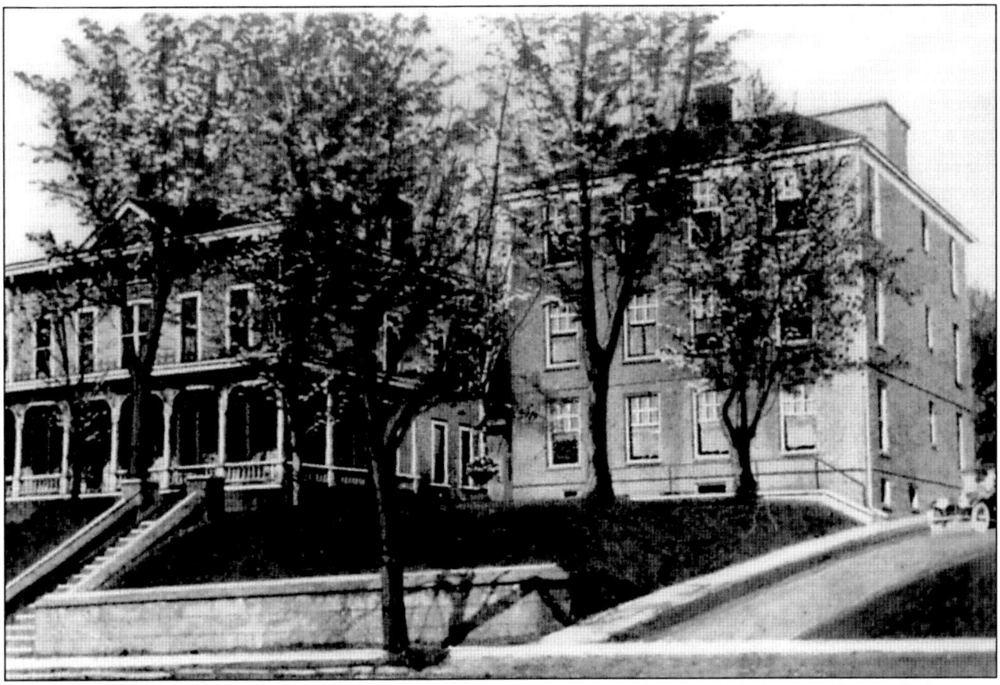

SANITARIUM IN MOUNT VERNON. The Mount Vernon Developmental Center formerly known as the State Sanitarium is located on beautiful grounds just east of Mount Vernon and north of Route 36. This photograph shows early buildings, probably *c.* 1920s. (Photograph courtesy of the Knox County Agricultural Museum.)

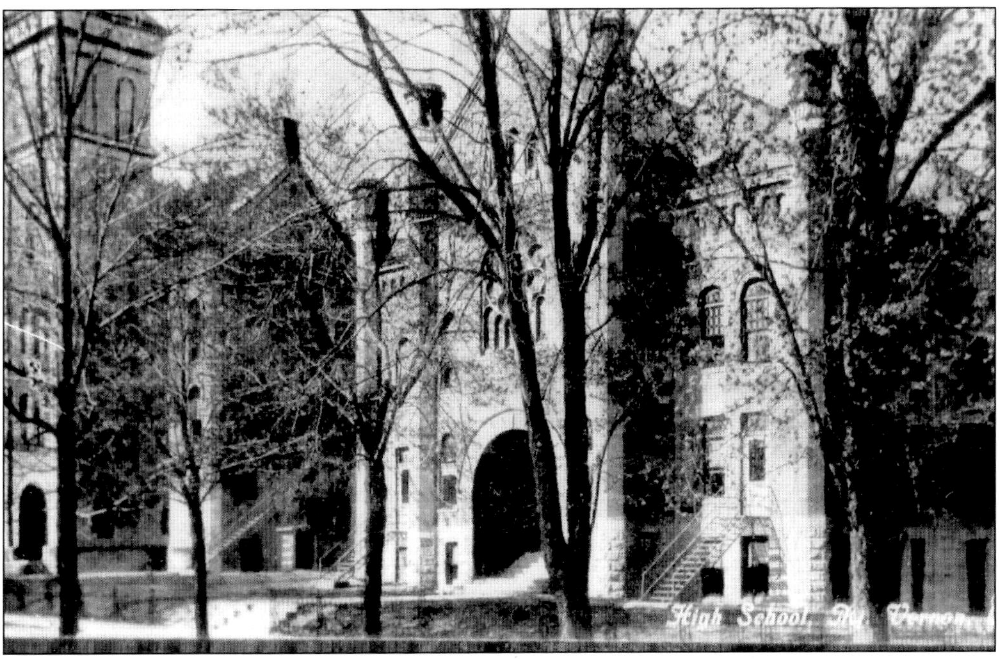


THE HIGH SCHOOL. This castle-like home for the Mount Vernon High School was used as such in the early 20th century. (Photograph courtesy of the Knox County Agricultural Museum.)

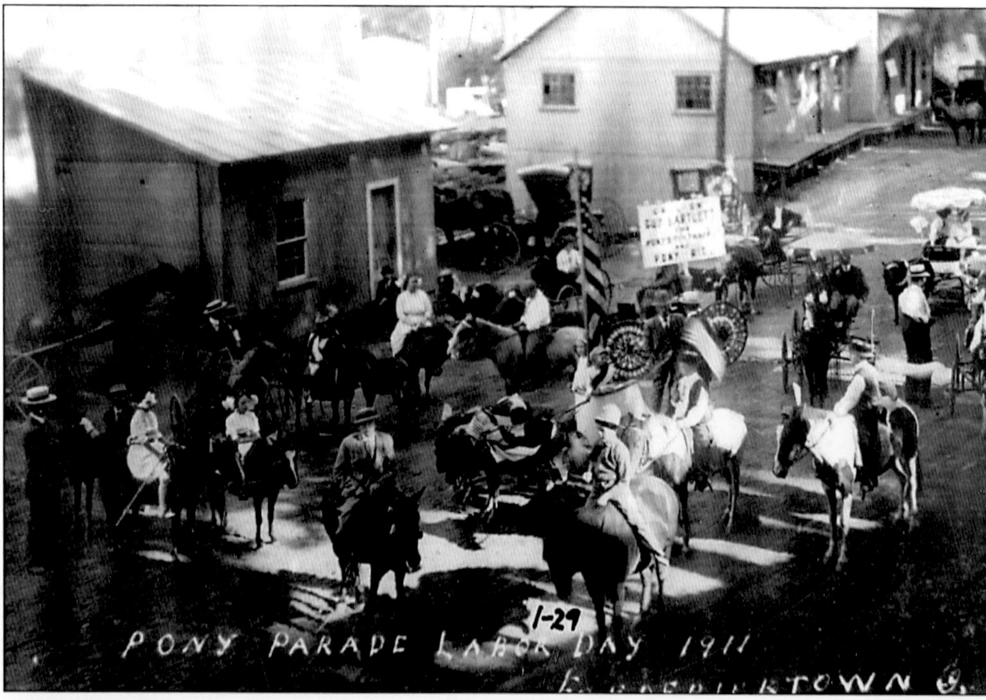


**LABOR DAY FUN.** Fredericktown has had an annual fall celebration for many years. These ponies paraded in 1911. The celebration later became the Tomato Show. (Photograph courtesy of the Fredericktown Historical Society.)

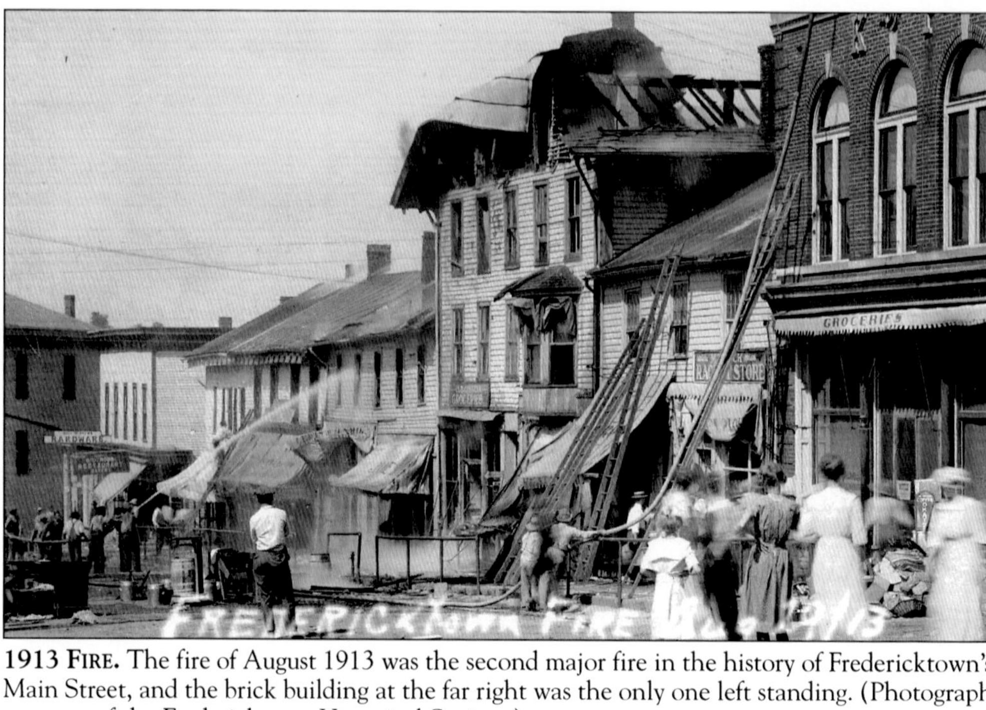


**1913 FIRE.** The fire of August 1913 was the second major fire in the history of Fredericktown's Main Street, and the brick building at the far right was the only one left standing. (Photograph courtesy of the Fredericktown Historical Society.)

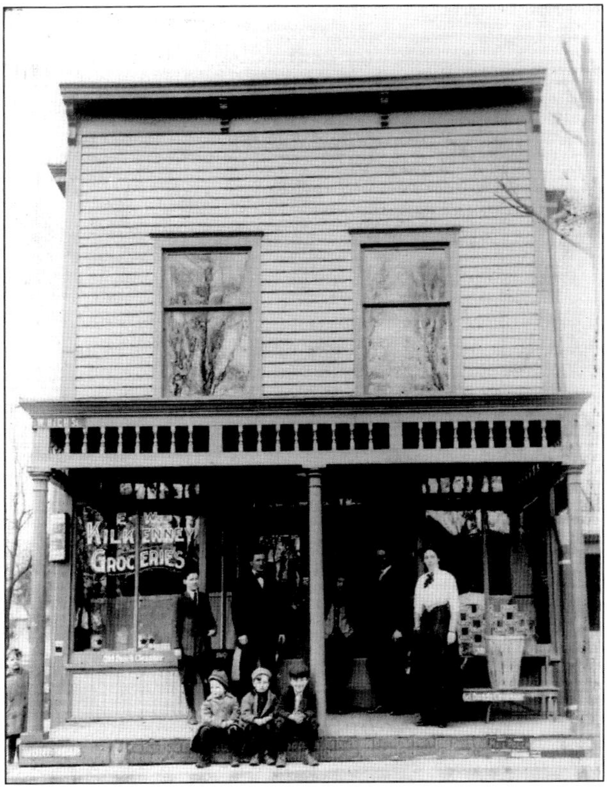


**KILKENNEY GROCERIES.** A neat and prosperous grocery store from Mount Vernon in the early part of the 1900s was Kilkenney Groceries. WMVO, formed in 1951, featured Charlie Kilkenney as a popular host. Helen Zelkowitz was one of the founders of the radio station and still works supporting preservation and other causes in Mount Vernon. (Photograph courtesy of the Knox County Agricultural Museum.)

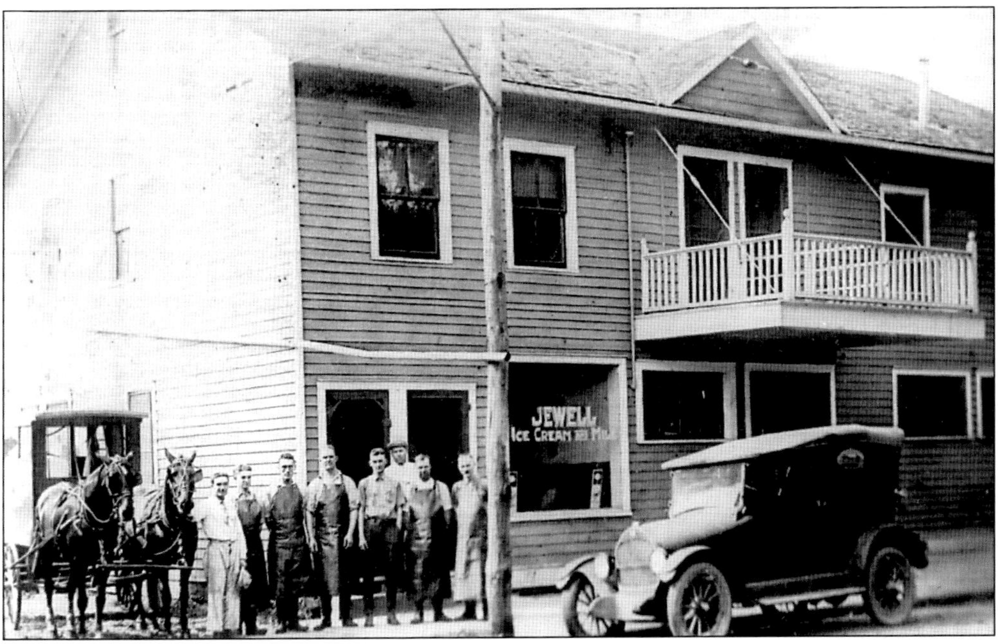


**A TRANSITION PHOTOGRAPH.** This was probably taken a few years after the Jewell Ice Cream and Milk Company began operation in Mount Vernon in 1912. The horse-powered delivery wagon would soon give way to trucks. (Photograph courtesy of the Knox County Agricultural Museum.)

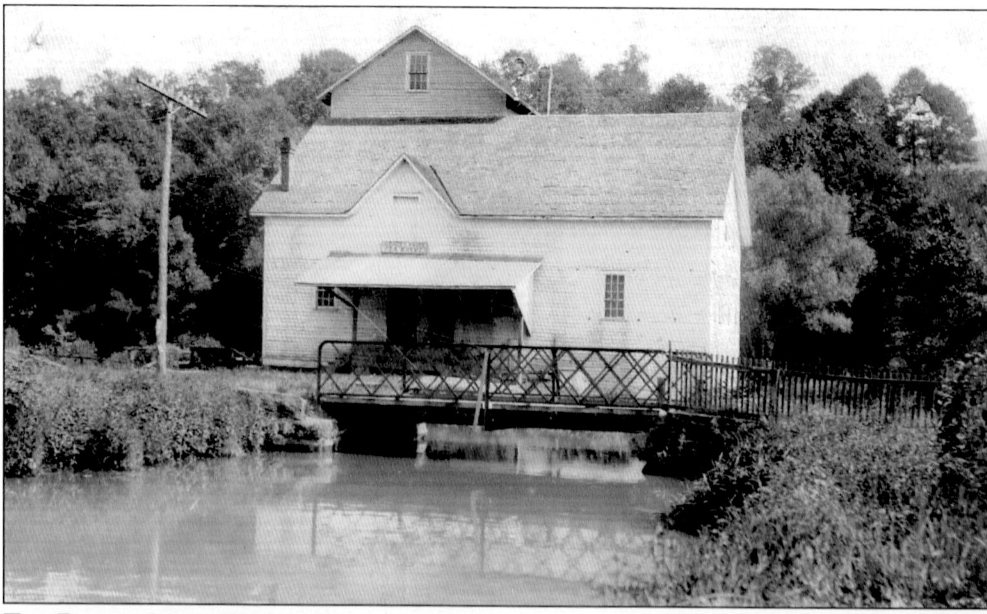

**THE BUTLER MILL.** "Highest Price for Wheat" reads the sign above the entrance to this well-maintained mill in Butler, just north of the Knox County border and northeast of Ankenytown. (Photograph courtesy of the Knox County Agricultural Museum.)

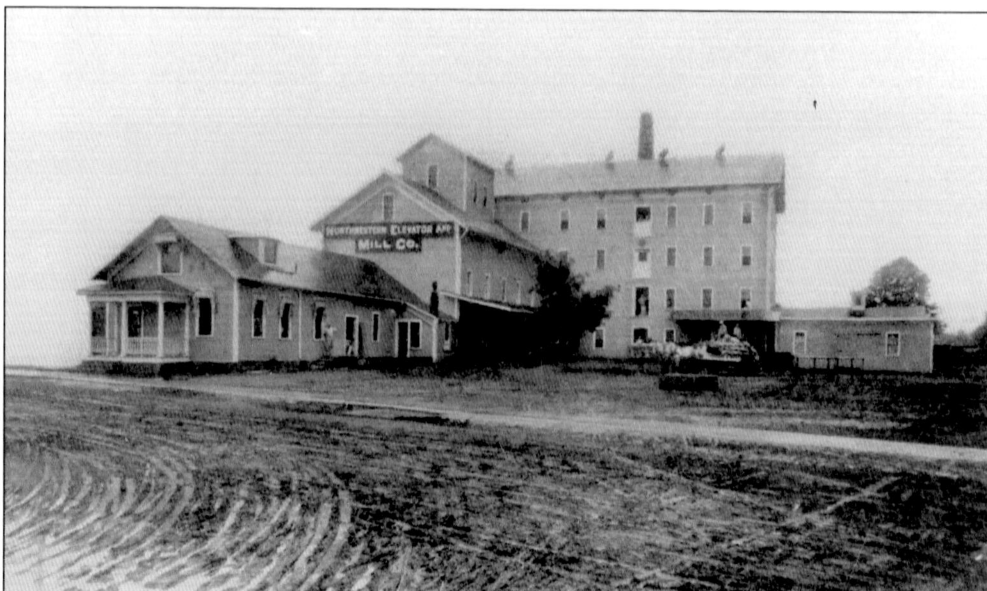

**NORTHWESTERN ELEVATOR AND MILL COMPANY.** This mill lasted from c. mid-1800s until the 1950s. Farmers brought in their wheat and received large sacks of white flour in return. (Photograph courtesy of Richard A. Cochran.)

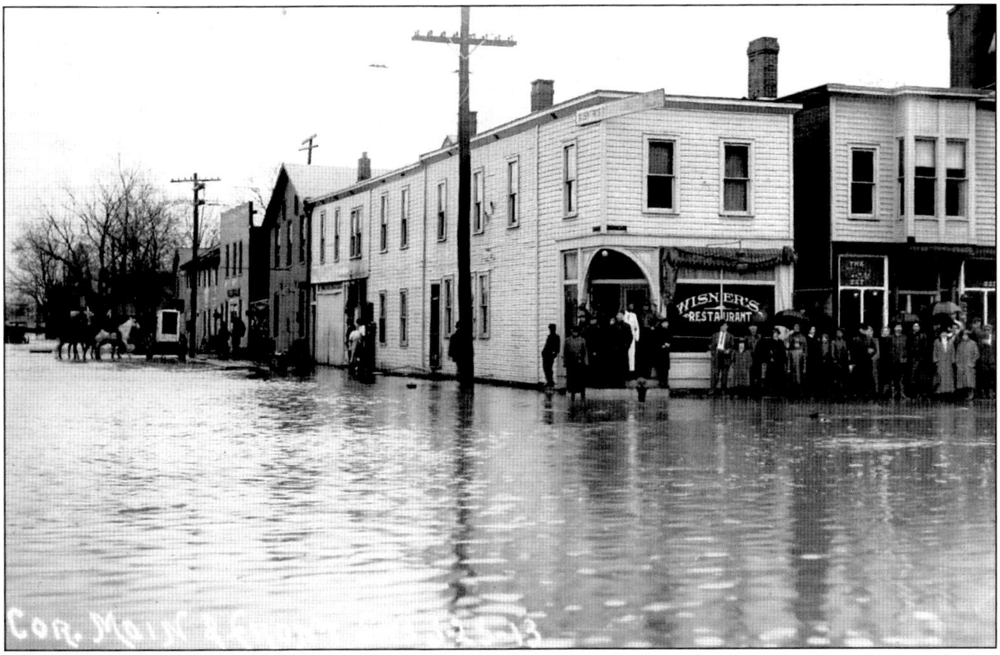


**WISNER'S RESTAURANT.** This building, on the corner of Front and Main Streets in Mount Vernon, is shown during the flood of March 25, 1913. Local historians believe that Front Street was later re-named Ohio Avenue. (Photograph courtesy of John and Vivian Lahmon.)

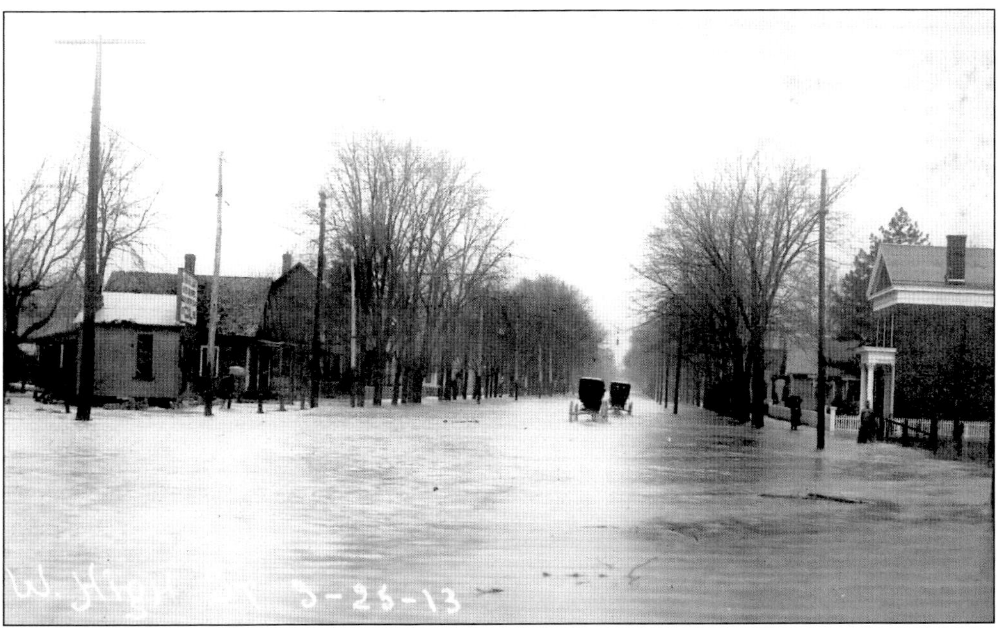

**WEST HIGH STREET IN THE 1913 FLOOD.** This photograph was taken looking west from a spot close to the present B&O railroad crossing. The brick building on the right is now the Mount Vernon Inn at 601 West High Street. (Photograph courtesy of John and Vivian Lahmon.)

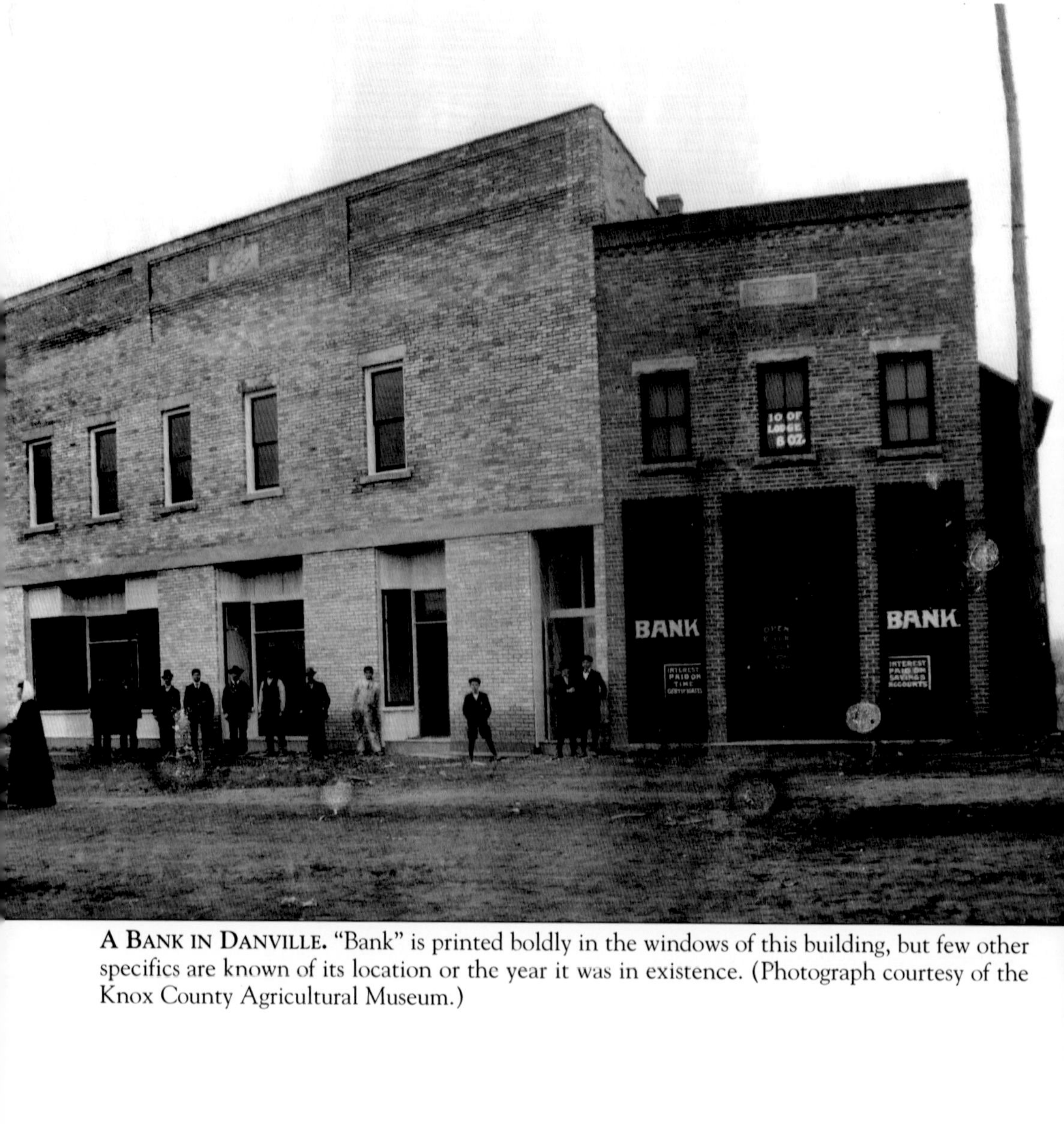


**A Bank in Danville.** "Bank" is printed boldly in the windows of this building, but few other specifics are known of its location or the year it was in existence. (Photograph courtesy of the Knox County Agricultural Museum.)

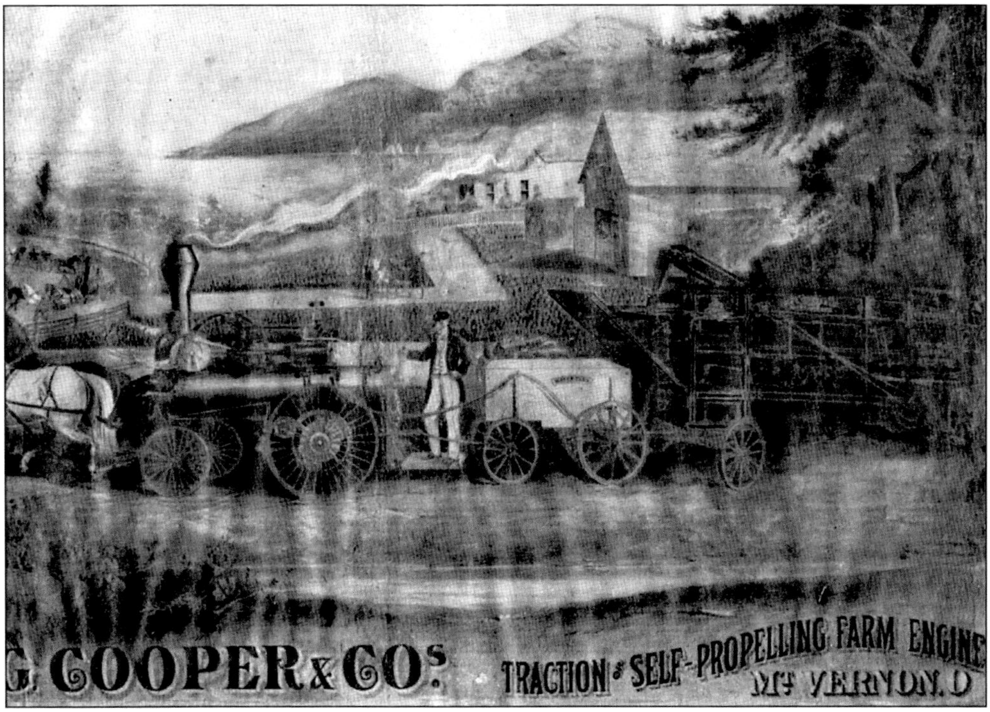


**THE FIRST TRACTOR?** A newspaper proclaims "G. Cooper & Co." as the manufacturers of the first "traction & self-propelling farm engine." Before that, engines were mounted on a wagon pulled by horses. (Photograph courtesy of the Knox County Agricultural Museum.)

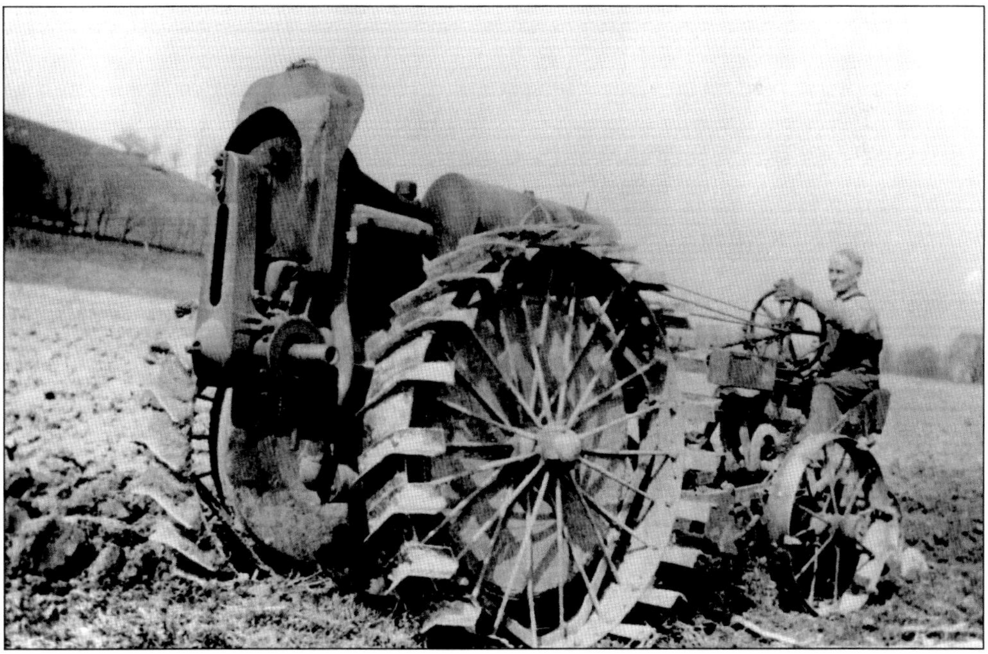

**LATER VERSION.** This huge tractor is much later than Cooper's. It is most likely an early 20th century Minneapolis Moline. (Photograph courtesy of the Knox County Agricultural Museum.)

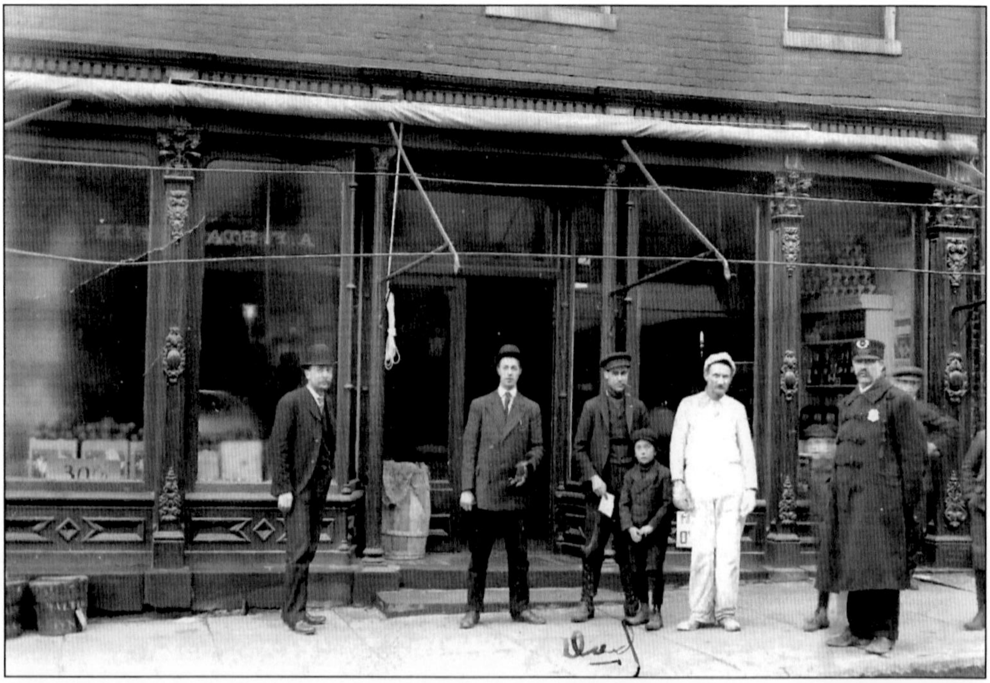

**EMPLOYEES OUTSIDE BARBER AND COMPANY.** Employees assemble for a photograph outside their store on the west side of North Main Street (opposite Stauffer's) next to the Mount Vernon Public Square, *c.* 1912. (Photograph courtesy of John and Vivian Lahmon.)

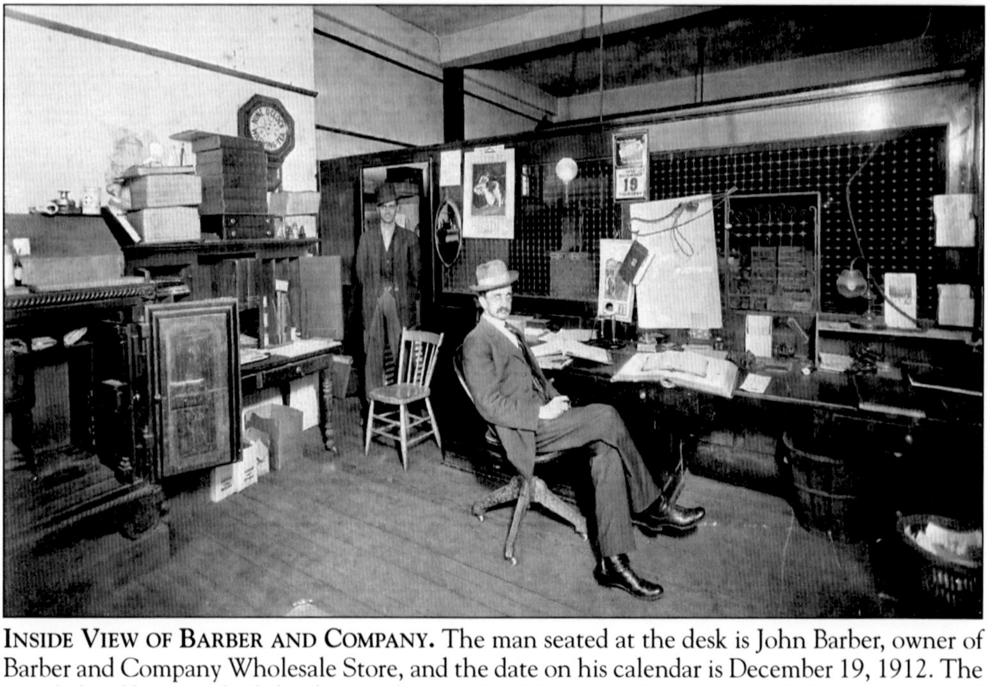

**INSIDE VIEW OF BARBER AND COMPANY.** The man seated at the desk is John Barber, owner of Barber and Company Wholesale Store, and the date on his calendar is December 19, 1912. The man behind him on the left is his employee, Friend Benjamin Jones, Vivian Lahmon's maternal grandfather. (Photograph courtesy of John and Vivian Lahmon.)

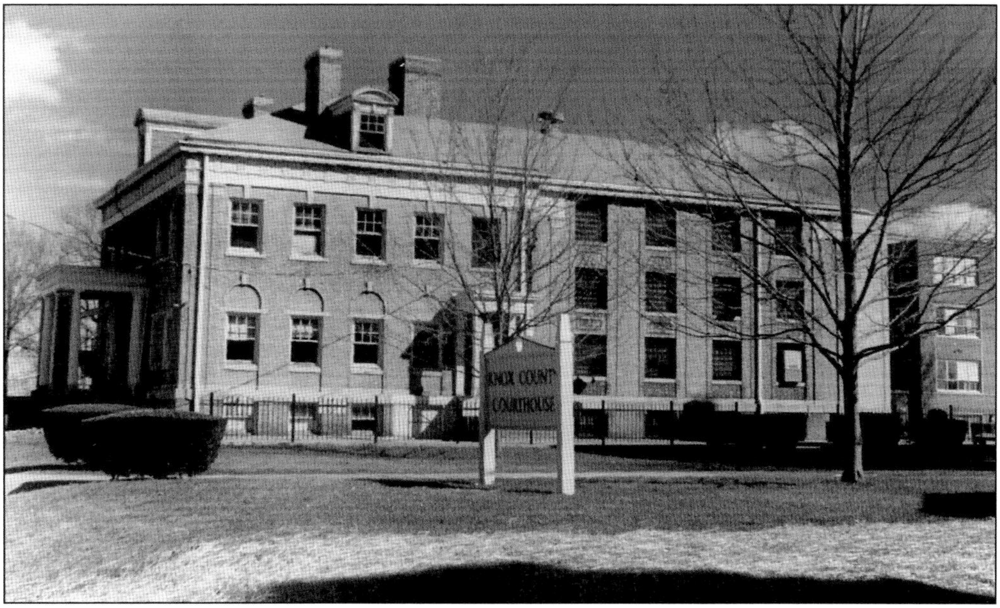

**1913 JAIL IN 2004.** This is the white brick Knox County jail built in 1913 where Paul Lynde lived with his family in the 1930s. Paul Newman spent a night here while he was a Kenyon student. (Photograph by D.E. Boyd.)

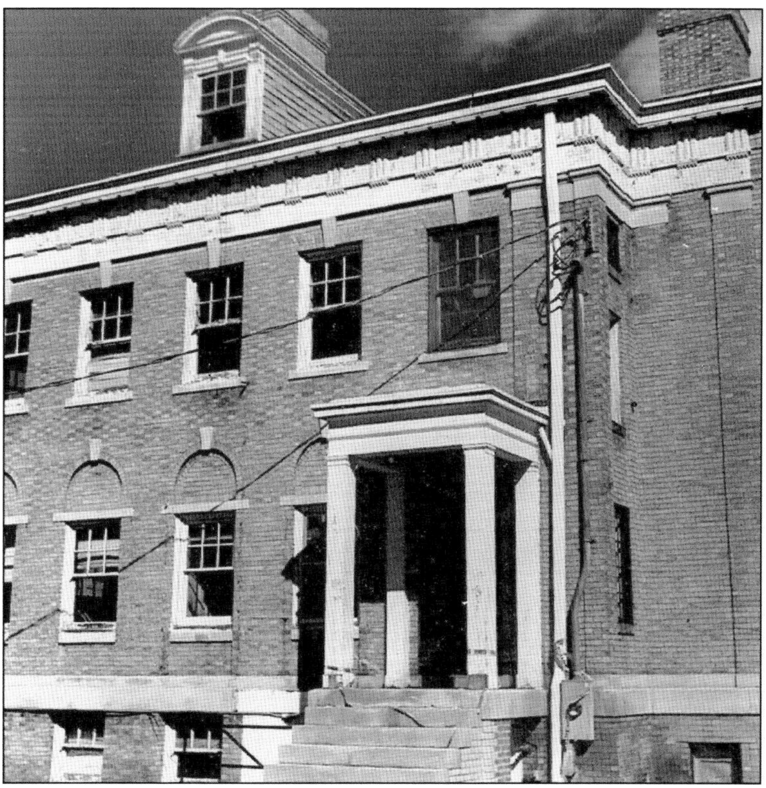

**PAUL LYNDE, COMEDIAN.** Paul's father, Hoy, served as Knox County Sheriff from 1929 to 1933. It is said Paul felt badly about living in the jail and would take various routes home from school to keep his friends from knowing. Paul starred in numerous films and on Hollywood Squares, c. 1960s–70s. (Photograph by D.E. Boyd.)

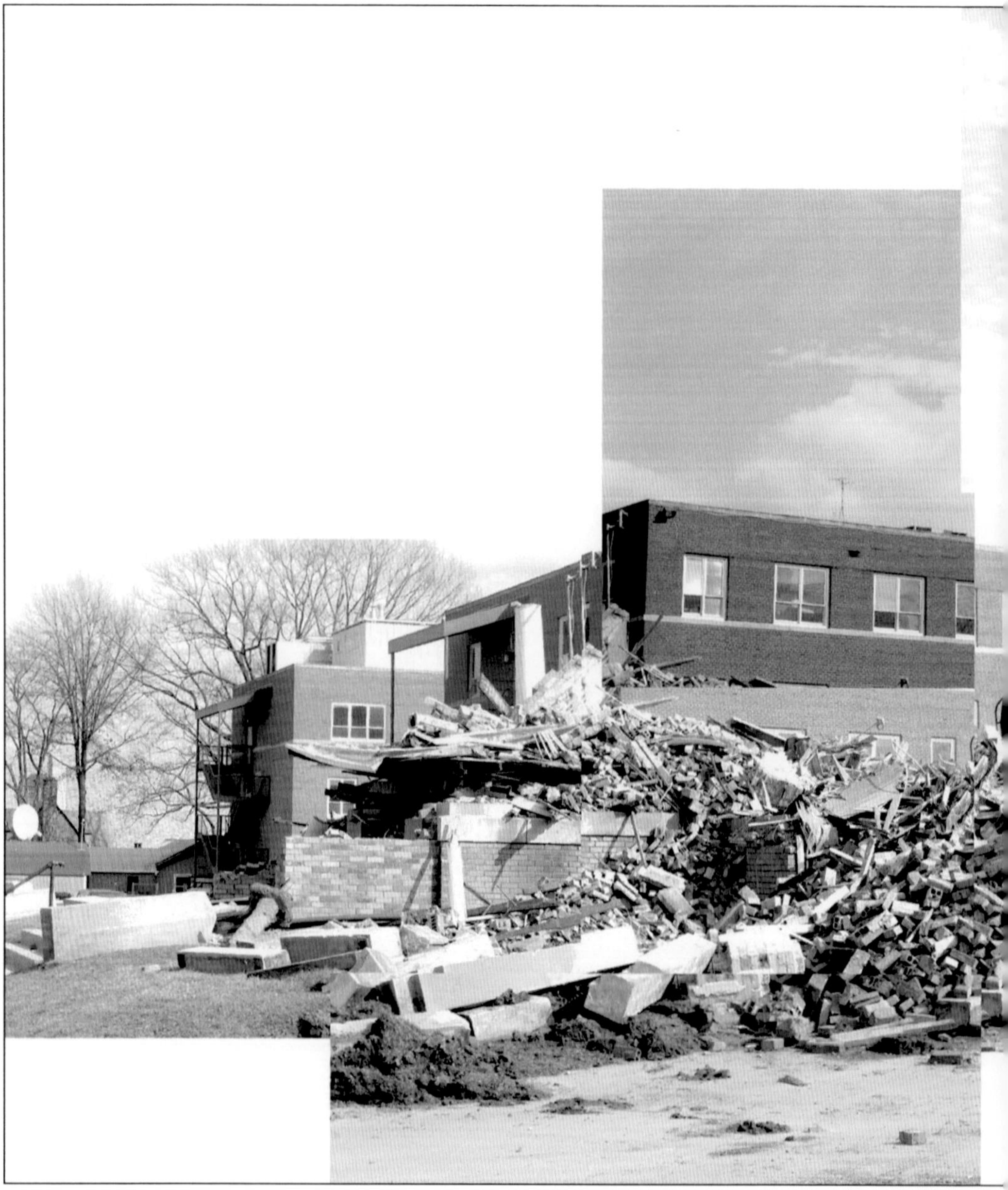

**1913 Jail After Demolition.** In this dramatic photographic collage by Crispin Webb in 2004, we see the destruction of a county landmark. The Knox County Renaissance Foundation, Inc., tried to preserve the building, but the majority of the Knox County Commissioners felt

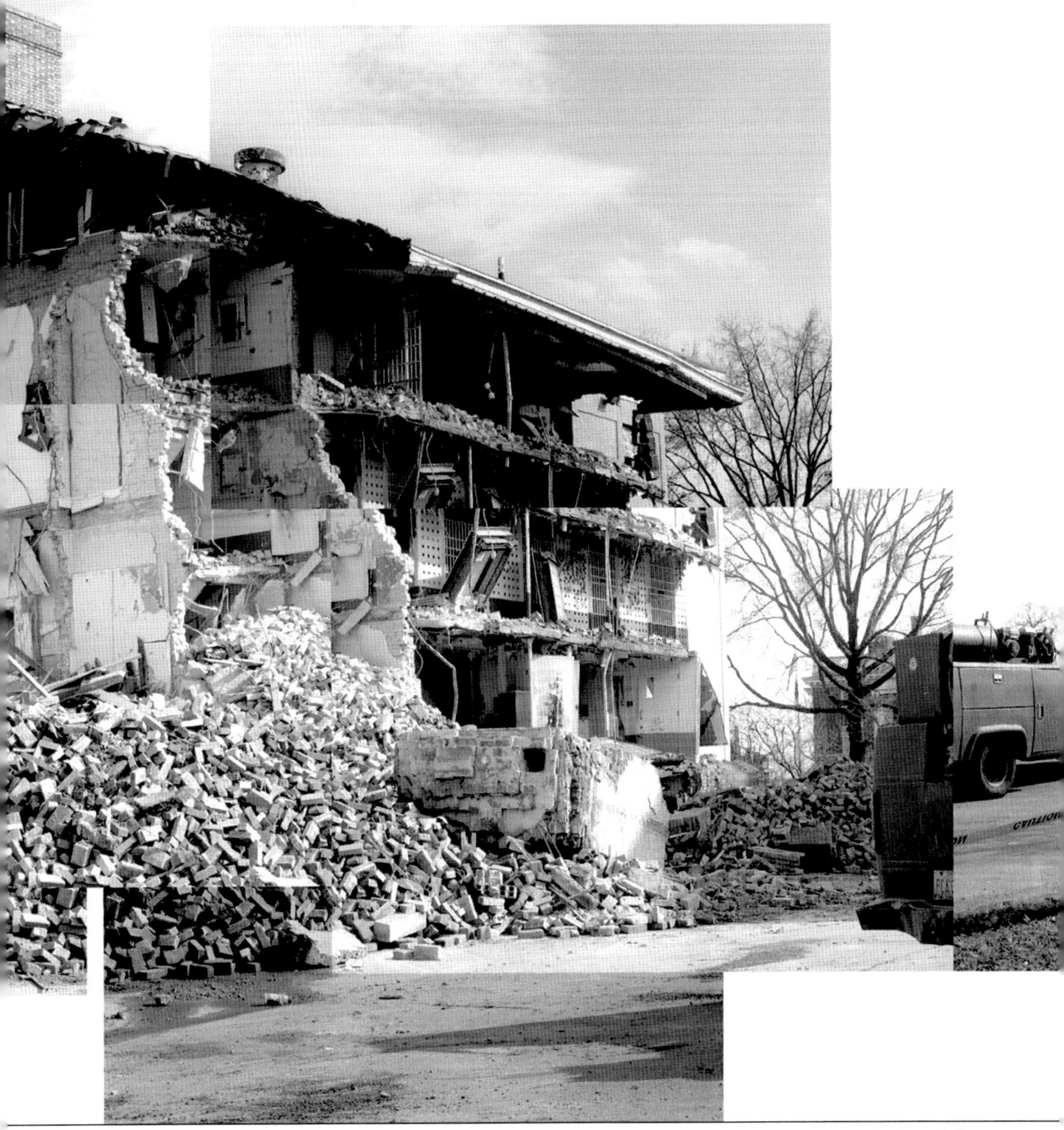

the building should be razed to make parking spaces between the Court House and the old Mercy Hospital Building on East High Street in Mount Vernon.

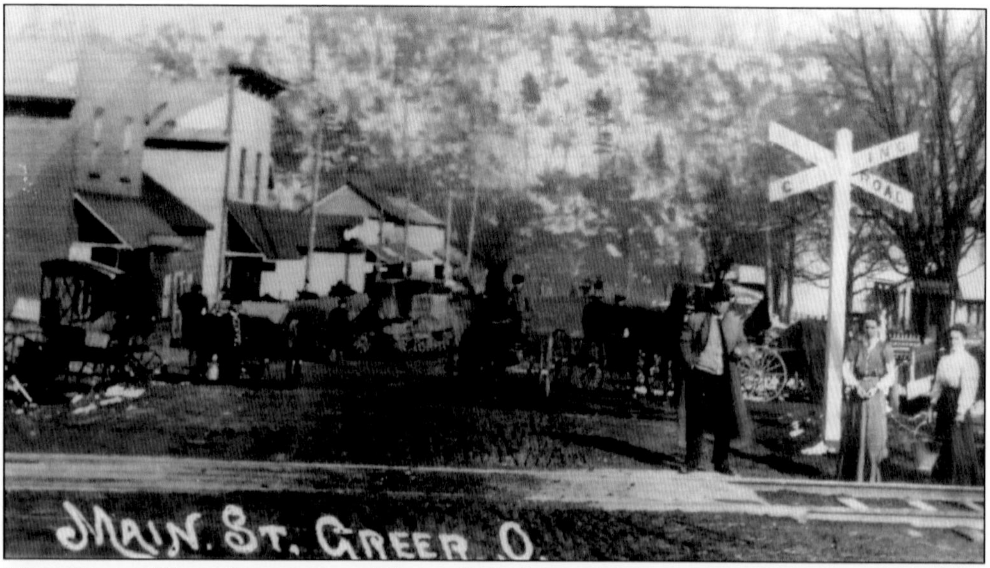


**MAIN STREET VIEW, GREER, OHIO.** This *c.* 1900s photograph from Greer illustrates a lively scene in one of Knox County's most northeastern communities. Known to the state as Greer, locally it is called Brinkhaven. The town has undergone several name changes. (Photograph courtesy of the Knox County Agricultural Museum.)

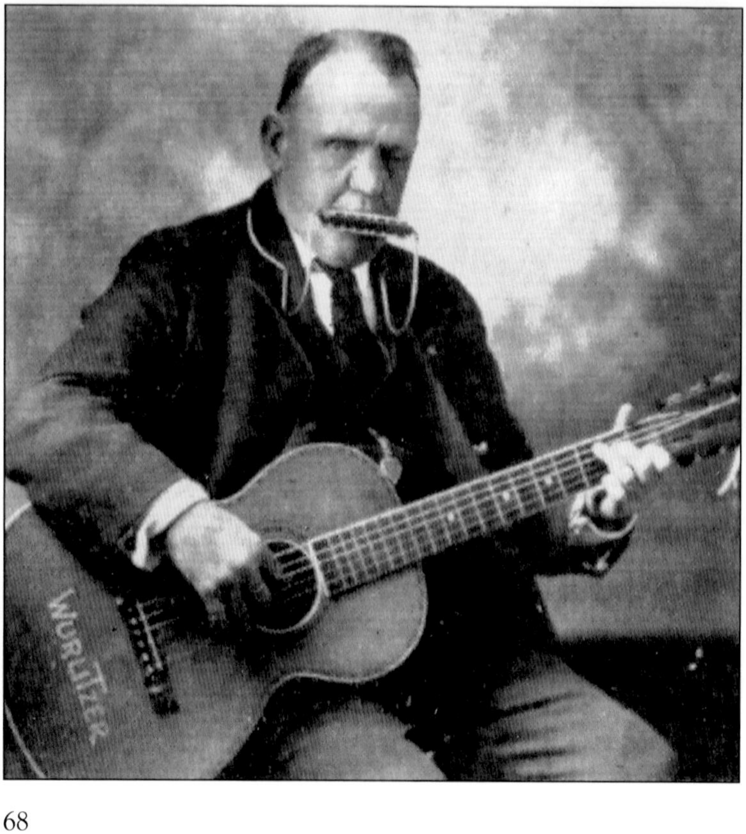


**MULTI-TALENTED.** William K. Wythe of 108 North Main Street in Mount Vernon was a popular musician of the early 20th century. (Photograph courtesy of Jeff Boucher of Flappers Bar & Grille.)

*Four*

# TRANSPORTATION

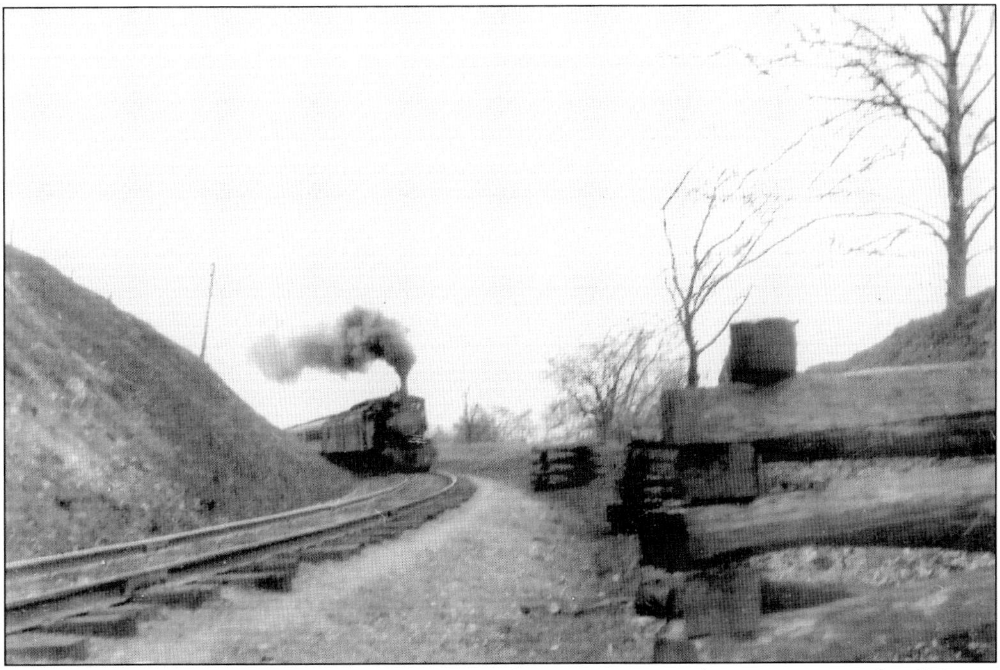

**AN OLD TRAIN.** This very old train photograph shows a train rounding a curve outside of Mount Vernon. Two major railroads served the city in their heyday, one traveling east to west and one from north to south. (Photograph courtesy of the Knox County Agricultural Museum.)

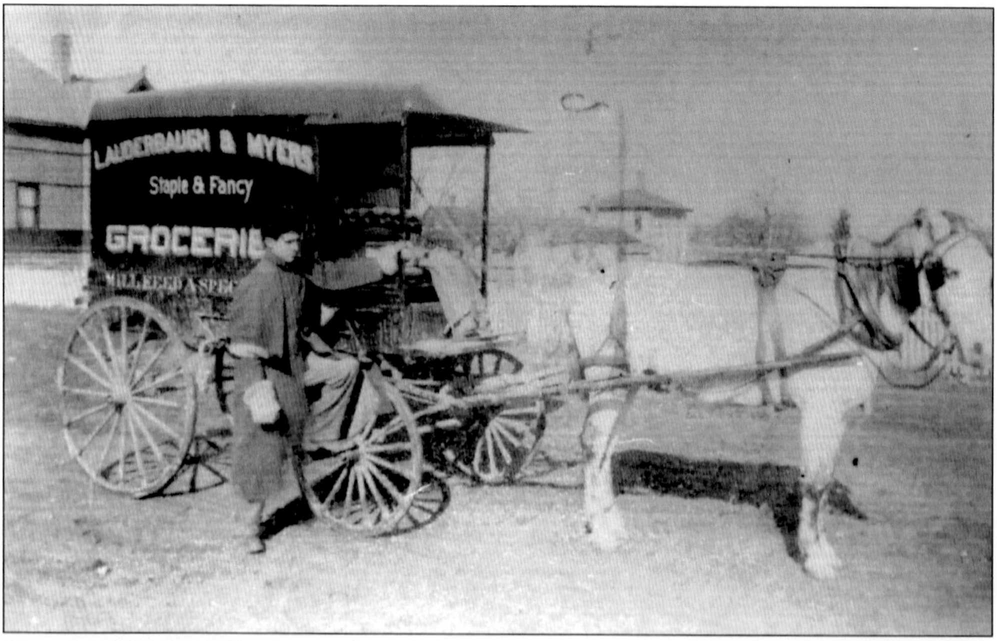


GROCERY WAGON. The wagon driver is wearing a dust coat and gloves as he poses for this photograph, c. 1890. (Photograph courtesy of the Knox County Agricultural Museum.)

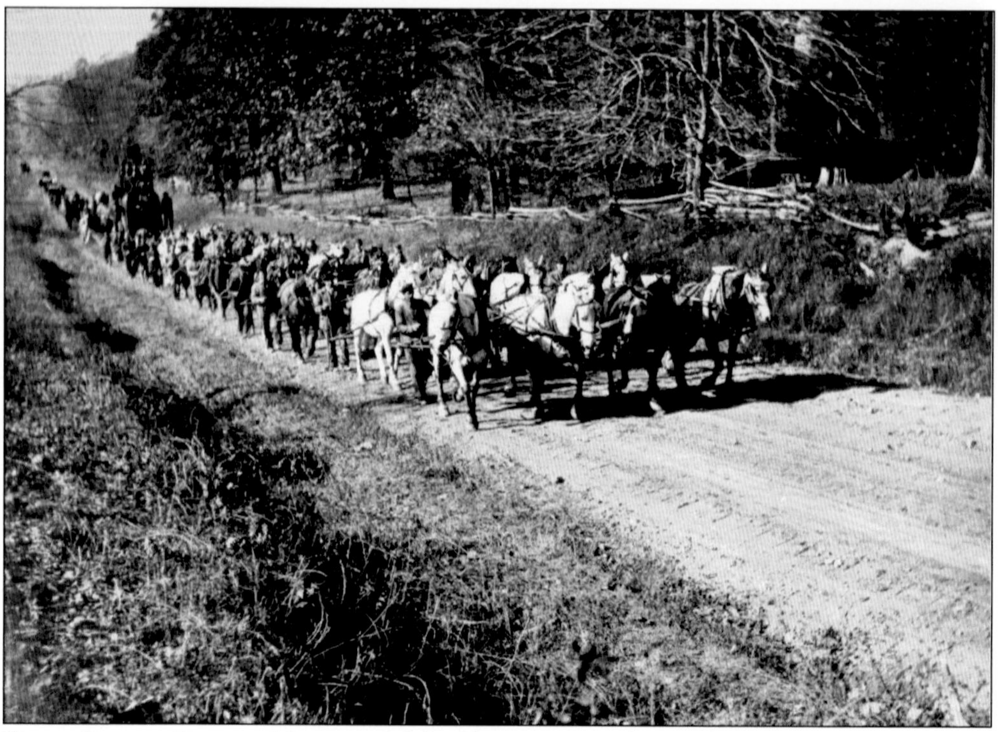

HORSE POWER. Coopers deliver one of their large engines along a dusty road in Knox County, c. 1920. (Photograph courtesy of the Knox County Agricultural Museum.)

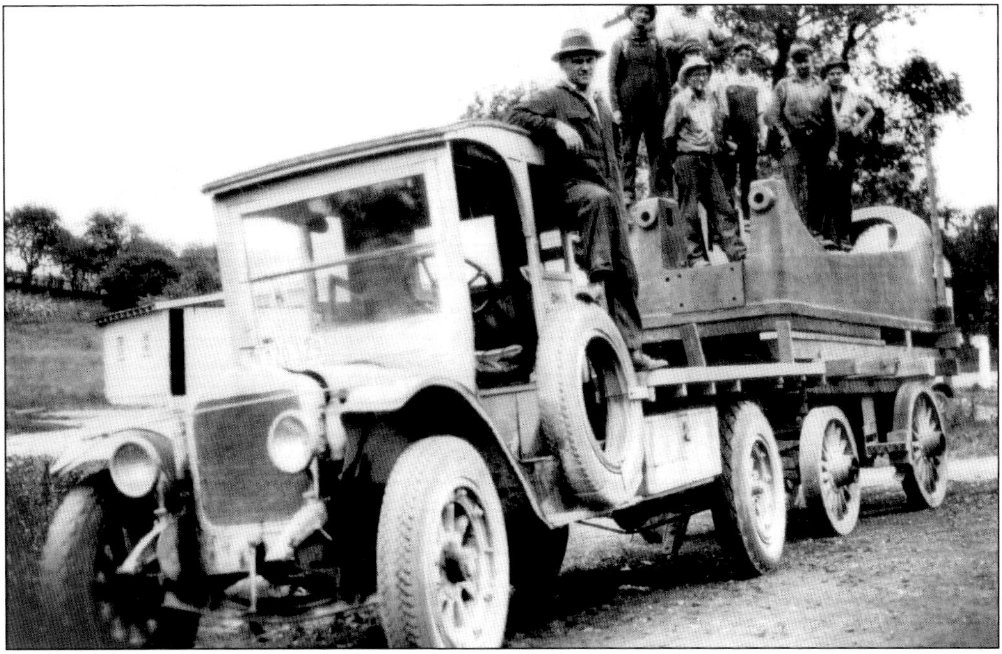

**BIG TRUCK.** This photograph shows the difference in the method of delivering a Cooper engine after big trucks were developed. (Photograph courtesy of the Knox County Agricultural Museum.)

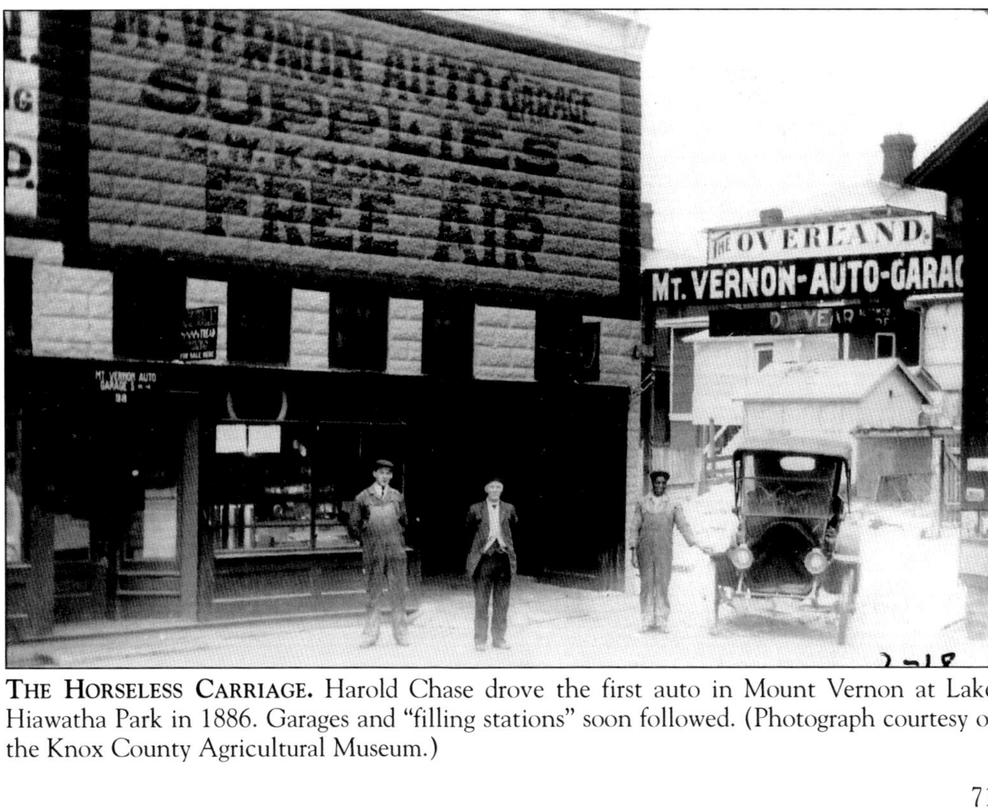


**THE HORSELESS CARRIAGE.** Harold Chase drove the first auto in Mount Vernon at Lake Hiawatha Park in 1886. Garages and "filling stations" soon followed. (Photograph courtesy of the Knox County Agricultural Museum.)

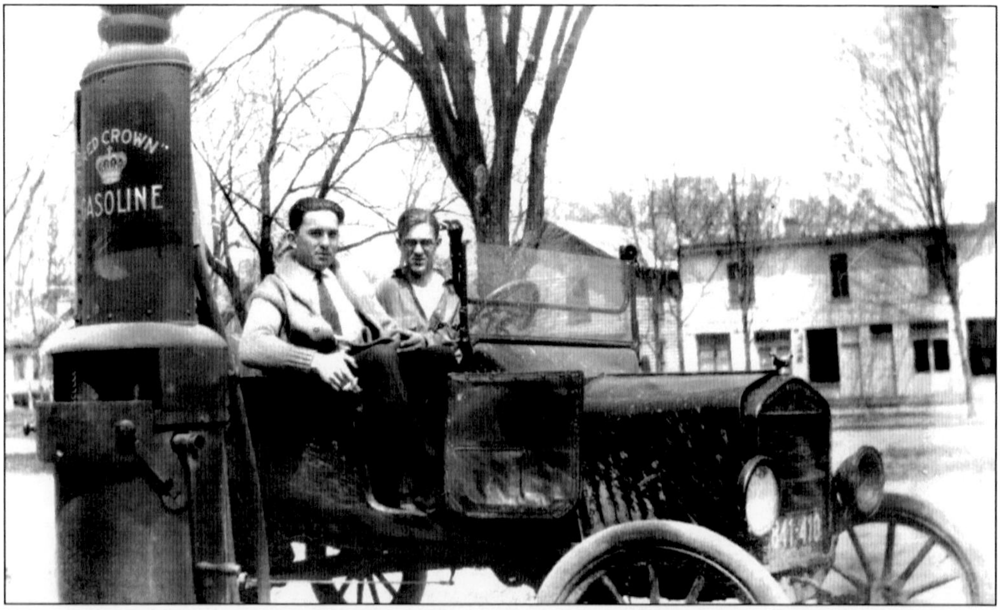

**CHEAP GAS?** It's hard to guess how much gas cost on Gaskin Avenue in Gambier when Robert Decan, left, and John Dangler, right, were photographed. Both were members of the Class of 1924–25 of Kenyon College, Gambier, Ohio. (Photograph courtesy of the Olin Library, Kenyon College, Greenslade Special Collections and Archives.)

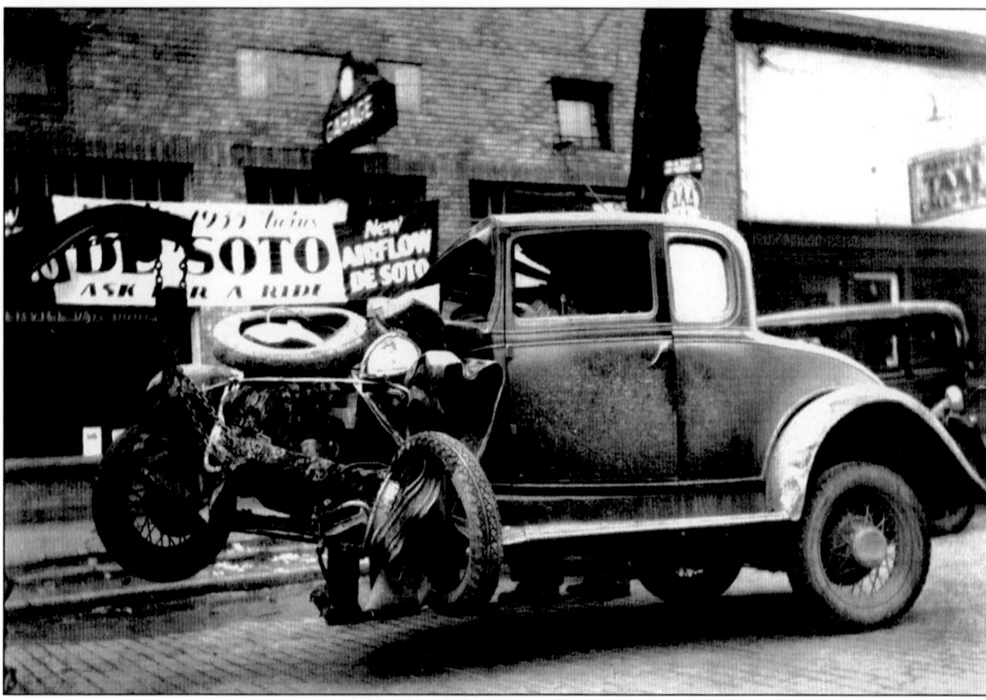


**AN EARLY AUTO ACCIDENT.** Mount Vernon has its share of "fender benders," and as the population increases, more are sure to happen. This accident occurred in the 1930s. (Photograph courtesy of Jeff Boucher of Flapper's Bar & Grill.)

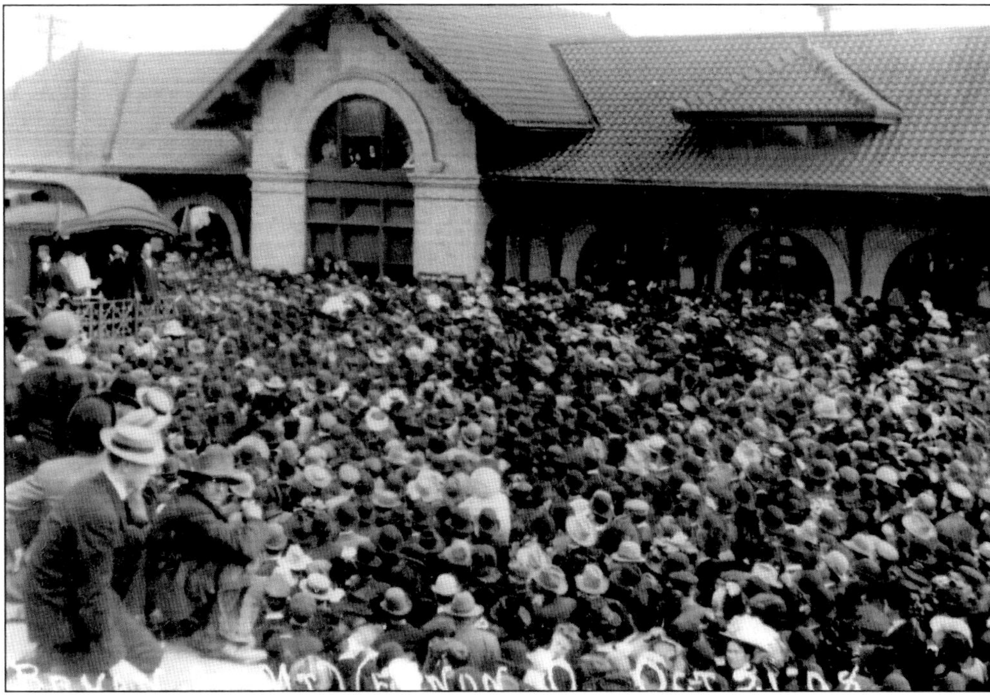

**William Jennings Bryan in 1908.** Bryan spoke from the back of a train to a huge crowd at the B&O station in Mount Vernon on October 28. Taft was elected president later that year. (Photograph courtesy of the Knox County Agricultural Museum.)

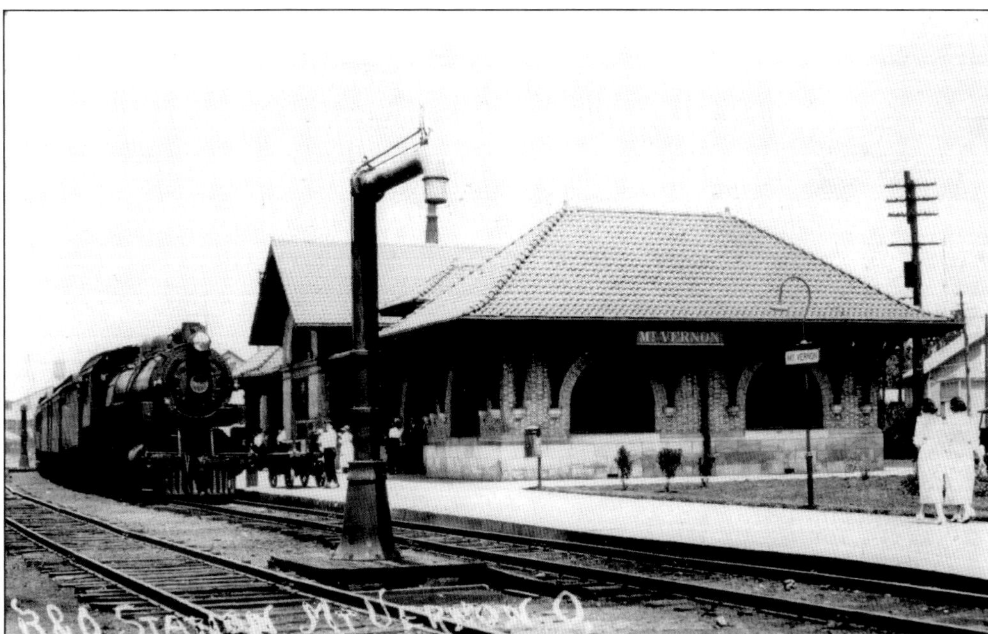


**B&O Station on West High Street.** This prosperous-looking building still exists in Mount Vernon and is being restored by volunteers with encouragement and help from the city. (Photograph courtesy of the Knox County Agricultural Museum.)

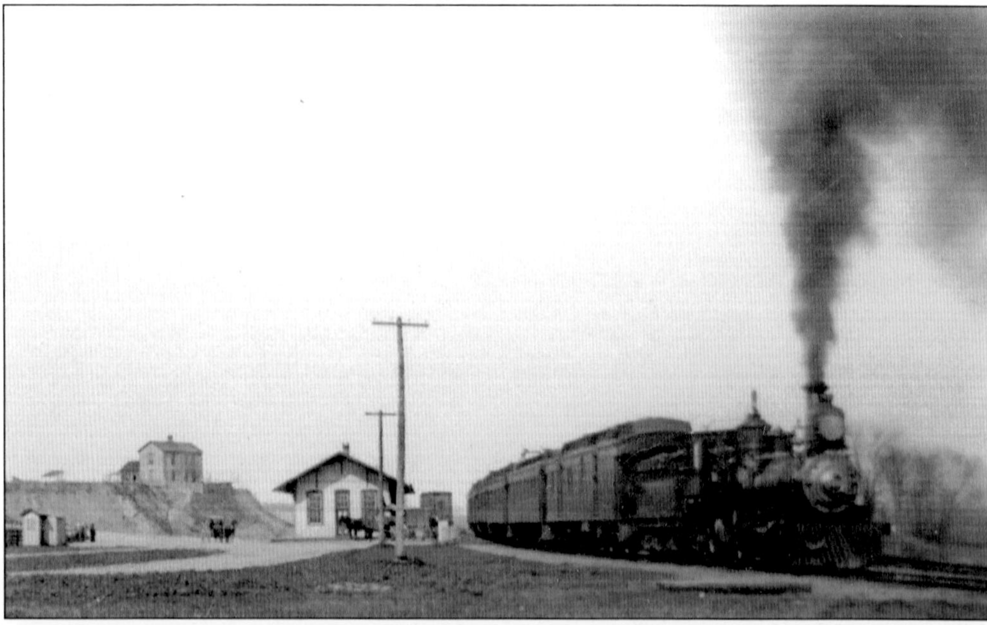

**CA&C Railroad at Bangs.** This small town five miles west of Mount Vernon on State Route 36 towards Columbus was a thriving community at one time and housed the "old folk's home." (Photograph courtesy of the Knox County Agricultural Museum.)

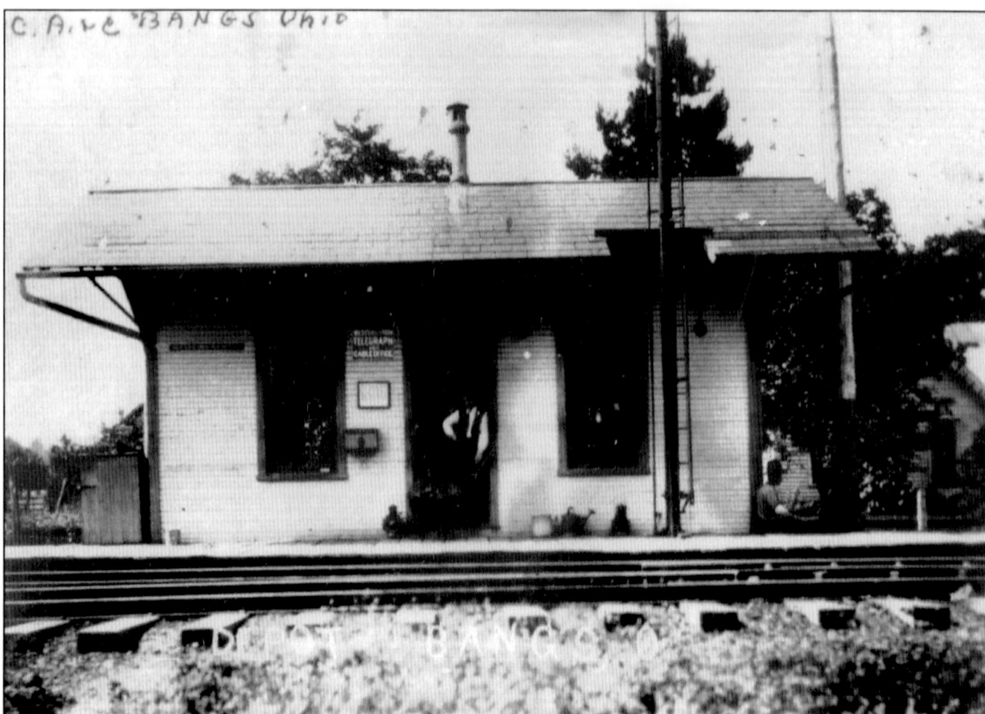


**The Depot at Bangs.** A closer look at the depot shows the station agent/telegraph operator relaxing. (Photograph courtesy of the Knox County Agricultural Museum.)

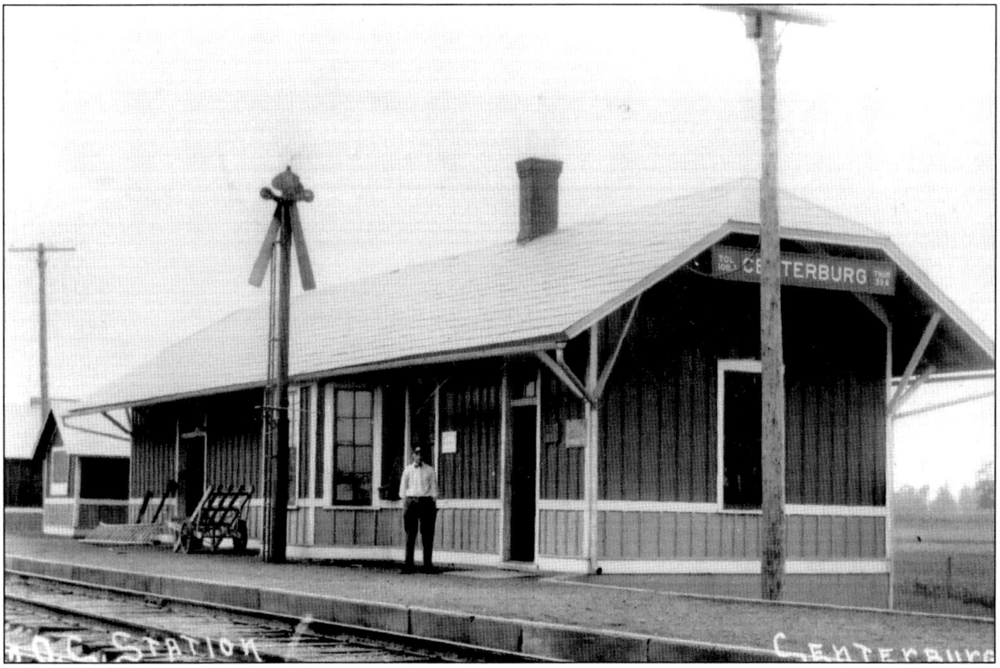


**AO&C AT CENTERBURG.** The Centerburg station seems somewhat more prosperous than the one at Bangs. Centerburg is 13 miles west of Mount Vernon on State Route 36 and is considered the geographical center of Ohio. (Photograph courtesy of the Knox County Agricultural Museum.)

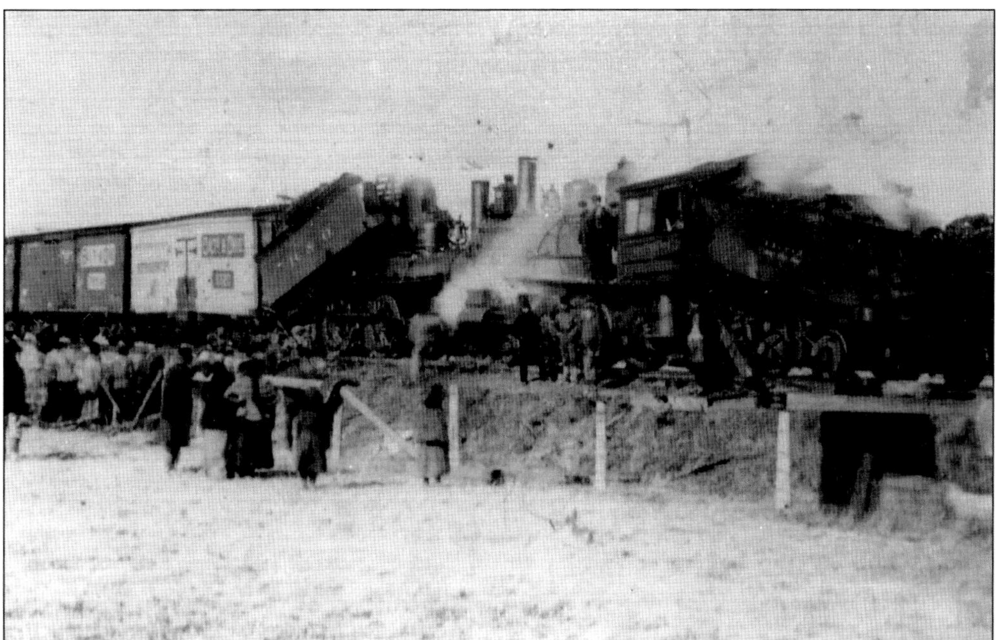

**TRAIN WRECK.** A B&O engine collided head on with another train. Such events drew quite a crowd. (Photograph courtesy of the Knox County Agricultural Museum.)

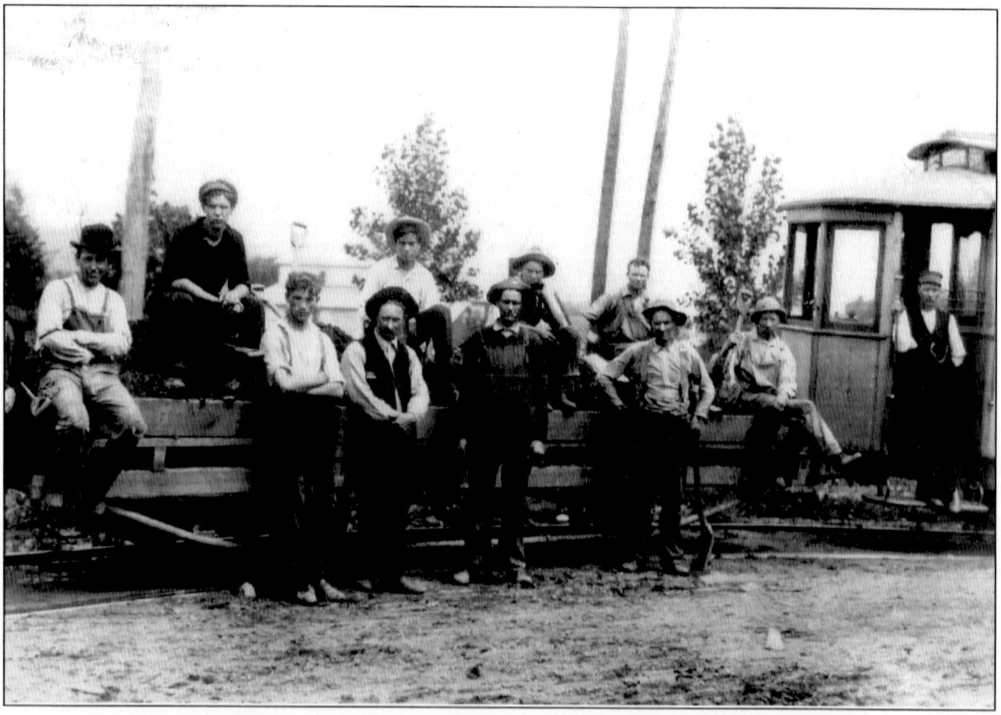

**CABLE CAR CREW.** Cable cars and their tracks needed plenty of attention. This fact probably led to their abbreviated use in Mount Vernon and other major cities. (Photograph courtesy of the Knox County Agricultural Museum.)

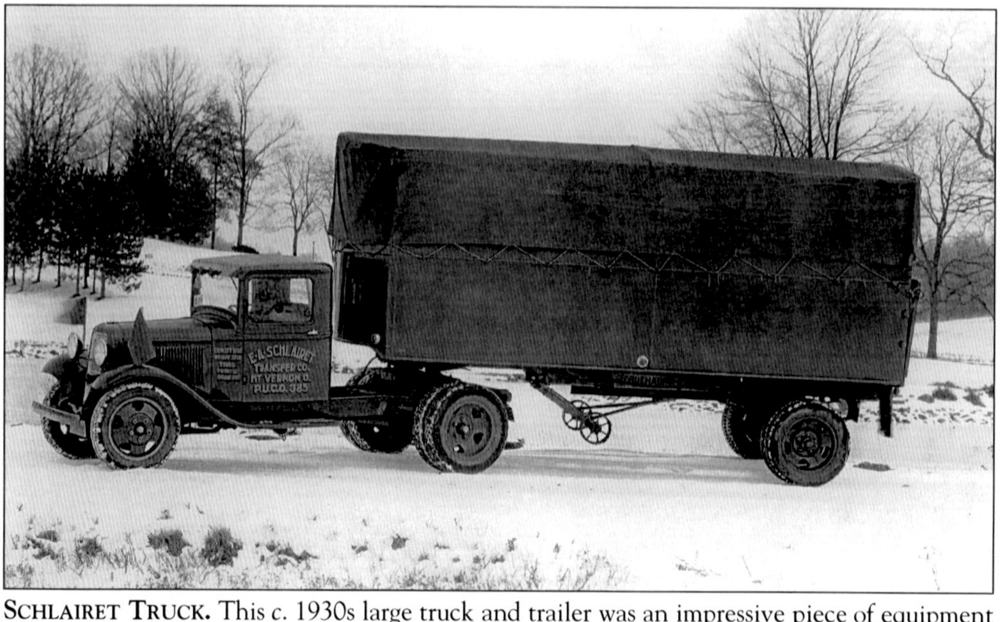


**SCHLAIRET TRUCK.** This *c.* 1930s large truck and trailer was an impressive piece of equipment in its time. The company was one of the largest trucking companies in Mount Vernon and central Ohio for many years. (Photograph courtesy of Ken Blubaugh.)

# *Five*

# World War I and the Depression Era

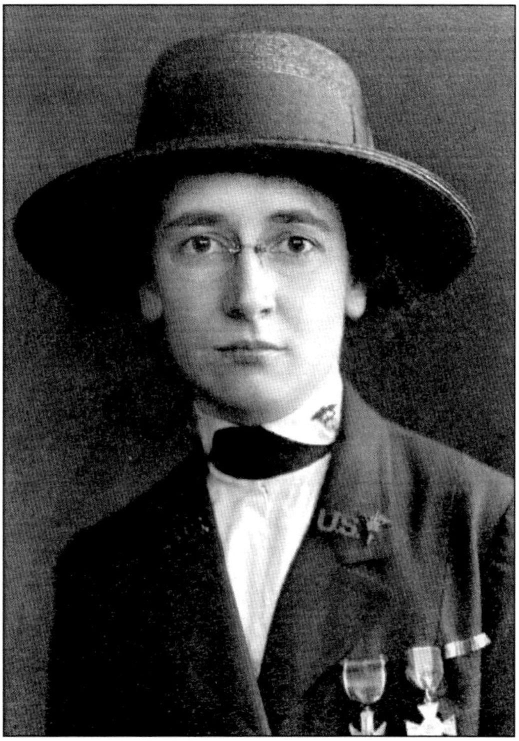

**World War I Nurse.** Helen G. McCelland, from Fredericktown, wears the uniform she wore while serving as a nurse during World War I. (Photograph courtesy of the Fredericktown Historical Society.)

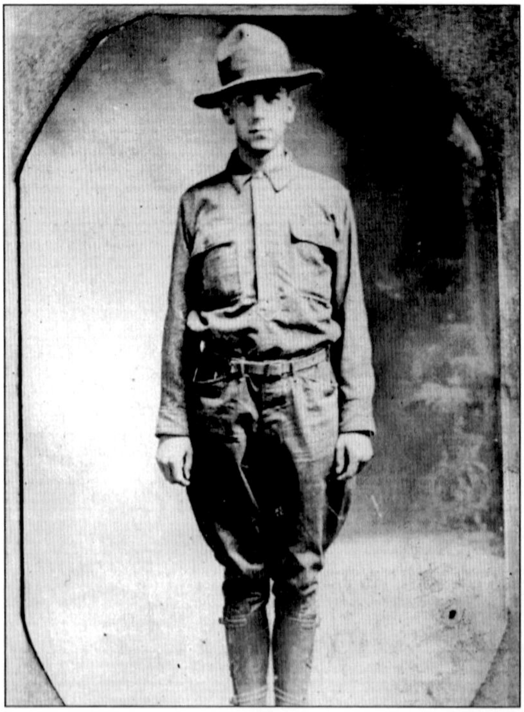

**A "DOUGHBOY" IN UNIFORM.** Albert Newman, of near Gambier, poses for the camera during WWI. Thirty-one people from Knox County were killed in WWI. (Photograph courtesy of Anita V. Lahmon.)

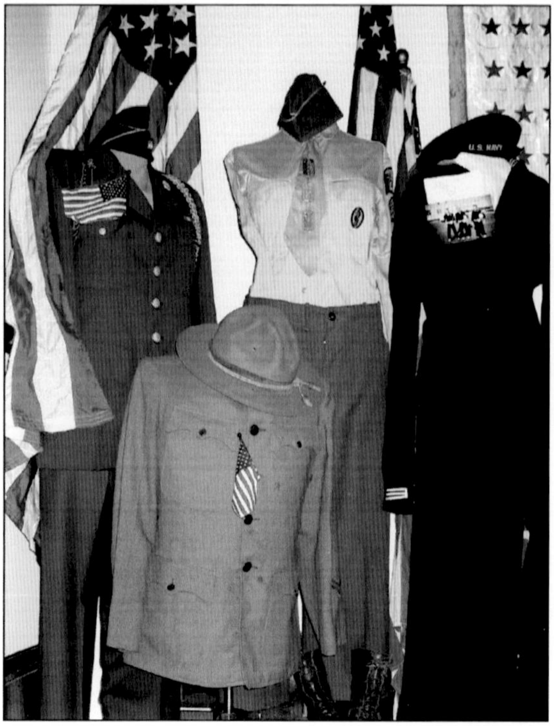



**WORLD WAR UNIFORMS AND FLAGS.** This grouping of flags and uniforms is located in the Fredericktown Historical Museum. (Photograph by D.E. Boyd.)

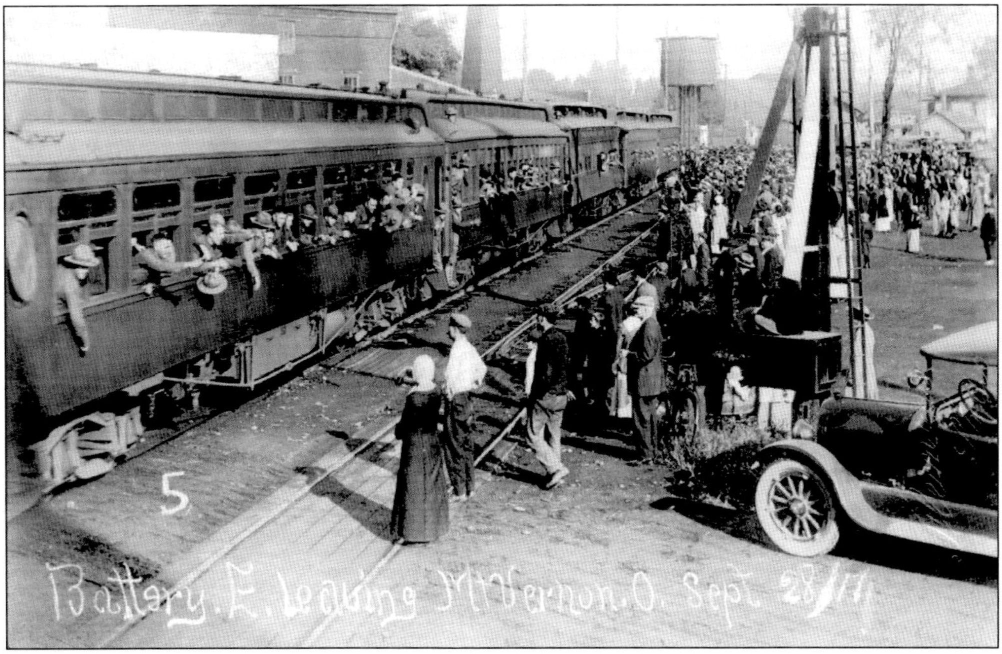


**WW I RECRUITS.** September 28, 1917, saw the mass exodus of Mount Vernon recruits for Battery E of WW I at the B&O train station. It was a well-attended event. Thirty-one men from Knox County died in the first World War. (Photograph courtesy of Margie and David Grubaugh.)

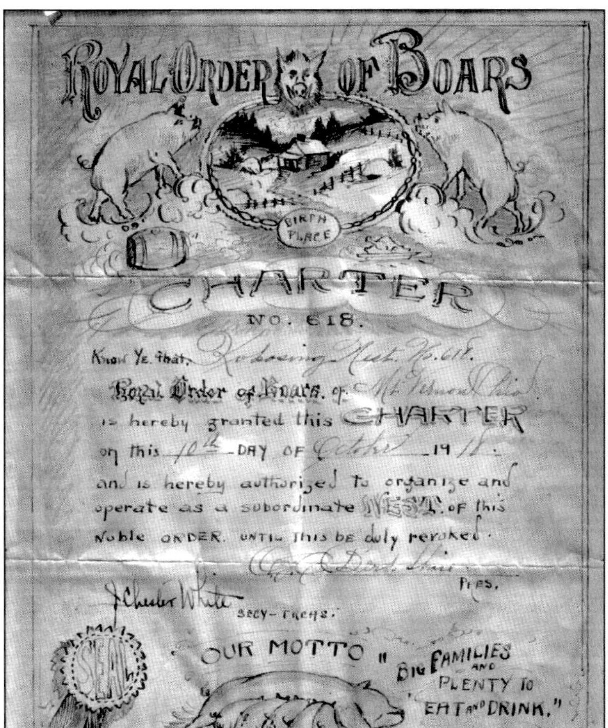


**THE BOAR SOCIETY.** This hand-drawn and hand-lettered fake certificate was created out of a good-natured sense of humor in prevalent use among Mount Vernon citizens of the time (1918), perhaps to relieve the pressures of war. (Certificate courtesy of the Knox County Agricultural Museum.)

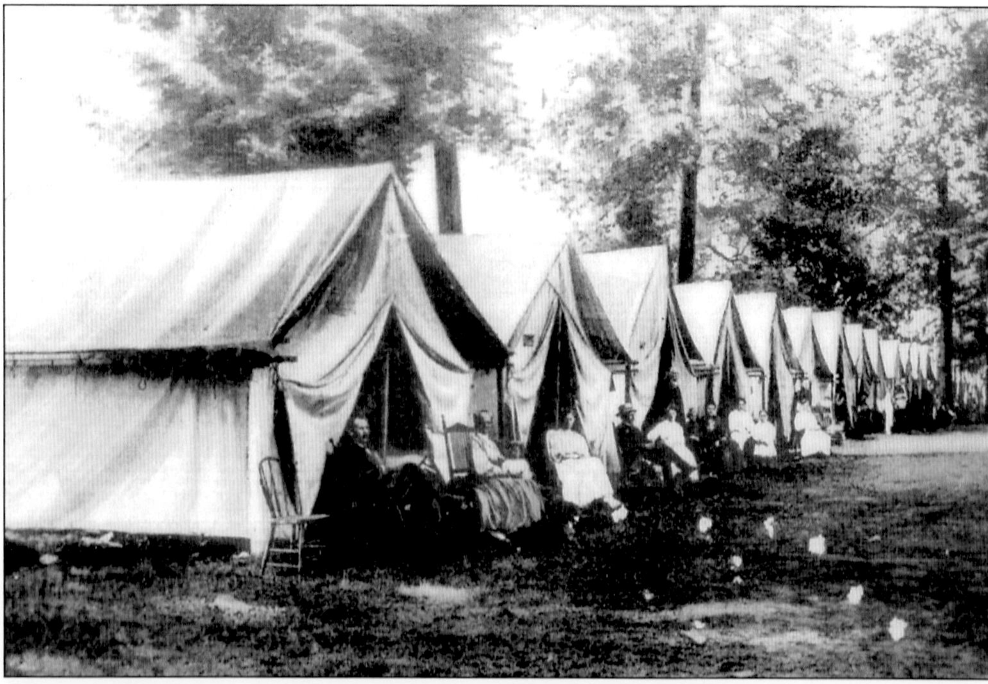

**Tents at Camp Sychar.** The Seventh Day Adventist church held camp meetings in Mount Vernon on Sychar Road. There are permanent camp buildings now, which are still used by the church. (Photograph courtesy of the Knox County Agricultural Museum.)

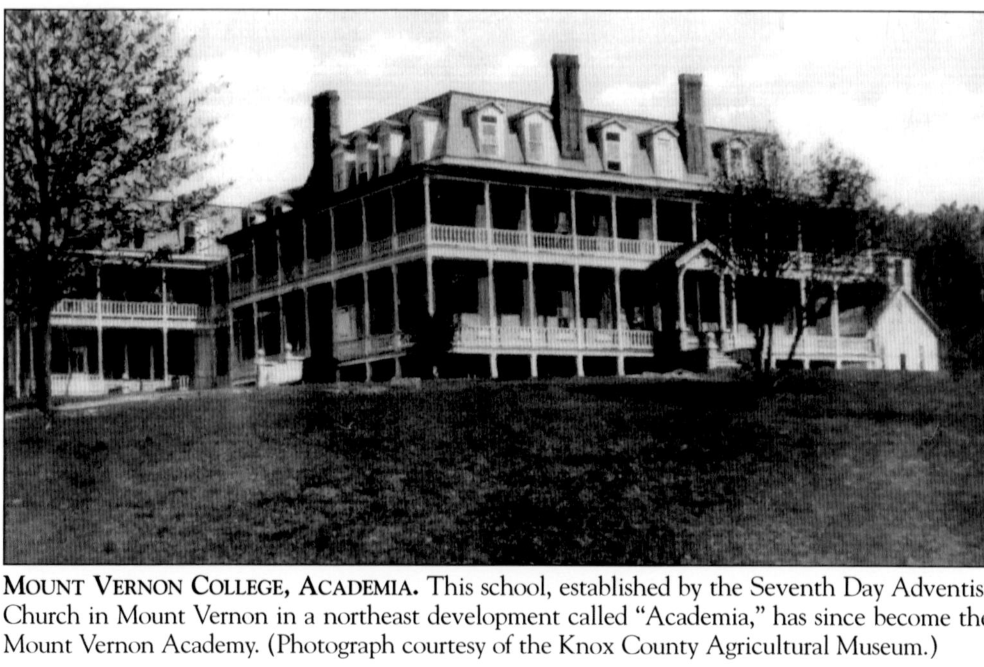

**Mount Vernon College, Academia.** This school, established by the Seventh Day Adventist Church in Mount Vernon in a northeast development called "Academia," has since become the Mount Vernon Academy. (Photograph courtesy of the Knox County Agricultural Museum.)

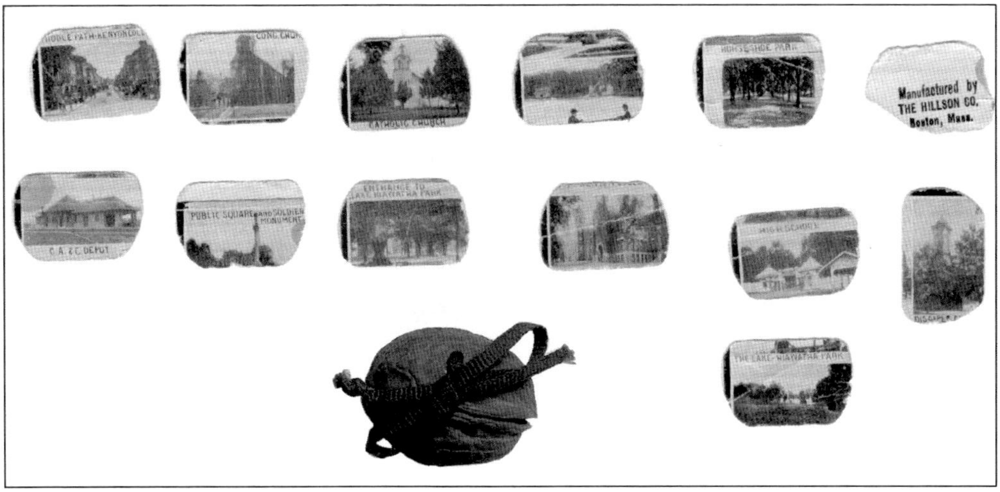


**MOUNT VERNON IN A NUTSHELL.** Tiny photographs of Mount Vernon scenes were packed into this walnut shell and tied with a ribbon in this *c.* 1920s promotional piece. (Photograph courtesy of Margie and David Grubaugh.)

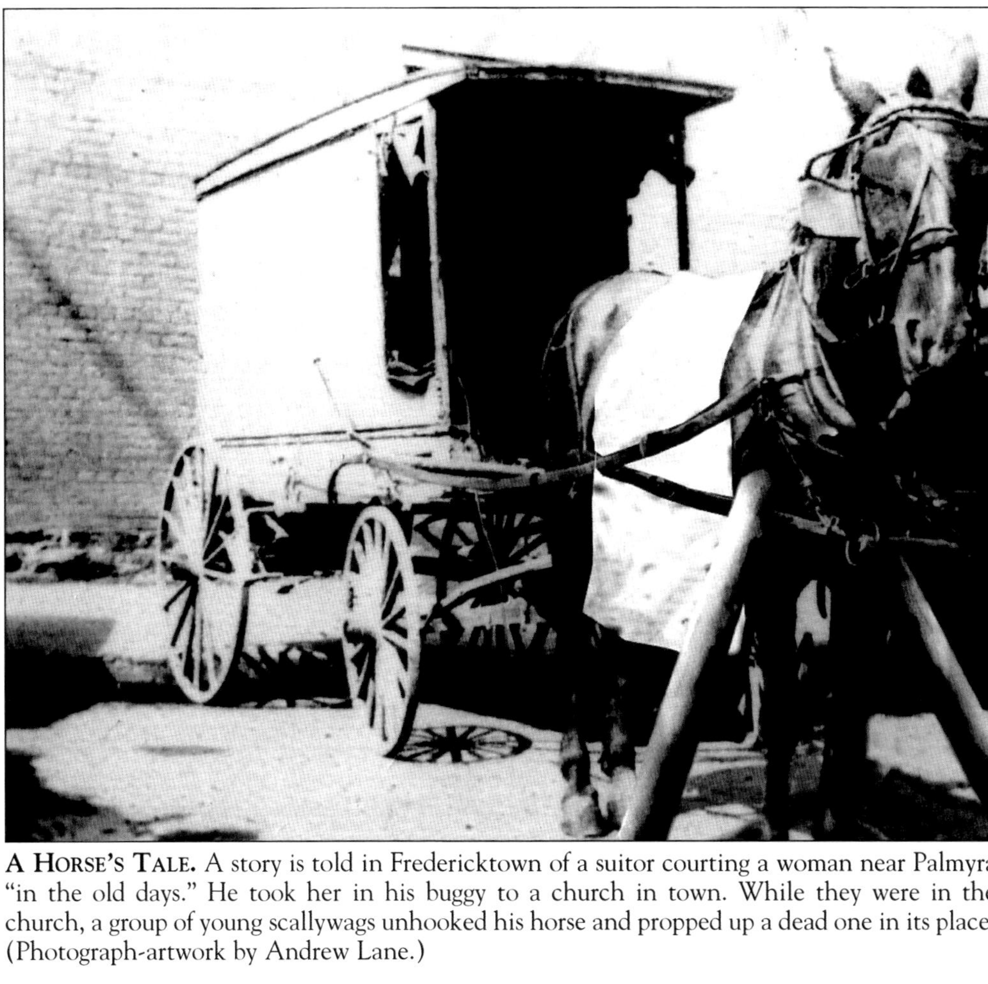

**A HORSE'S TALE.** A story is told in Fredericktown of a suitor courting a woman near Palmyra "in the old days." He took her in his buggy to a church in town. While they were in the church, a group of young scallywags unhooked his horse and propped up a dead one in its place. (Photograph-artwork by Andrew Lane.)

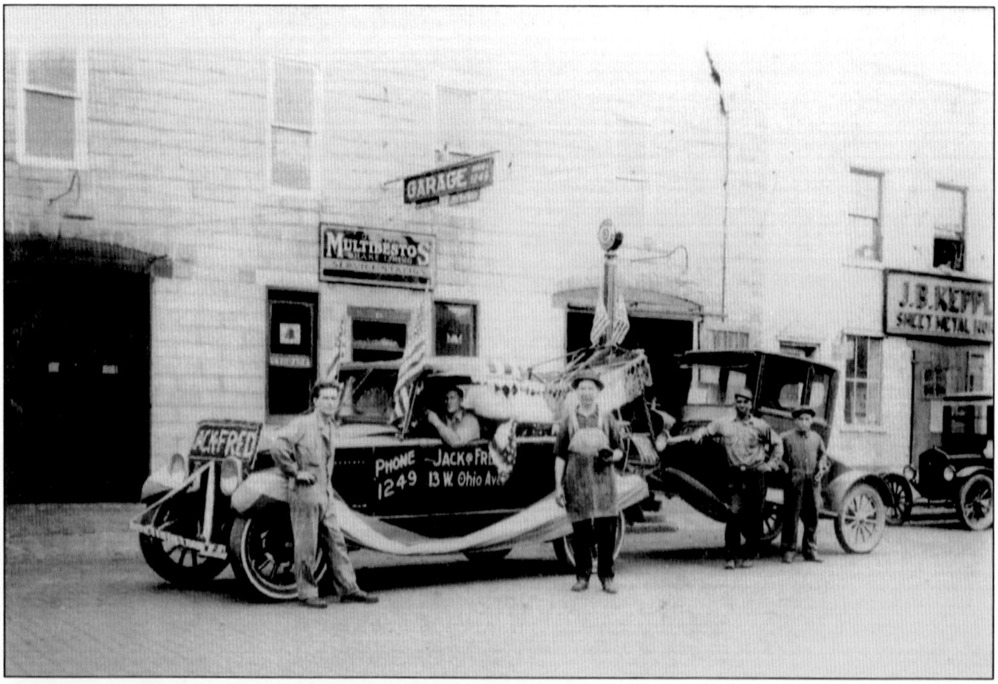


**TOWING A WRECK.** Car accidents require a tow truck. Garages, service stations, tire shops, and body shops all appeared as the demand increased. Kepple's Sheet Metal (on the far right) still exists and does business in Mount Vernon. (Photograph courtesy of the Knox County Agricultural Museum.)

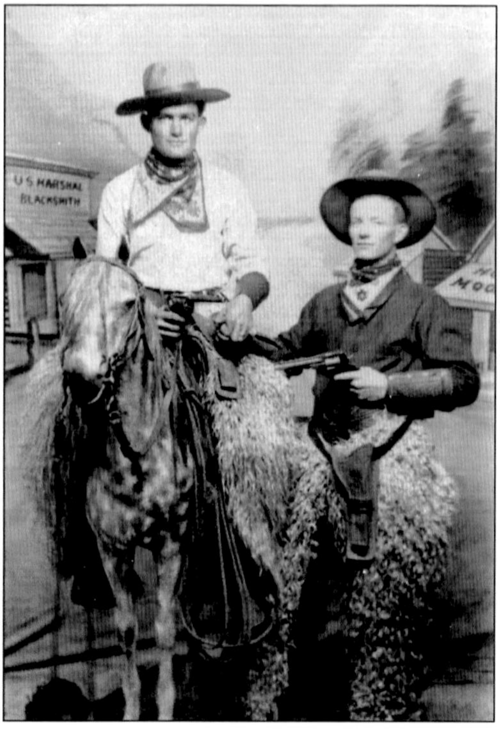


**COWBOYS AND MOVIES.** B-grade westerns ruled the screens, and movies cost 25¢ or less during most of the first half of the 20th century. A story is told around town of one enterprising theater owner, Mose Blackburn, who invented the shutter that stopped movies from flickering. Apparently, he was out on the street trying to drum up business for a passion play movie, and he shouted out, "Come one, come all, this is the last time Jesus Christ will be seen in Fredericktown!" (Photograph courtesy of the Knox County Agricultural Museum.)

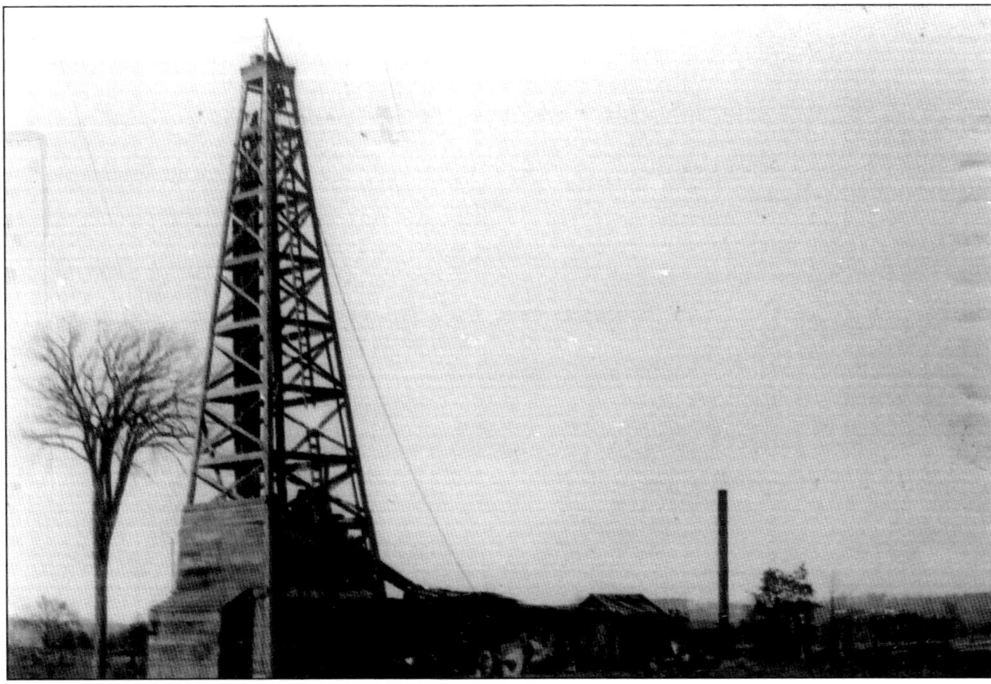

**Knox County Oil.** One of the great attractions for industries such as glass and foundries was the abundance of cheap gas in the area. (Photograph courtesy of the Knox County Agricultural Museum.)

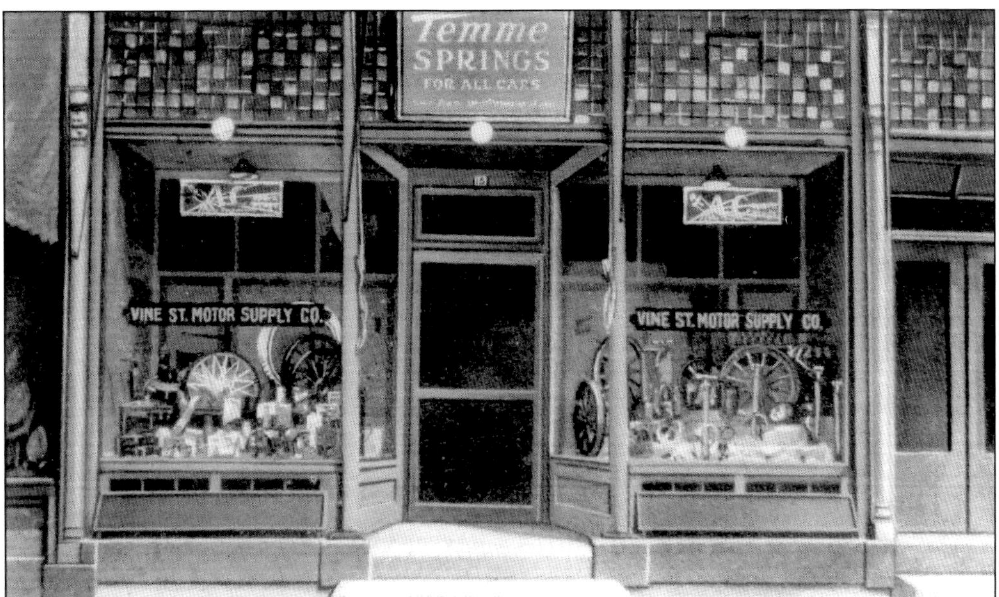


**A Typical Store Front.** Mount Vernon was a bustling area of growth after WWI, until the Great Depression. This store was presumably on West Vine Street (1928). (Photograph courtesy of the Knox County Agricultural Museum.)

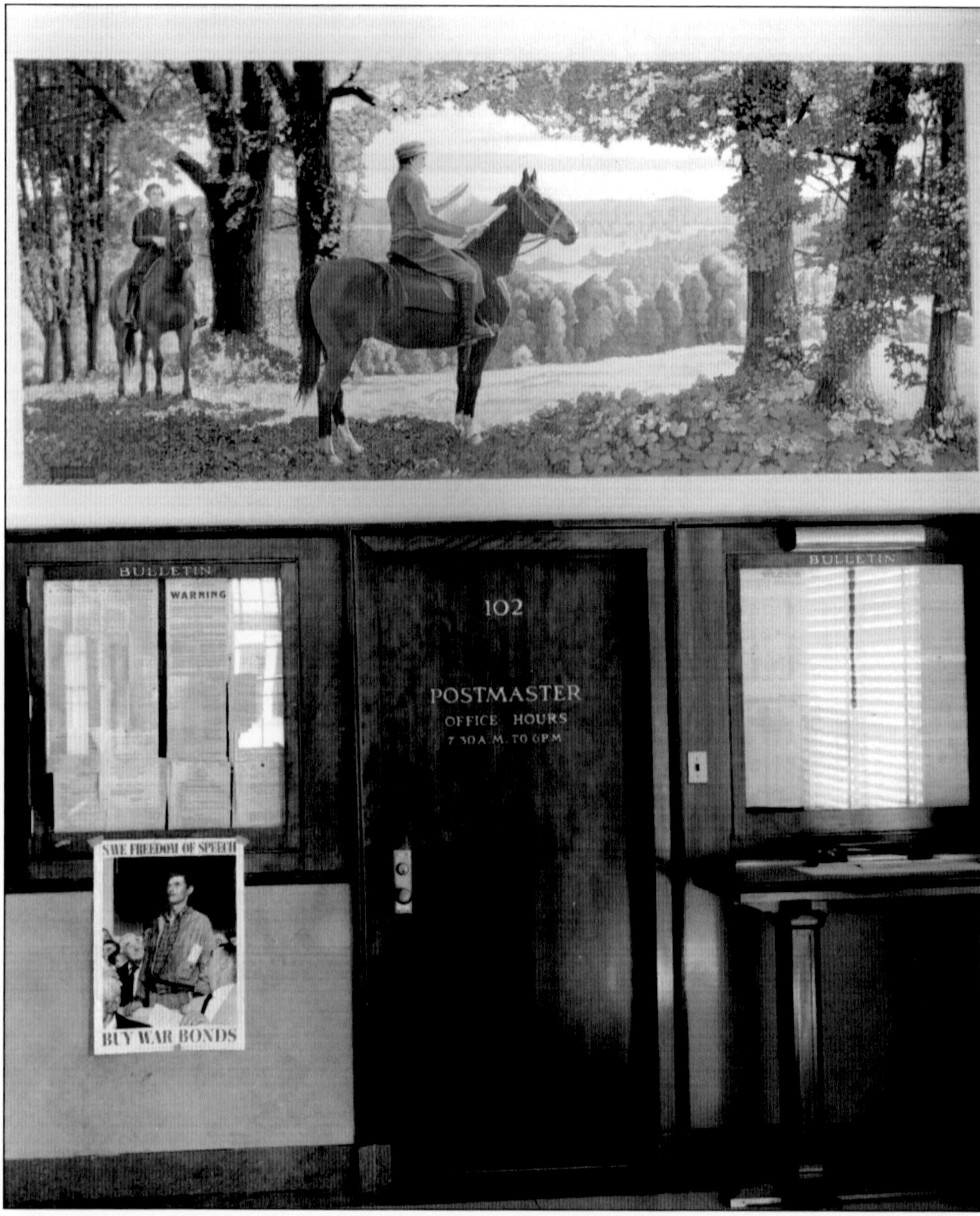


**WPA PROJECT.** During the Great Depression, the Works Progress Administration (WPA) created jobs for people in many fields, even the arts. This mural painted by Norris Rhaming, Kenyon College art professor in the late 1930s, still exists in the Gambier Post Office. Bishop Chase, Kenyon's founder, is shown on his horse in the center of the painting saying, "Well, this will do!" as he takes in the beautiful scene, July 24, 1825. Behind Chase is Henry B. Curtis, Mount Vernon lawyer, who guided Chase in his search. (Photograph and quote from The Papers of Philander Chase courtesy of the Olin Library, Kenyon College, Greenslade Special Collections and Archives.)

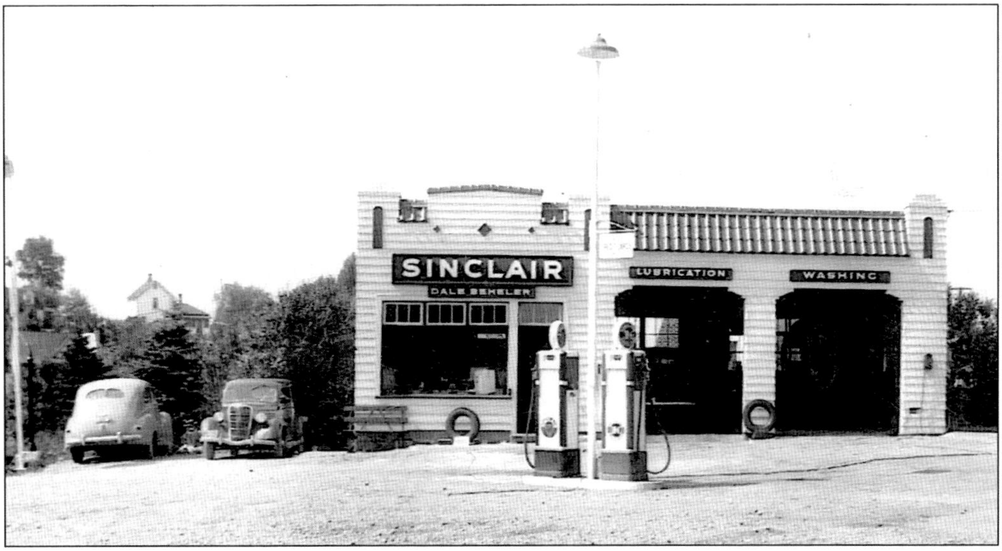


**DALE BEHELER'S SINCLAIR STATION.** Dale Beheler, president of the Fredericktown Historical Society, graduated from Fredericktown High School in 1946. He worked for H.P. Bowers at the Sinclair Station until it came up for lease. Dale and his father then operated it at the junction of South Main, Sixth Street, and Columbus Road in 1949, 1950, and 1951. (Photograph courtesy of the Fredericktown Historical Society.)

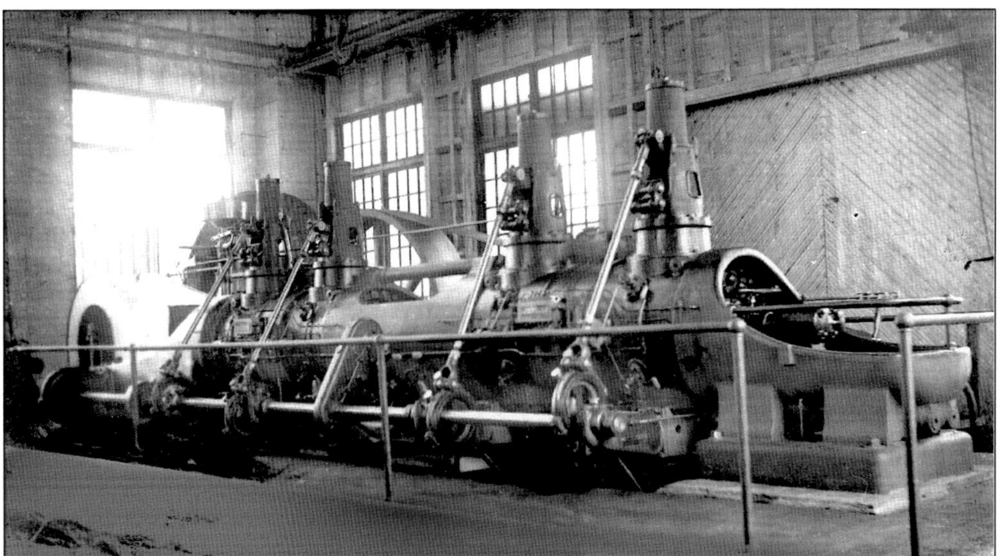

**COOPER COMPRESSOR.** This large Cooper engine is typical of many the company produced in their Mount Vernon plant. Such engines were used extensively to pump oil and gas in Knox County and later in oil producing areas such as Texas. (Photograph courtesy of the Knox County Agricultural Museum.)

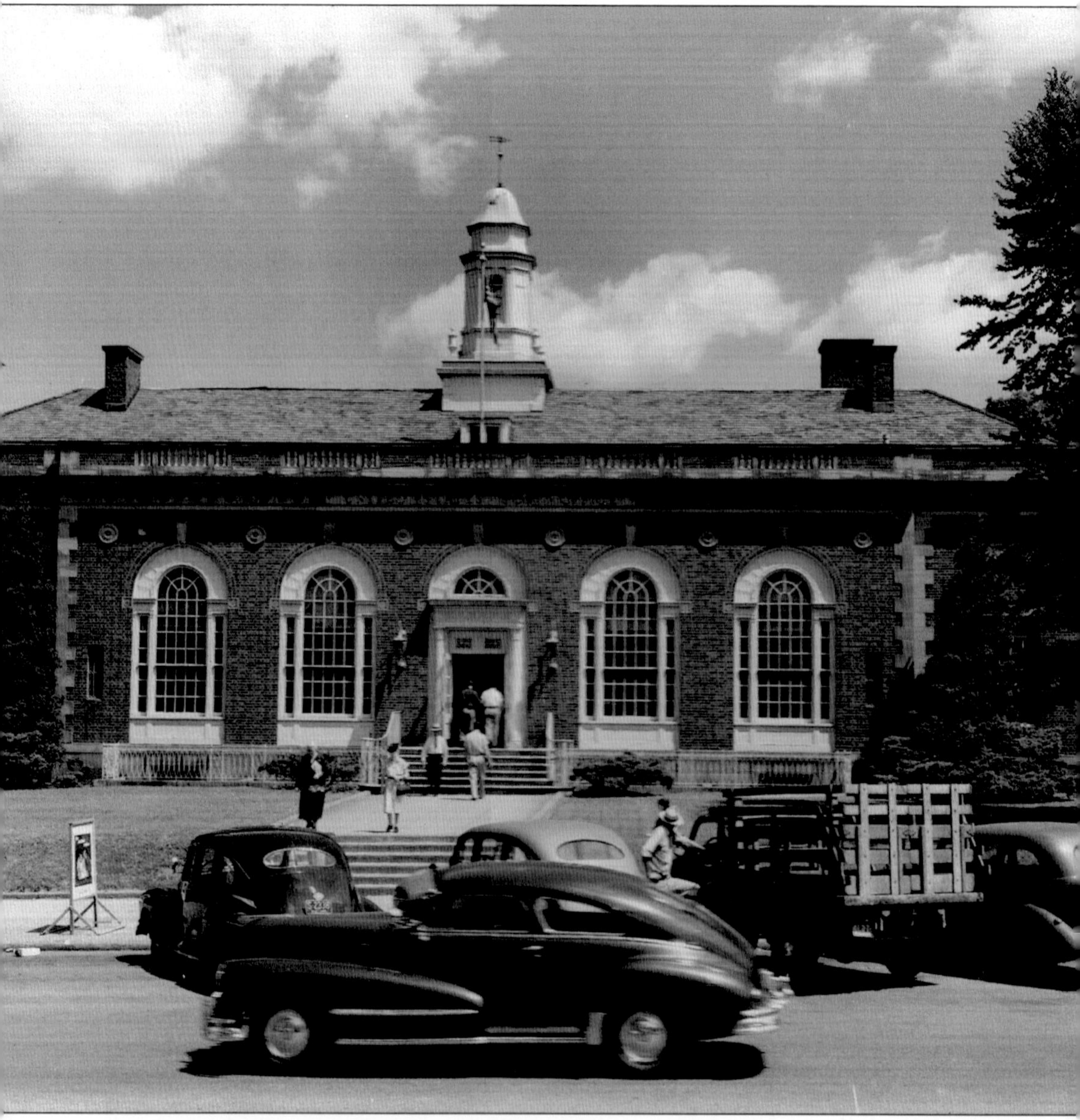

**The New Mount Vernon Post Office.** This new colonial-style post office was built on West High Street in the 1930s. It was remodeled in 2003. (Photograph by Joe Munroe of the Department of State, International Press Division, photographic branch; photograph courtesy of Sip's Coffee House in downtown Mount Vernon.)

# *Six*

# World War II and Beyond

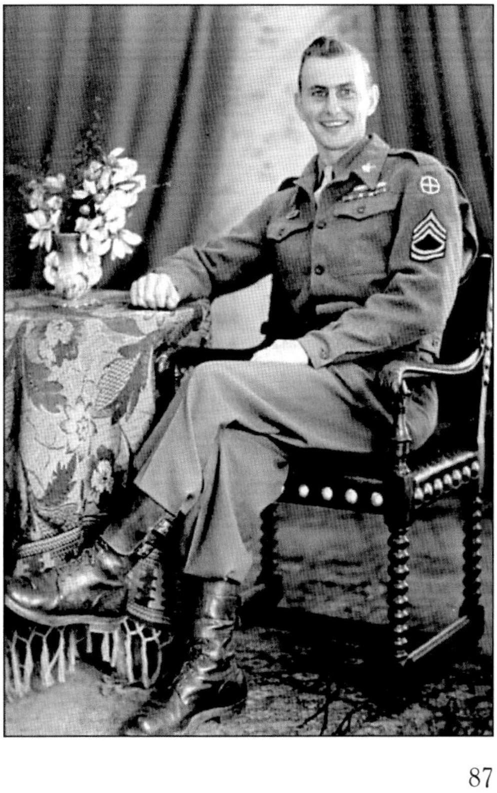

**A Soldier Poses for His Family.** Charles Douglas Welch of Fredericktown served in the 134th infantry, 35th Division in WWII. (Photograph courtesy of the Fredericktown Historical Society.)

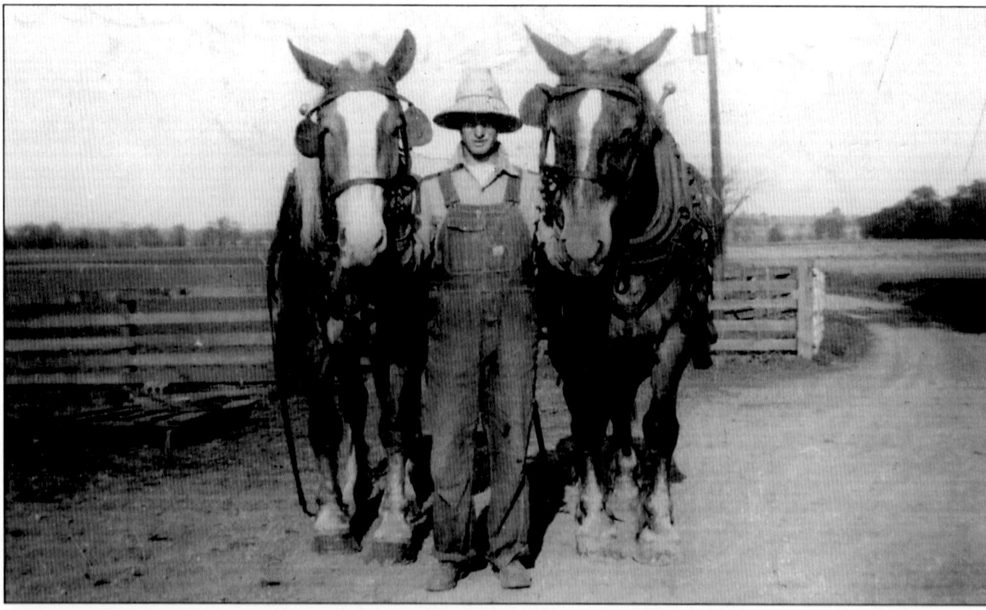

**A FARM BOY IN WW II.** Russell Rockwell, Anita Lahmon's cousin, is shown with a team of horses prior to enlistment. Sadly, he was killed in the war in December of 1944. One hundred and twenty-three people from Knox County died in the war. (Photograph courtesy of Anita V. Lahmon.)

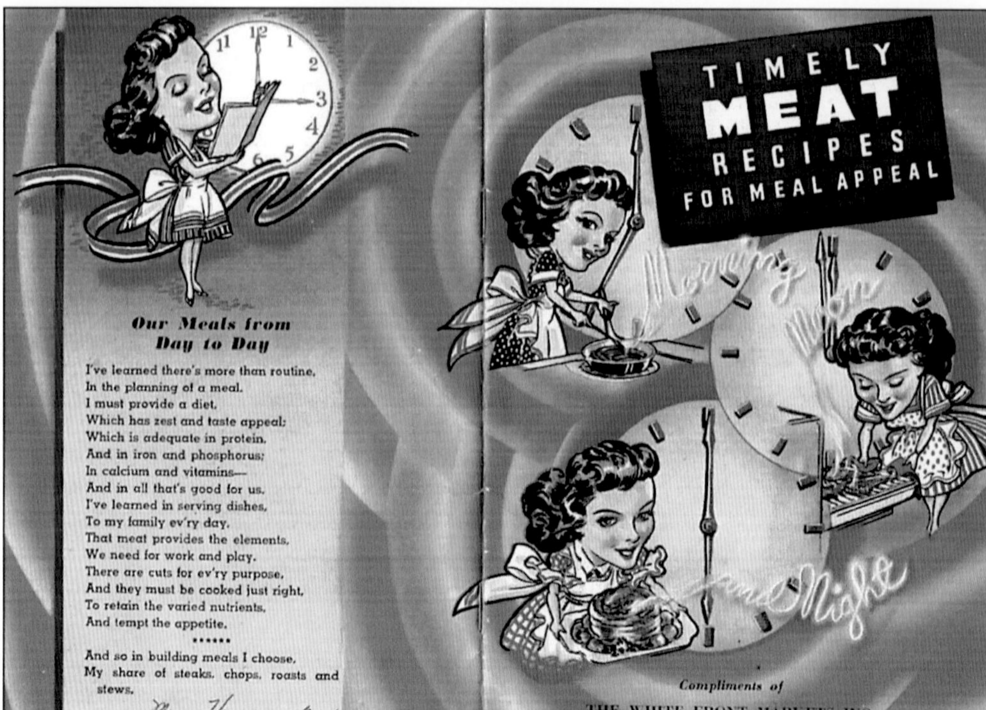


**TIMELY MEATS RECIPES, C. WWII.** The War was not just about soldiers. The home front was involved in rationing, doing more with less, and keeping spirits up. (Photograph of recipe loaned by Jack and Donna Martin, Howard, Ohio.)

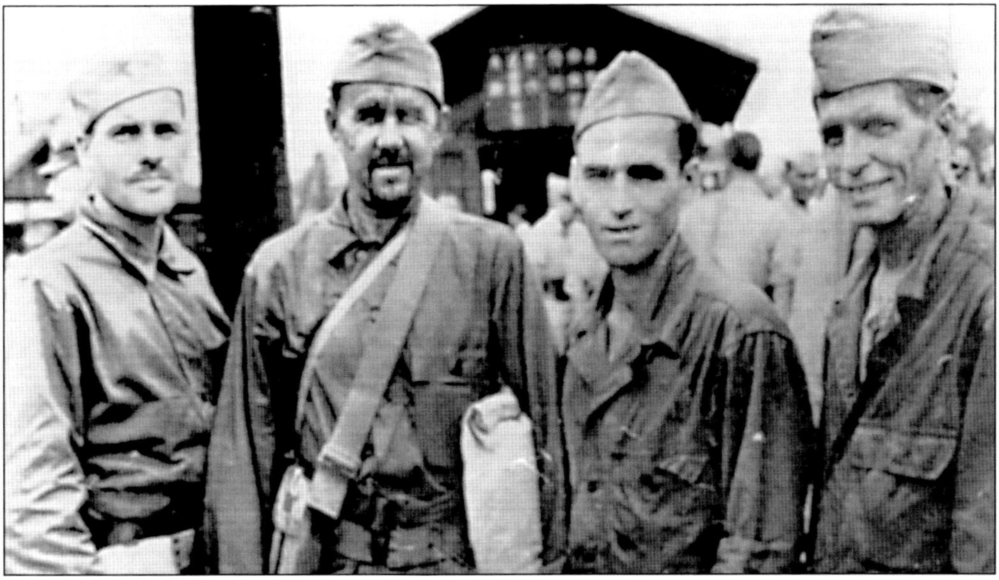

**Survivors of the Bataan Death March, World War II.** The men pictured above survived the Bataan Death March, enduring three and a half years of starvation and hard labor: (left to right) Robert W. Levering of Fredericktown, Ohio, and author of *Horror Trek*; Carl F. Kolodzik; Robert Rose; and William Brady. Levering went on to serve as a U.S. Representative for several years. His great-great grandfather was an early settler near Waterford, just west of Fredericktown. (Photograph courtesy of Usher Levering from the book, *Horror Trek*.)

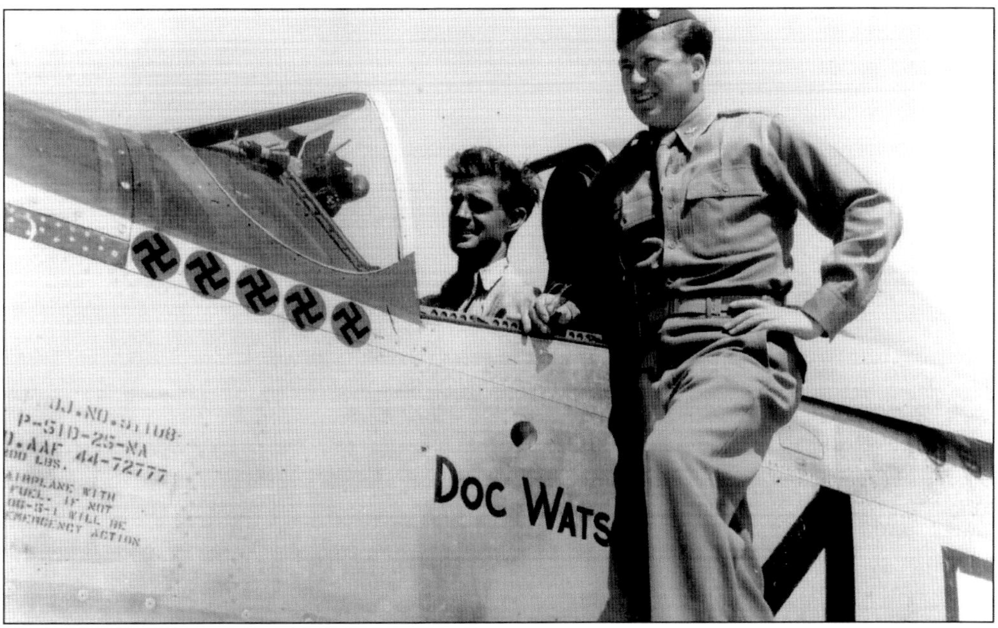


**World War II Ace.** Ralph "Doc" Watson from Centerburg is seen here on the wing of his P-51 Mustang in 1944. There are five swastikas on the fuselage indicating the number of planes he shot down in air-to-air combat to earn his "Ace" status. Watson joined the Army in 1937, earned his college degree, and retired a colonel. (Photograph and text from his children Bess and Ralph Jr.)

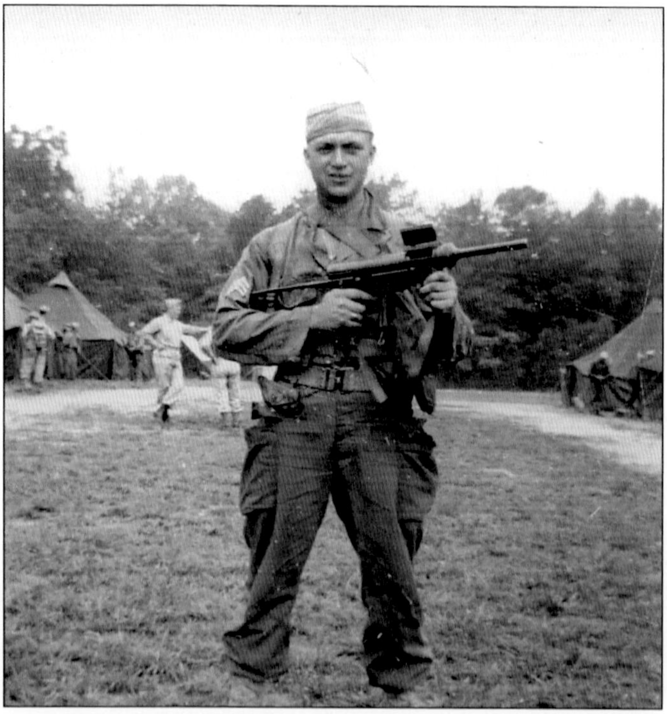

**MILITARY POLICEMAN, WW II.** Sergeant Walter H. Boyd holds his 45-caliber submachine gun at Fort Dix, New Jersey, in this 1945 photograph. (Photograph courtesy of Walter H. Boyd.)

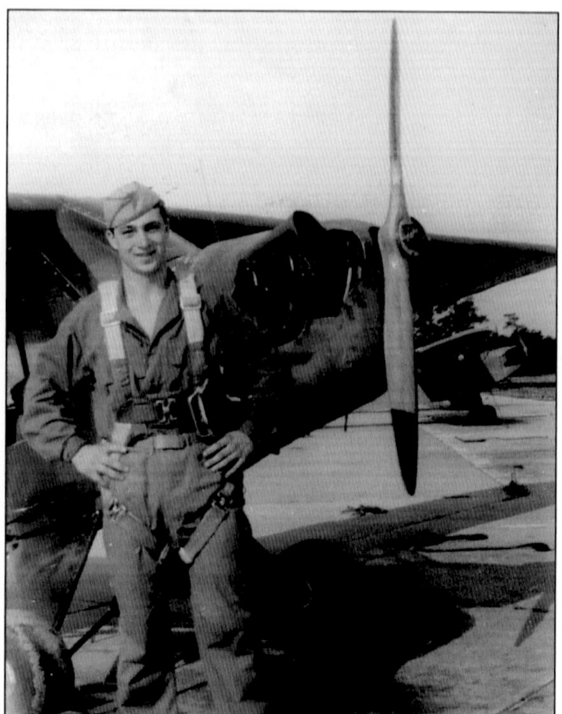

**WW II PILOT.** Brother to Walter, Paul Boyd, was in pilot's training when this photograph was taken. (Photograph courtesy of Walter H. Boyd.)

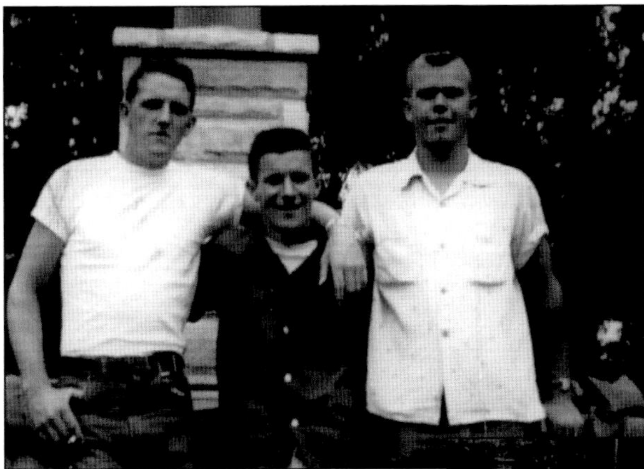

**THREE COUSINS OFF TO WAR.** Three Mount Vernon cousins were assigned to Company 197, 13th Battalion, 1st Regiment of the U.S. Navy. They are, left to right, James, Harry, and Roger Beckholt. They enlisted together in 1954 and served in the Vietnam War. (Photograph courtesy of Anita V. Lahmon.)

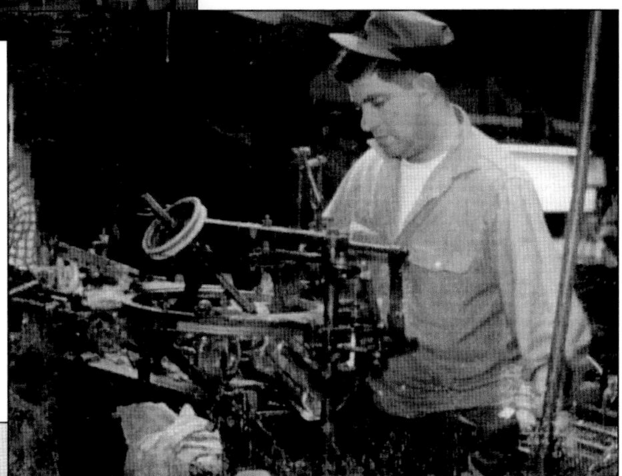

**AT WORK, POST-WAR.** Harry Beckholt, one of the three cousins, worked at Pittsburgh Plate for many years after leaving the service. (Photograph courtesy of Anita V. Lahmon.)

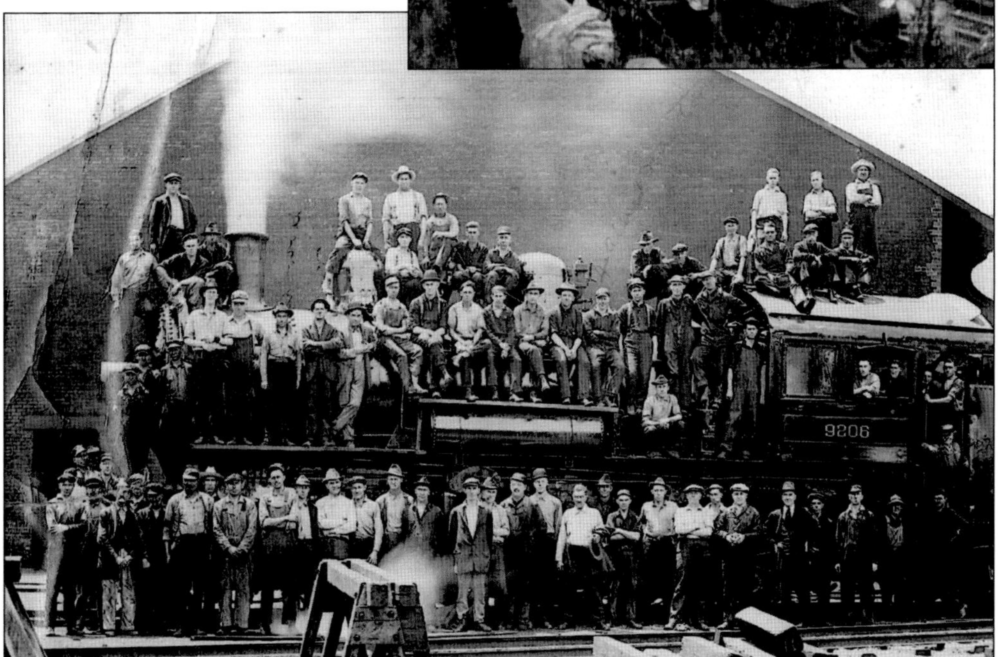


**LAMB GLASS WORKERS ON OLD 9206.** Albert Newton worked for Lamb Glass for over 32 years. He received a citation from President Reagan when he retired from the factory. He is in the middle of the photograph on the engine. (Photograph courtesy of Anita V. Lahmon.)

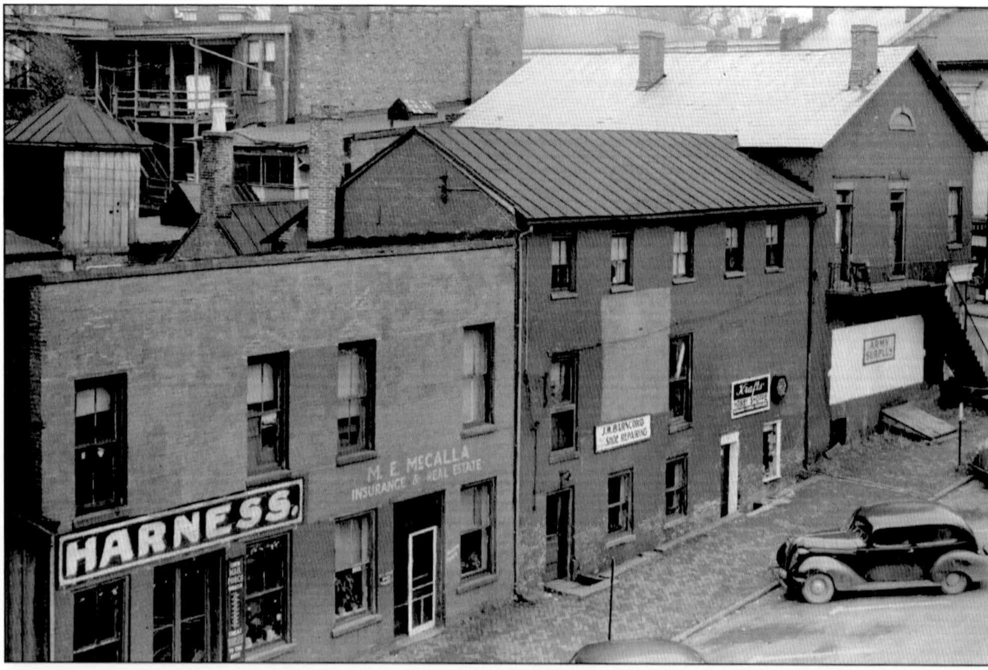


**NORTHWEST CORNER OF THE SQUARE.** This photograph was taken in the late 1940s or early 1950s, but there was still a harness shop active in Mount Vernon. Stauffer's clothing used to be in the shop on the far right corner. (Photograph courtesy of the Knox County Agricultural Museum.)

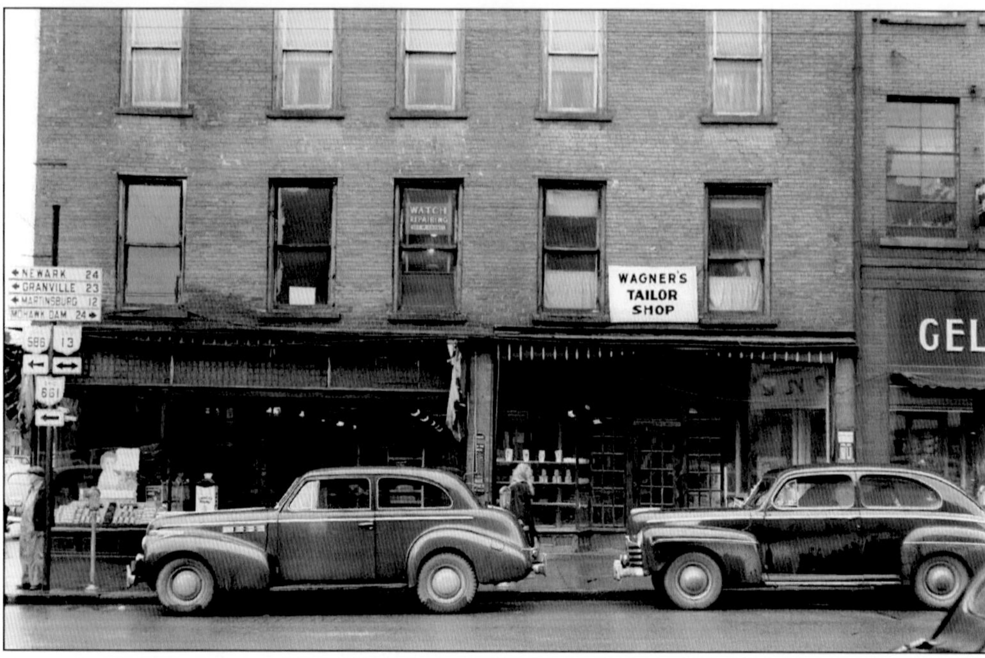


**PITKIN'S CORNER.** This is 135–7 South Main Street in Mount Vernon at the corner of Main and Gambier Streets, *c.* 1950. The sidewalks were so crowded on a Saturday night that you could hardly walk through them. (Photograph courtesy of Richard A. Cochran.)

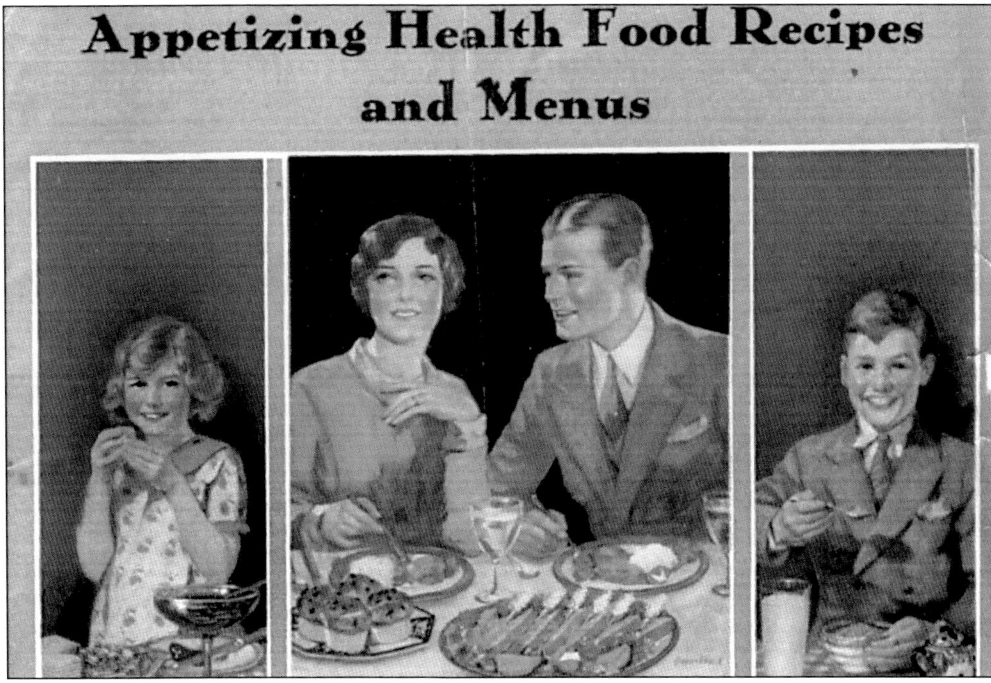


**PITKIN'S RECIPE BOOK.** Such items as this recipe book are now quite collectible, as are the memories of the good food and good times at Pitkin's produce and grocery store. (Image of book loaned by Margie and David Grubaugh.)

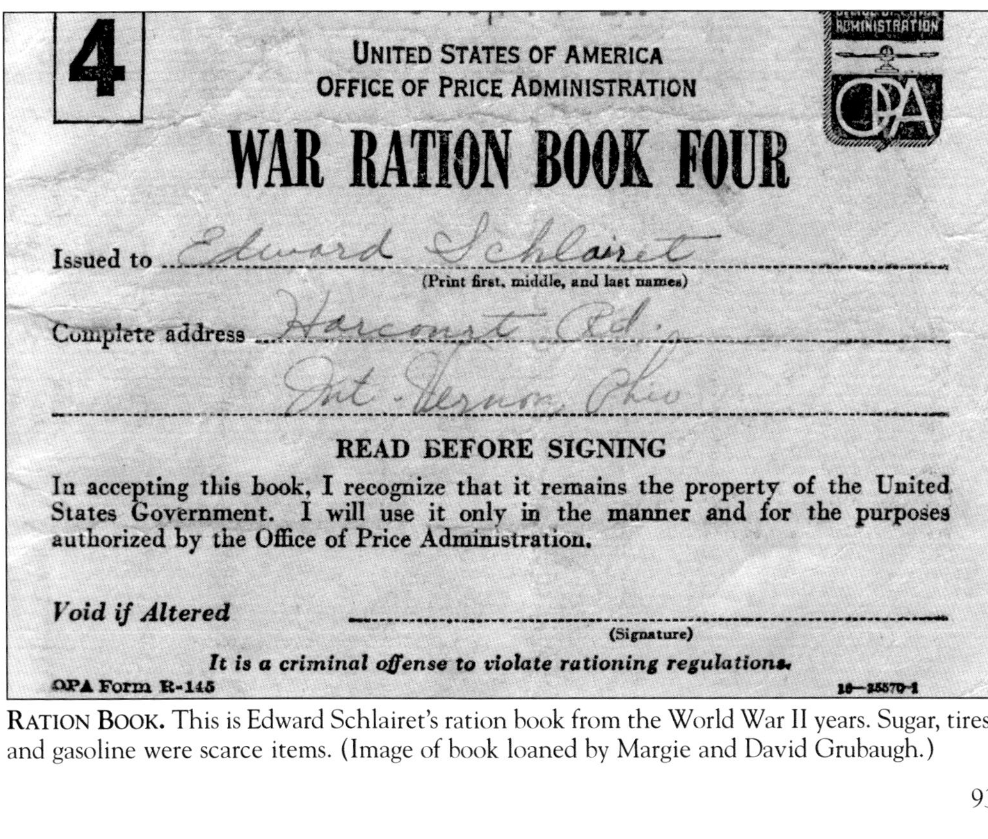
4

UNITED STATES OF AMERICA
OFFICE OF PRICE ADMINISTRATION

OPA

WAR RATION BOOK FOUR

Issued to Edward Schlairet
(Print first, middle, and last names)

Complete address Harcourt Rd.
Mt. Vernon, Ohio

READ BEFORE SIGNING

In accepting this book, I recognize that it remains the property of the United States Government. I will use it only in the manner and for the purposes authorized by the Office of Price Administration.

*Void if Altered* ............................................
(Signature)

*It is a criminal offense to violate rationing regulations.*

OPA Form R-145 16—35570-1

**RATION BOOK.** This is Edward Schlairet's ration book from the World War II years. Sugar, tires, and gasoline were scarce items. (Image of book loaned by Margie and David Grubaugh.)

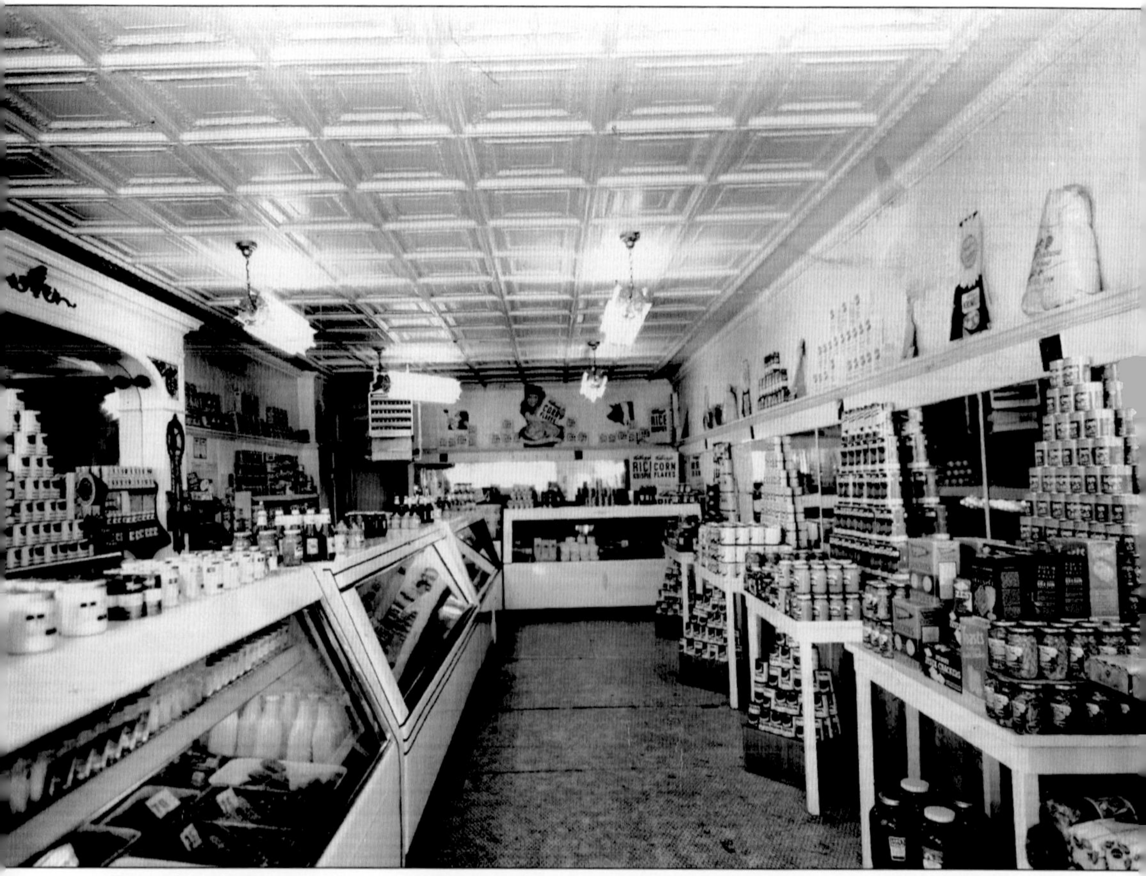

**The White Front Market.** This market, operated by Earl Martin, a trained meat cutter, was located under the Curtis Hotel on the southeast corner of the Square. Earl and Marie Martin also operated the Nook Restaurant at 2 East Ohio Avenue and South Main Street from the late 1940s to the late 1950s in Mount Vernon. (Photograph courtesy of Jack and Donna Martin of Howard, Ohio.)

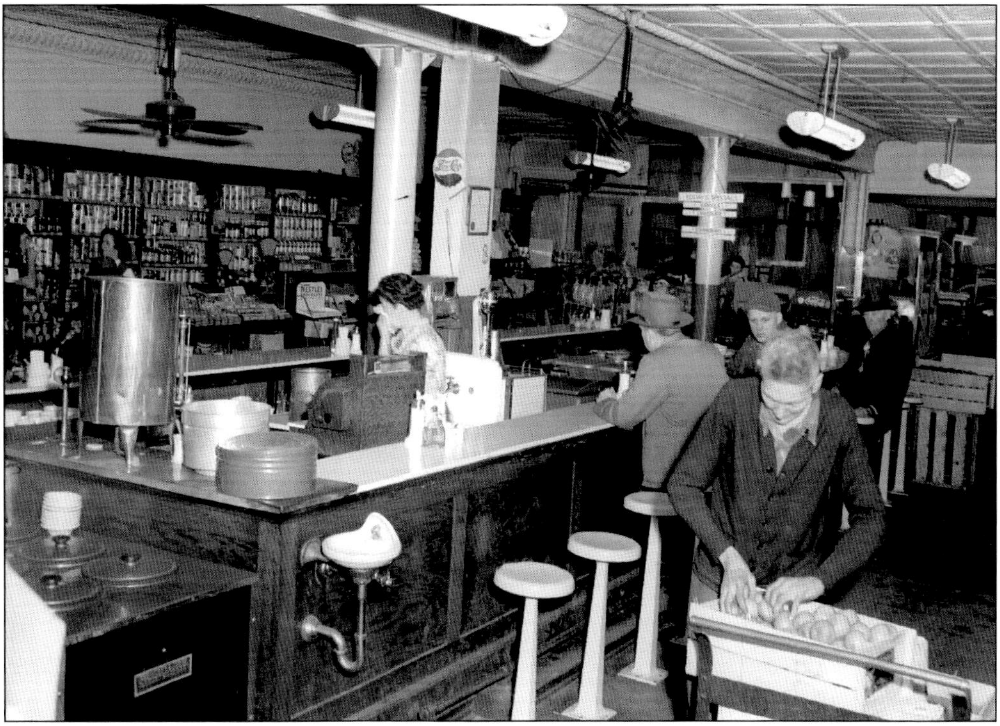

**PITKIN'S LUNCH COUNTER.** This photograph of Pitkin's was most likely taken in the late 1940s. Charlie Baughman is the only person identified. He is placing fruit out in the lower right of the photograph. (Photograph courtesy of Richard A. Cochran.)

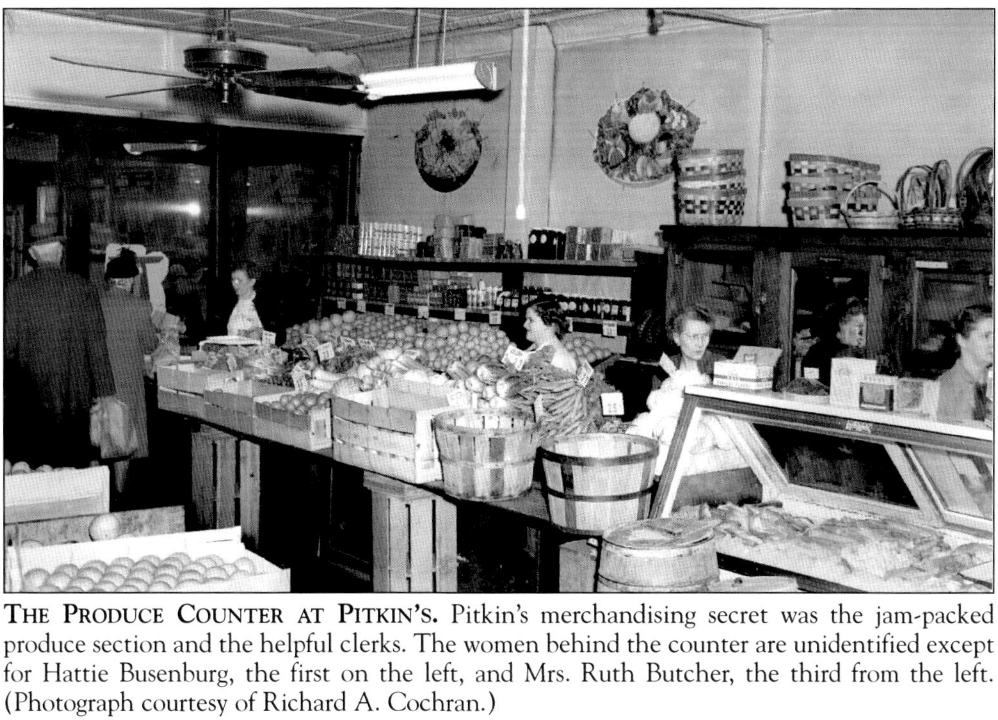

**THE PRODUCE COUNTER AT PITKIN'S.** Pitkin's merchandising secret was the jam-packed produce section and the helpful clerks. The women behind the counter are unidentified except for Hattie Busenburg, the first on the left, and Mrs. Ruth Butcher, the third from the left. (Photograph courtesy of Richard A. Cochran.)

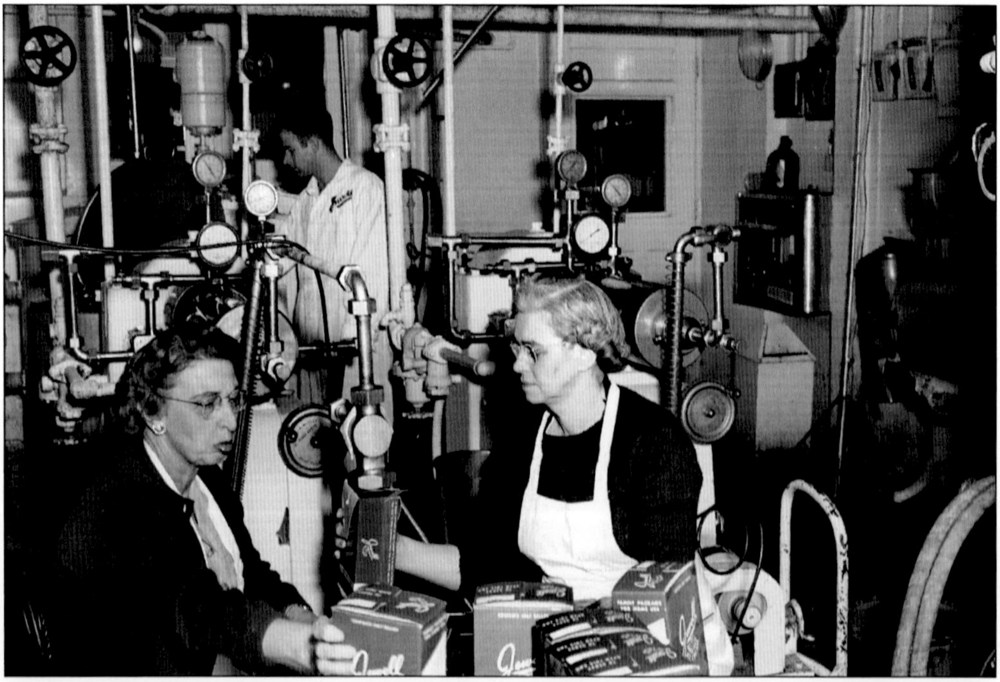

**Jewell's Ice Cream Plant.** Jewell existed in Mount Vernon from 1912 until the 1950s. This was taken toward that later date. The workers are unidentified. (Photograph by Guy E. Lipps, loaned by Richard A. Cochran.)

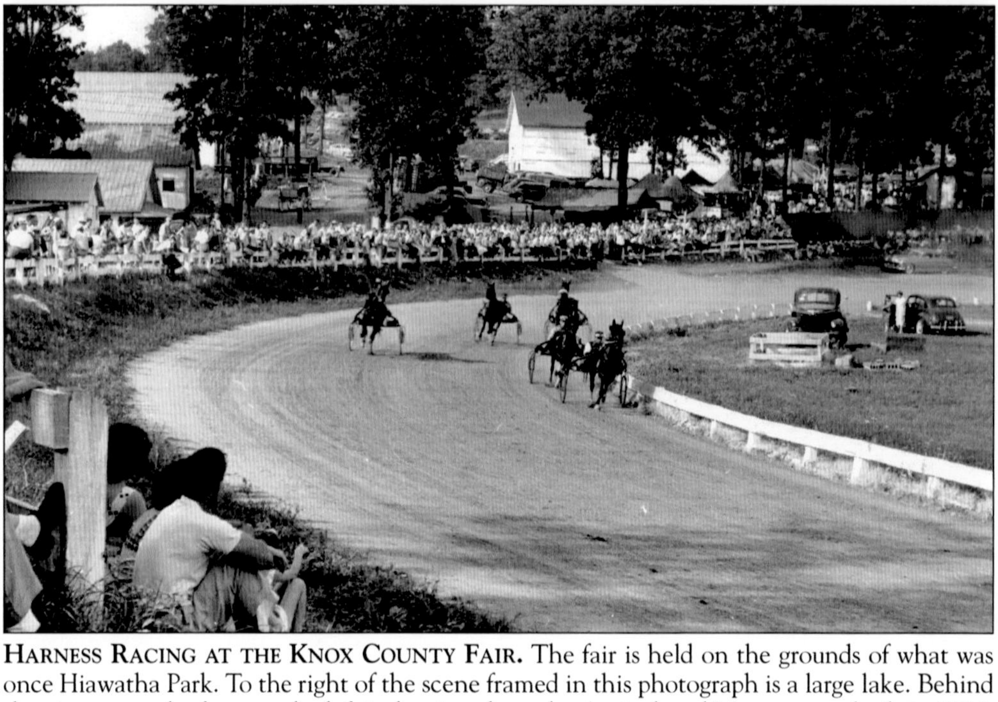

**Harness Racing at the Knox County Fair.** The fair is held on the grounds of what was once Hiawatha Park. To the right of the scene framed in this photograph is a large lake. Behind the viewers on the fence at the left is the site where the Agricultural Museum was built in 1984. (Photograph courtesy of Sip's Coffee House in downtown Mount Vernon.)

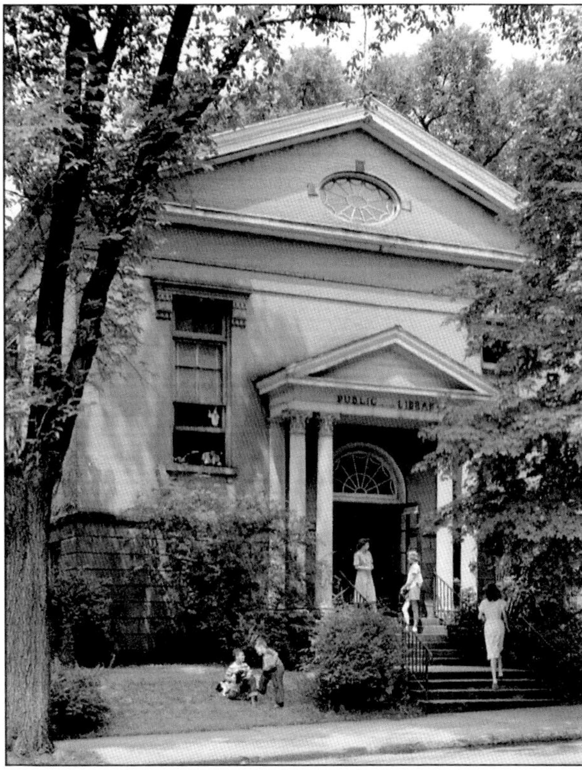

**THE LIBRARY EXTERIOR, 1965.** This photograph of the Mount Vernon Library was taken by the Ohio Department of Development c. 1965–66 to document the award of the "All-American City" designation to Mount Vernon. (Photograph courtesy of Sip's Coffee House in downtown Mount Vernon.)

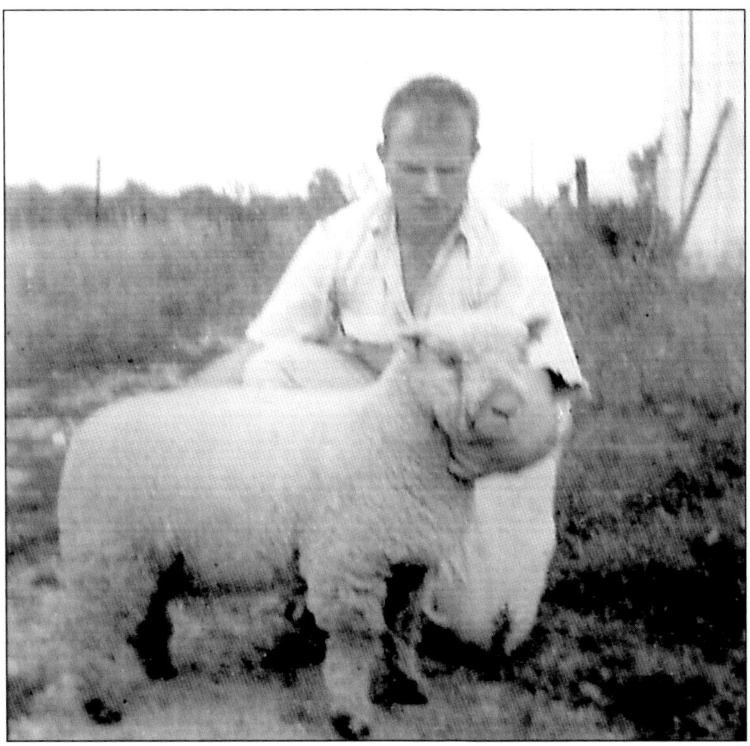

**PROMINENT SHOWMAN, WARREN WARD.** Warren started showing hogs at the Knox County Fair in 1929 when he was eight years old. He served on the Fair Board for 28 years and was a competitor for 50 years, mostly with Southdown sheep, such as the one he is holding in this 1940s photograph. (Photograph courtesy of Margene Ward.)

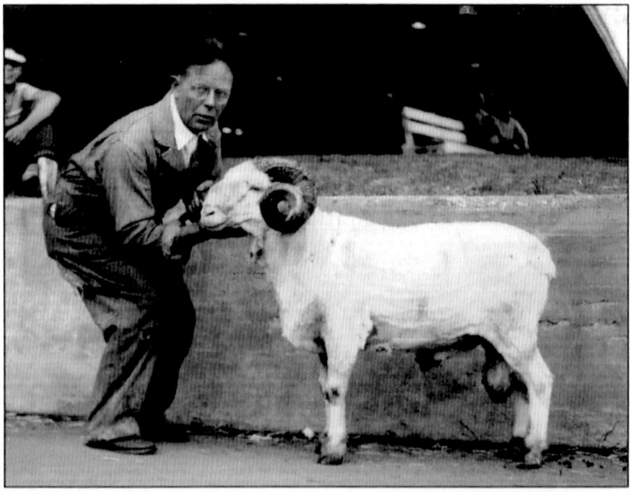

**Arthur Jewell of Centerburg Holds a Champion Merino Ram.** Jewell was a well-known Knox County sheep man. His Merino ram would have a fleece of long, oily wool, which was much prized in the manufacturing of wool clothing. Knox County was the largest sheep-producing county east of the Mississippi until the 1950s. (Photograph courtesy of the Knox County Agricultural Museum.)

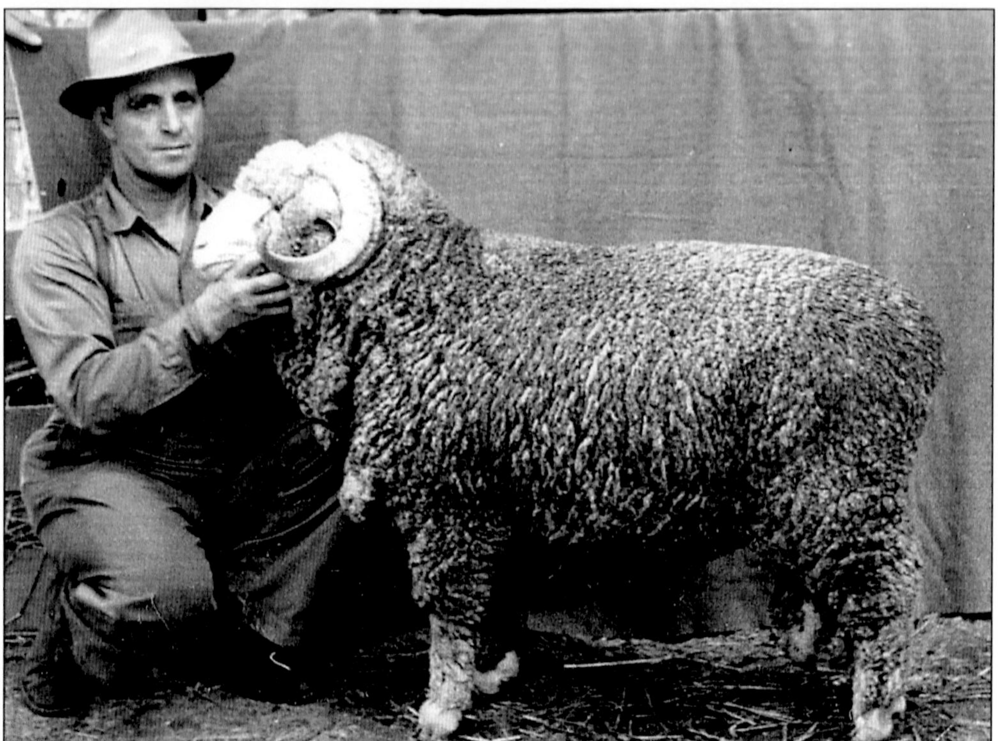

**Ram with His Wool On.** This unshorn ram appears as the sheep would normally appear. The man holding the ram is unidentified, but he was photographed at the Knox County Fair in the early 1950s. (Photograph courtesy of the Knox County Agricultural Museum.)

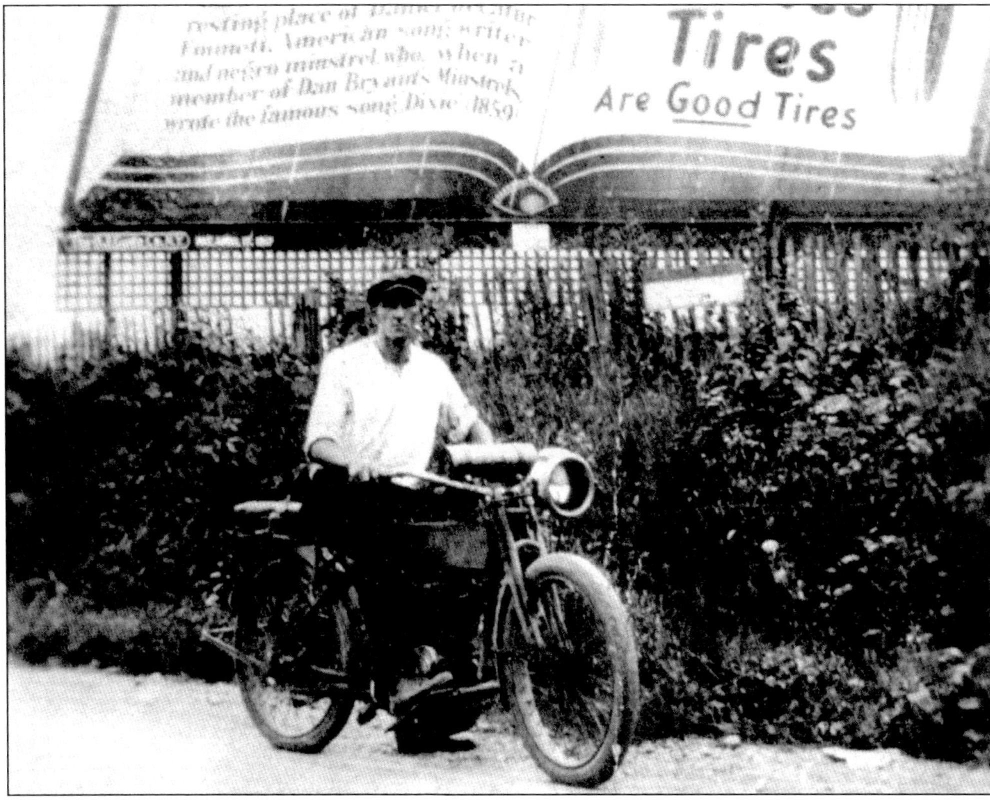


**OUTDOOR SIGN AND MOTORCYCLIST.** Pictured probably in the late 1930s or early 1940s, this outdoor advertising sign credits Dan Emmett with authoring "Dixie" in 1859. It also advertises United States Tires. (Photograph courtesy of Jeff Boucher at Flapper's Bar & Grille.)

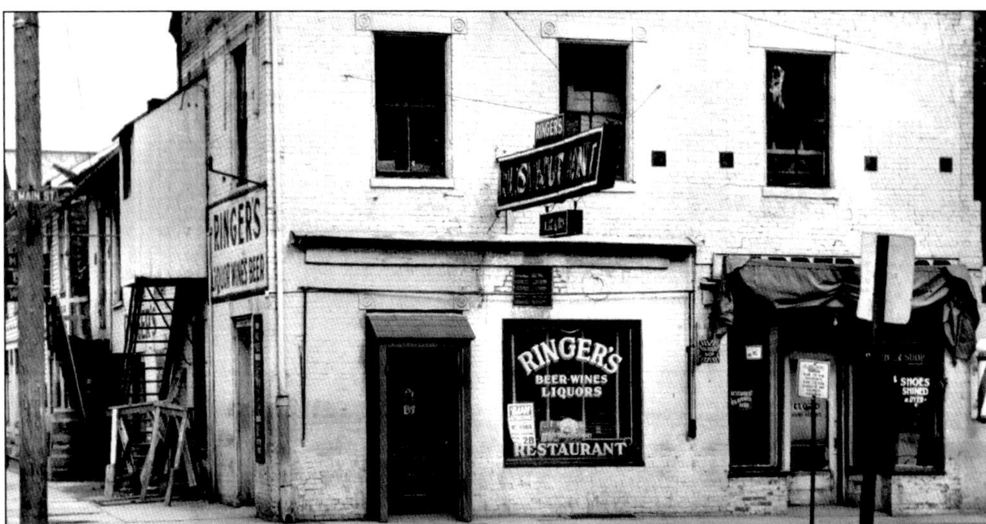


**RINGER'S IN 1944.** This restaurant was a popular eating spot in downtown Mount Vernon and maintained its antique lettering and look well into the 20th century. (Photograph courtesy of Jeff Boucher, Flapper's Bar & Grille.)

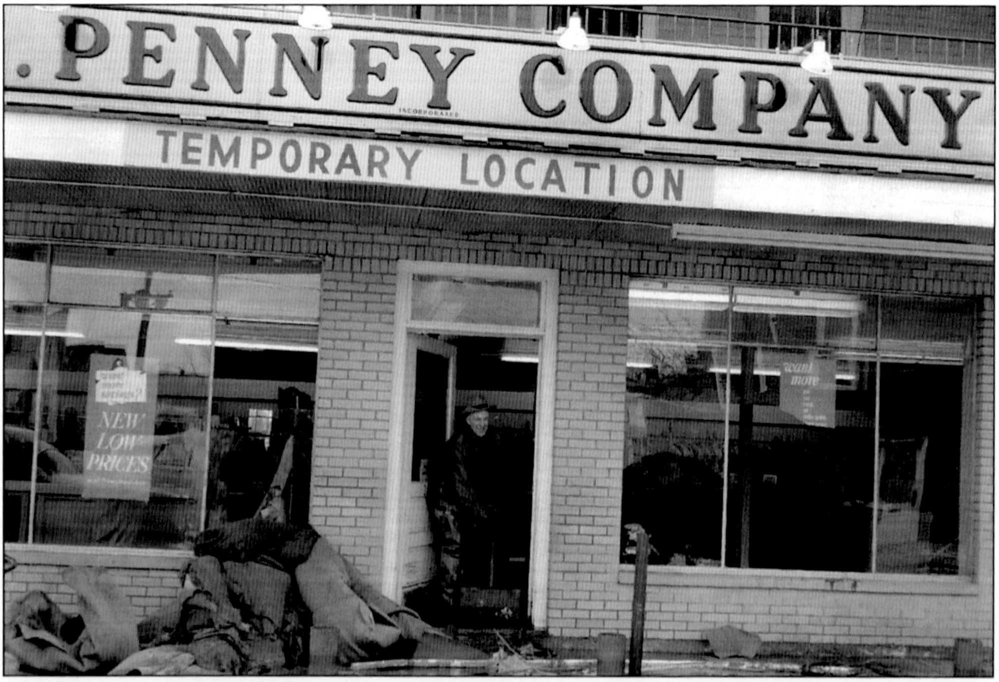


**J.C. PENNEY'S HAD TO MOVE.** This photograph from the flood of 1959 shows the problems it caused for downtown merchants. (Photograph by Gary Hewitt, courtesy of the Knox County Agricultural Museum.)

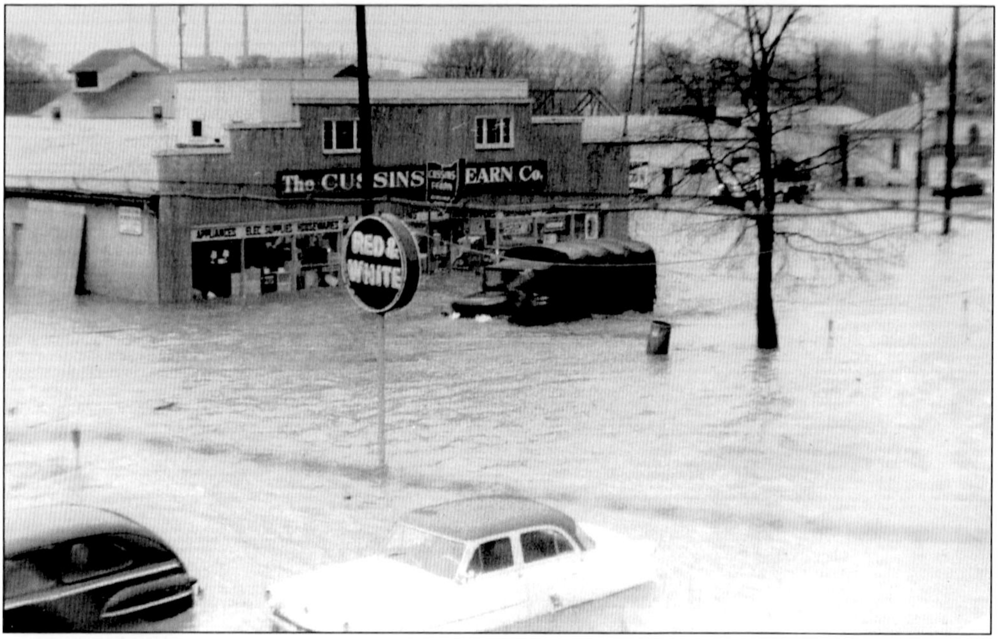


**CUSSINS & FEARN, RED AND WHITE.** The flood of 1959 was one of the last floods in Mount Vernon. Dikes were built later, and the Kokosing was dammed northwest of Fredericktown by the Army Corps of Engineers. (Photograph by Gary Hewitt, courtesy of the Knox County Agricultural Museum.)

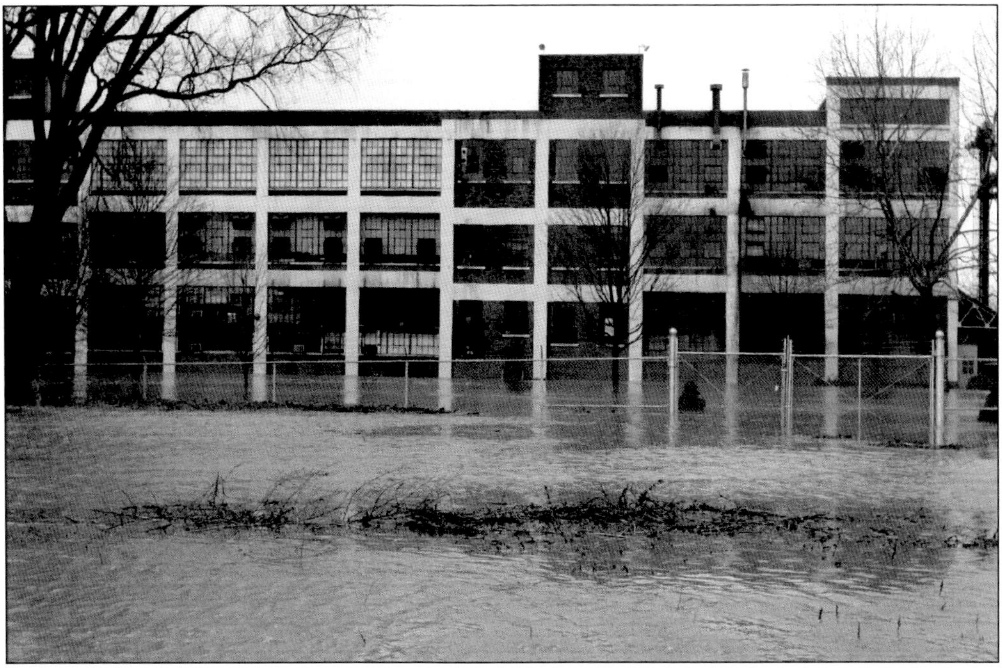

**SHELMAR FACTORY DURING THE FLOOD.** This photograph by Gary Hewitt shows how high the water rose in the 1959 flood of Mount Vernon, which was caused by six inches of rain falling on frozen ground. Shelmar produced a rubber-based plastic, which was used to wrap equipment and supplies shipped overseas during WWII. The company received the Army/Navy "E" Award based on their quality work and war efforts. (Photograph courtesy of the Knox County Agricultural Museum.)

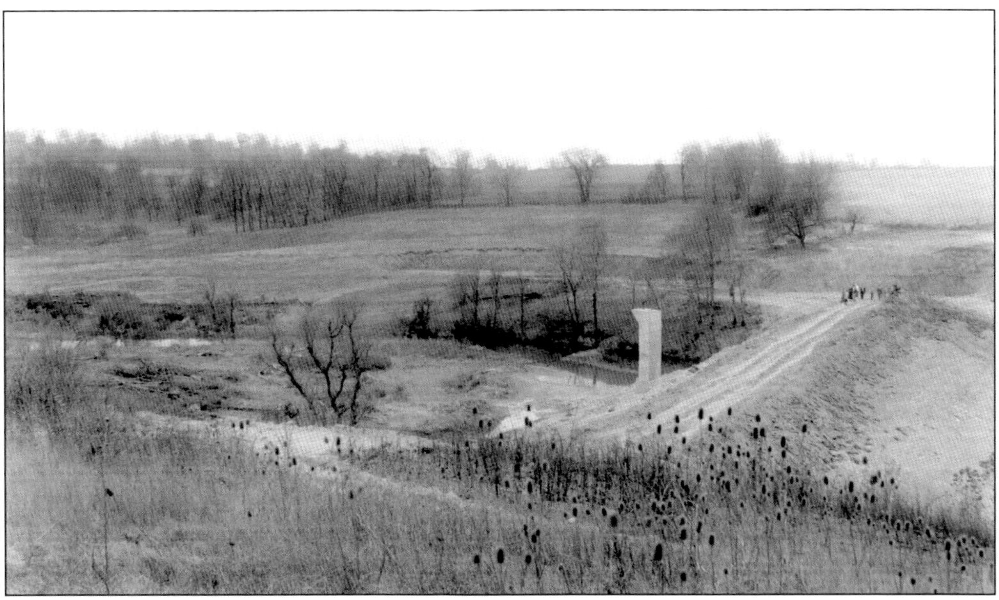

**KNOX LAKE DAM.** This photograph shows work underway to create a dam on Knox Lake to lessen flooding in Mount Vernon and the area. (Photograph courtesy of Knox County Agricultural Museum.)

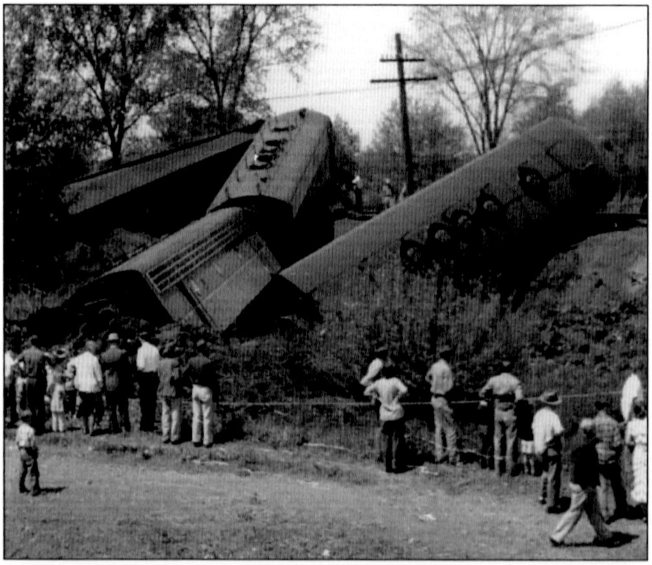

**1949 TRAIN WRECK.** These cars from the Pennsylvania Railroad derailed in South Vernon near where the Highway Garage is still located. The engineer probably missed a signal. (Photograph courtesy of Walter H. Boyd.)

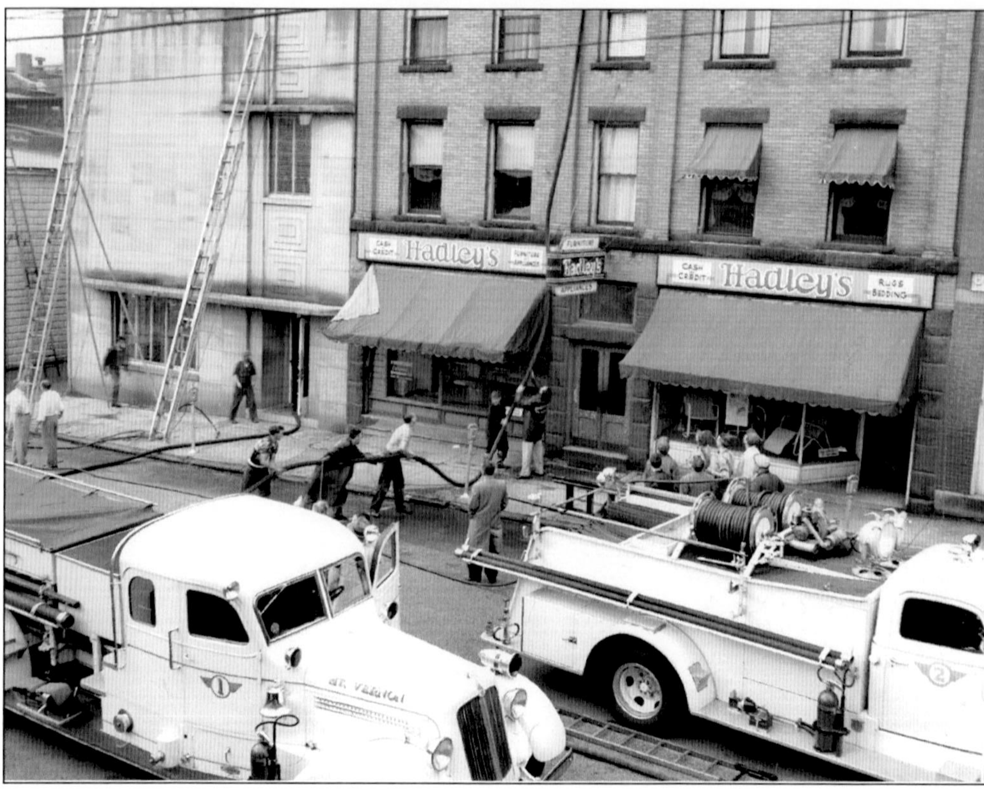


**FIRE IN TOWN.** Mount Vernon Fire Department fire trucks deal with a major fire on South Main Street in the 1950s. (Photograph courtesy of Richard A. Cochran.)

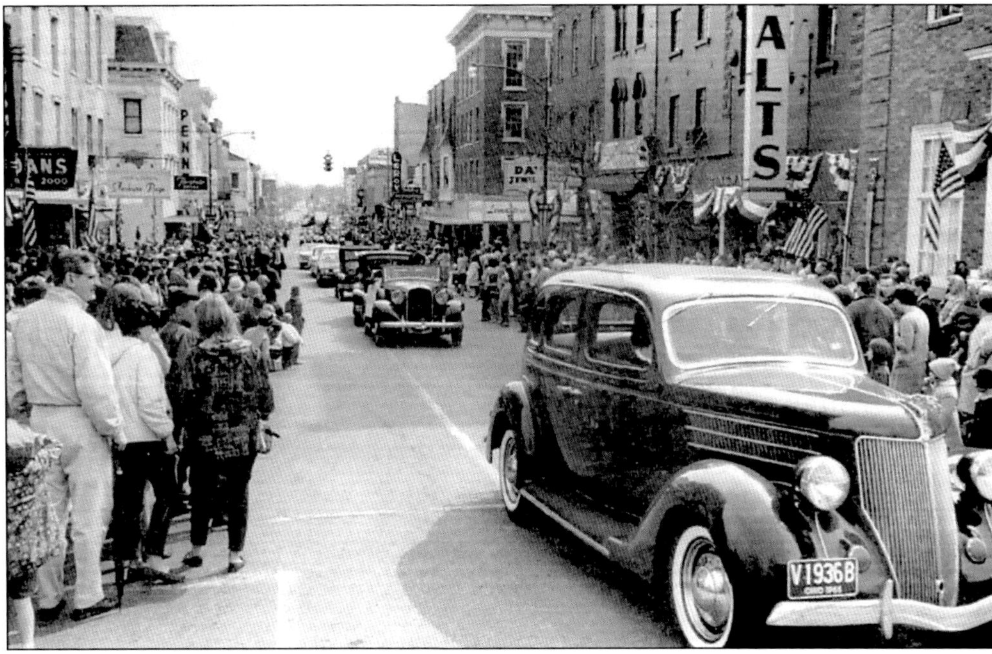


**ALL-AMERICAN CITY PARADE, APRIL 1966.** *Look Magazine* awarded Mount Vernon, Ohio, the distinction of being the "All-American City" and sent reporters and photographers to cover the city for an article. Since that honor was bestowed on Mount Vernon, city fathers have tried to maintain its high standards. (Photograph courtesy of Sip's Coffee House in downtown Mount Vernon.)

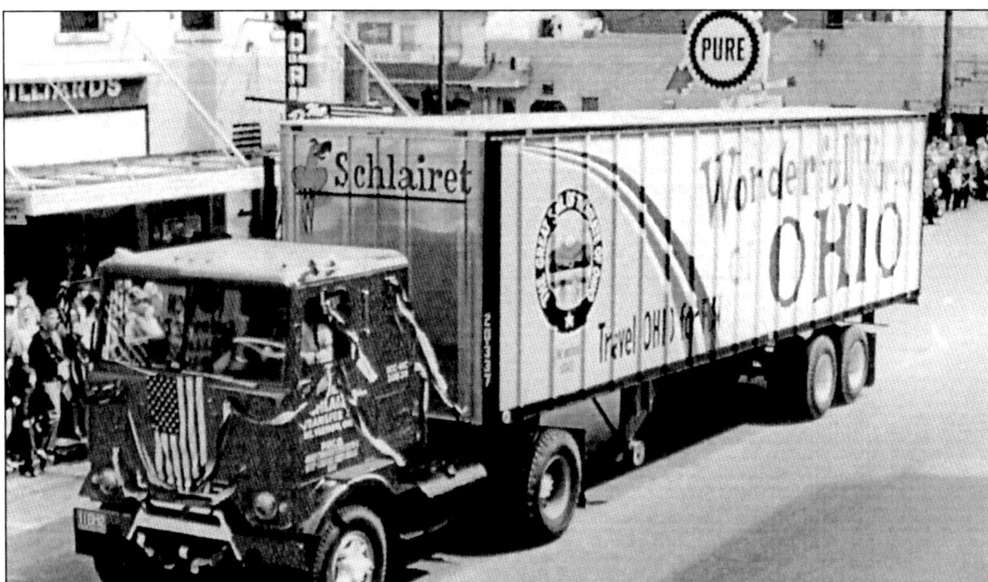


**SCHLAIRET TRUCKING IN C. 1960 PARADE.** E.A. Schlairet began trucking in 1917 in Mount Vernon when someone offered him $50 to haul a load to Columbus. He made the trip on a Sunday, but a flat tire cost him his profit. From that day until he died in 1960, Schlairet never trucked again on a Sunday. Mr. Schlairet had five sons, and they all worked in the business until it was sold in 1969. (Photograph courtesy of Ken Blubaugh.)

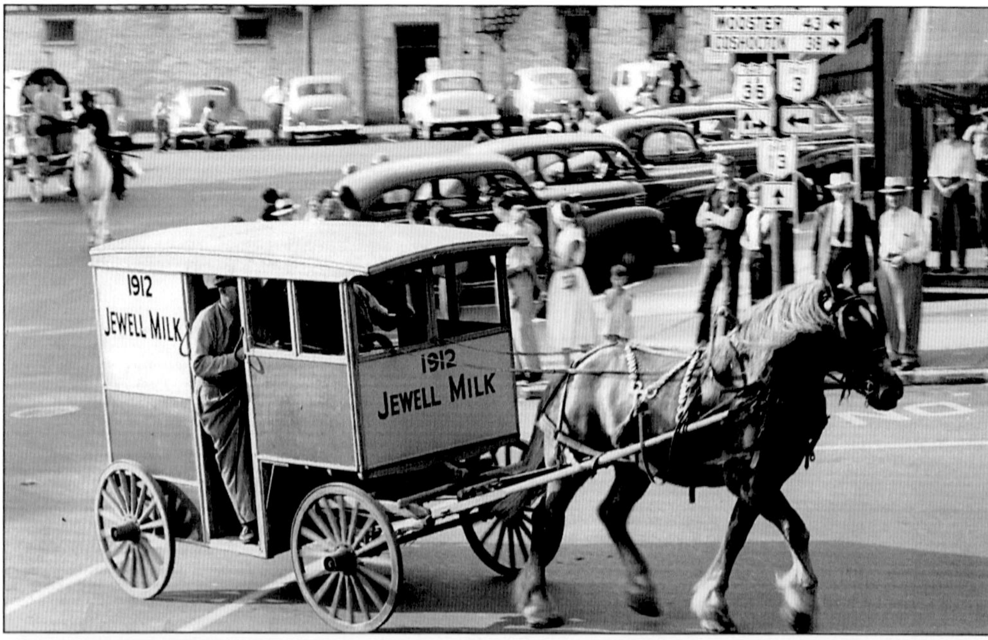


**1912 JEWELL MILK WAGON.** Two re-enactors drive a plow horse in this 1966 photograph of a parade crossing the Mount Vernon Square. (Photograph courtesy of the Knox County Agricultural Museum.)

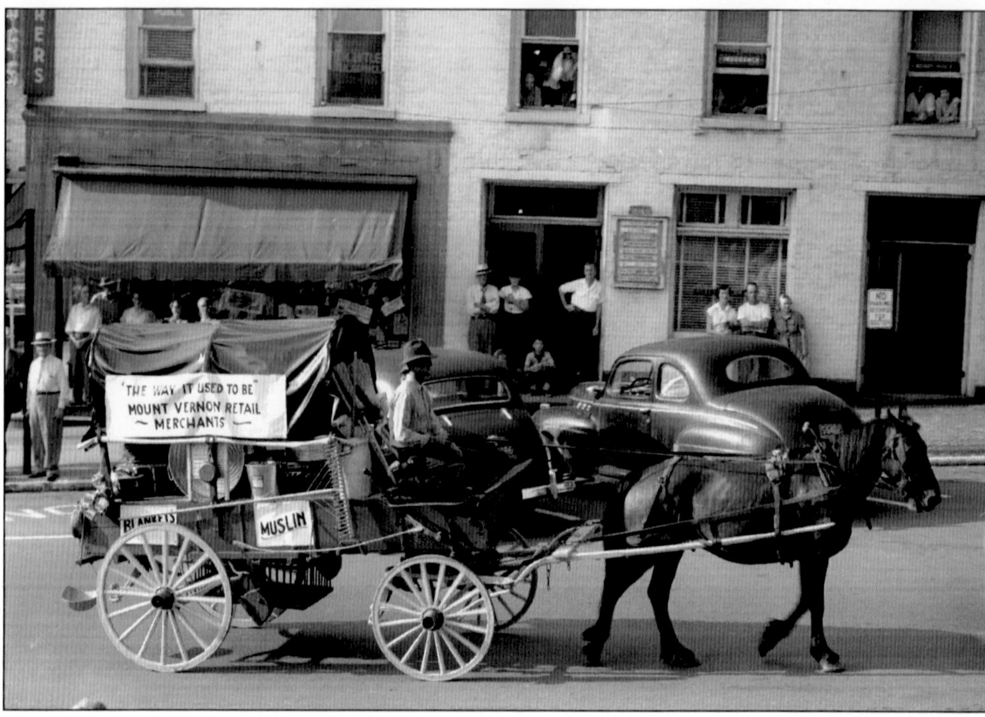


**THE WAY IT USED TO BE.** This photograph of the re-enactment of a typical early merchant is believed to have been taken at the All-American City parade. (Photograph courtesy of the Knox County Agricultural Museum.)

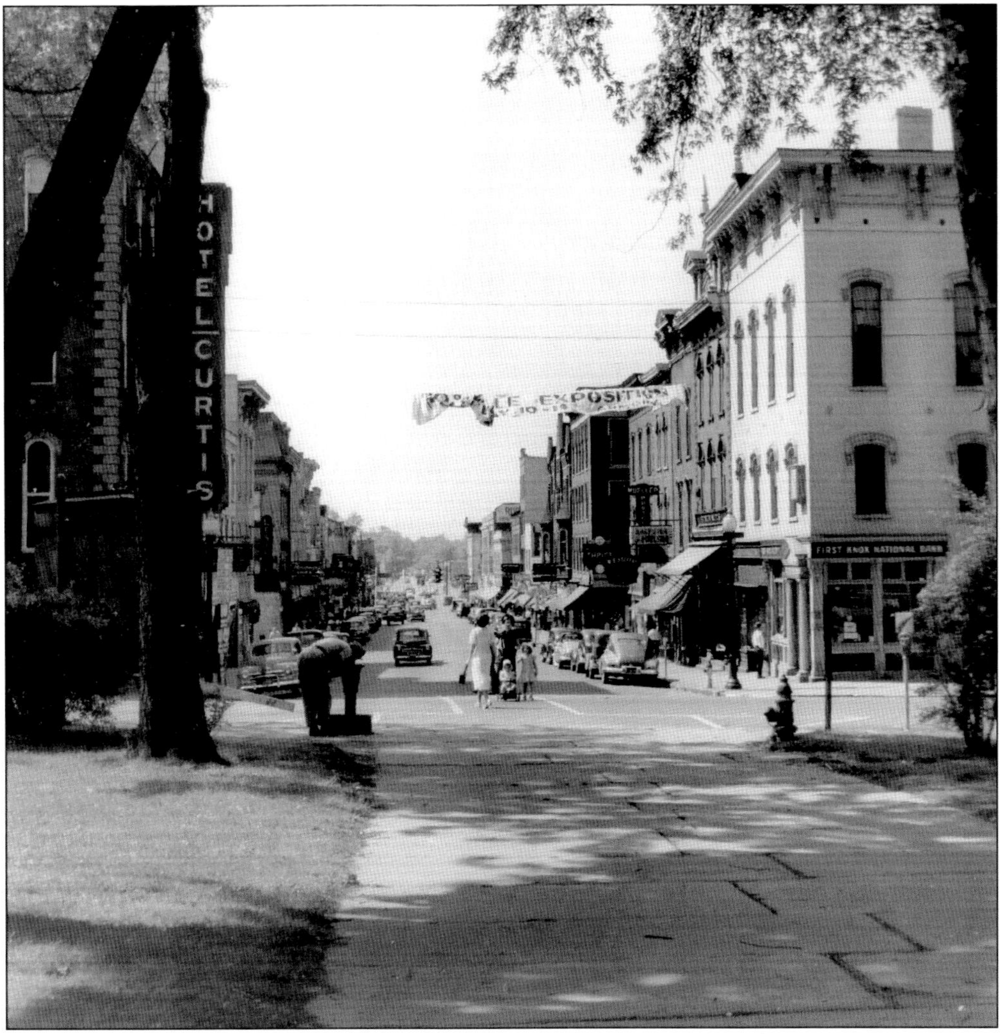


**TREE SHADED SCENE.** Large trees on the Square frame the view of South Main Street in 1966. First Knox Savings Bank is on the right. Curtis House has become "Hotel Curtis." (Photograph courtesy of Sip's Coffee House in downtown Mount Vernon.)

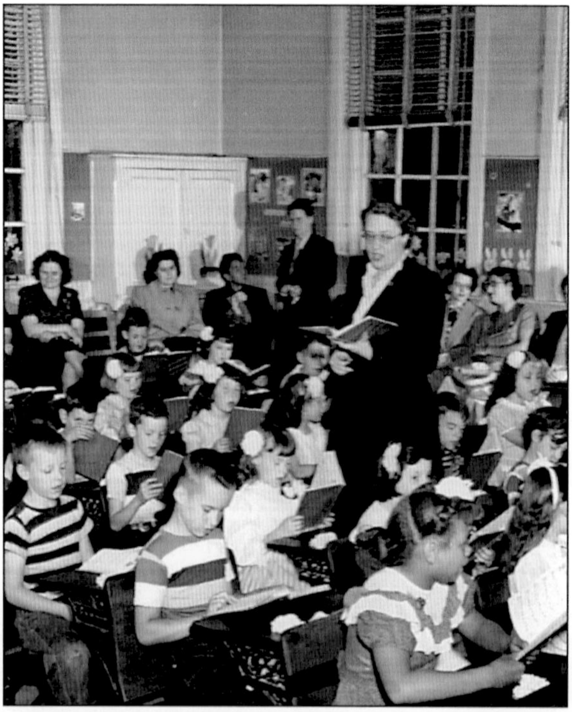

**TEACHING.** This state department photograph of a typical Mount Vernon school room in 1965–66 shows numerous parents and visitors. (Photograph courtesy of Sip's Coffee House in downtown Mount Vernon.)

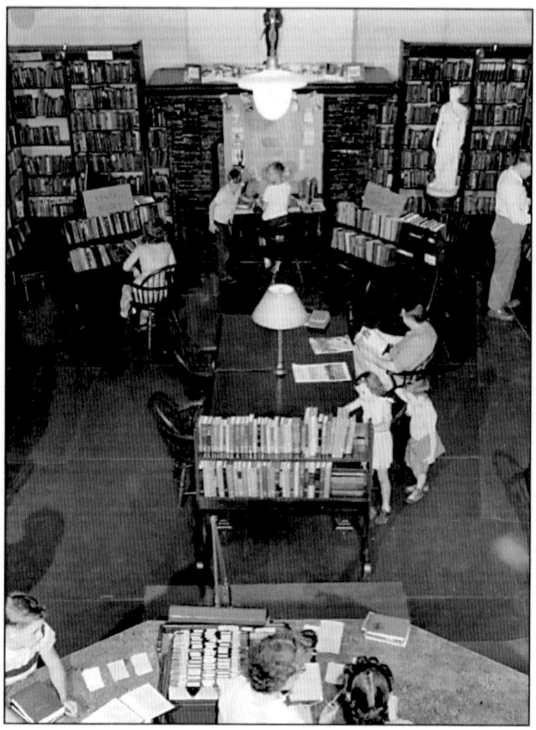

**LIBRARY IN 1965–66.** This is another photograph by the state department in conjunction with the All-American City celebration for Mount Vernon. The State of Ohio wanted to publicize the achievement. (Photograph courtesy of Sip's Coffee House in downtown Mount Vernon.)

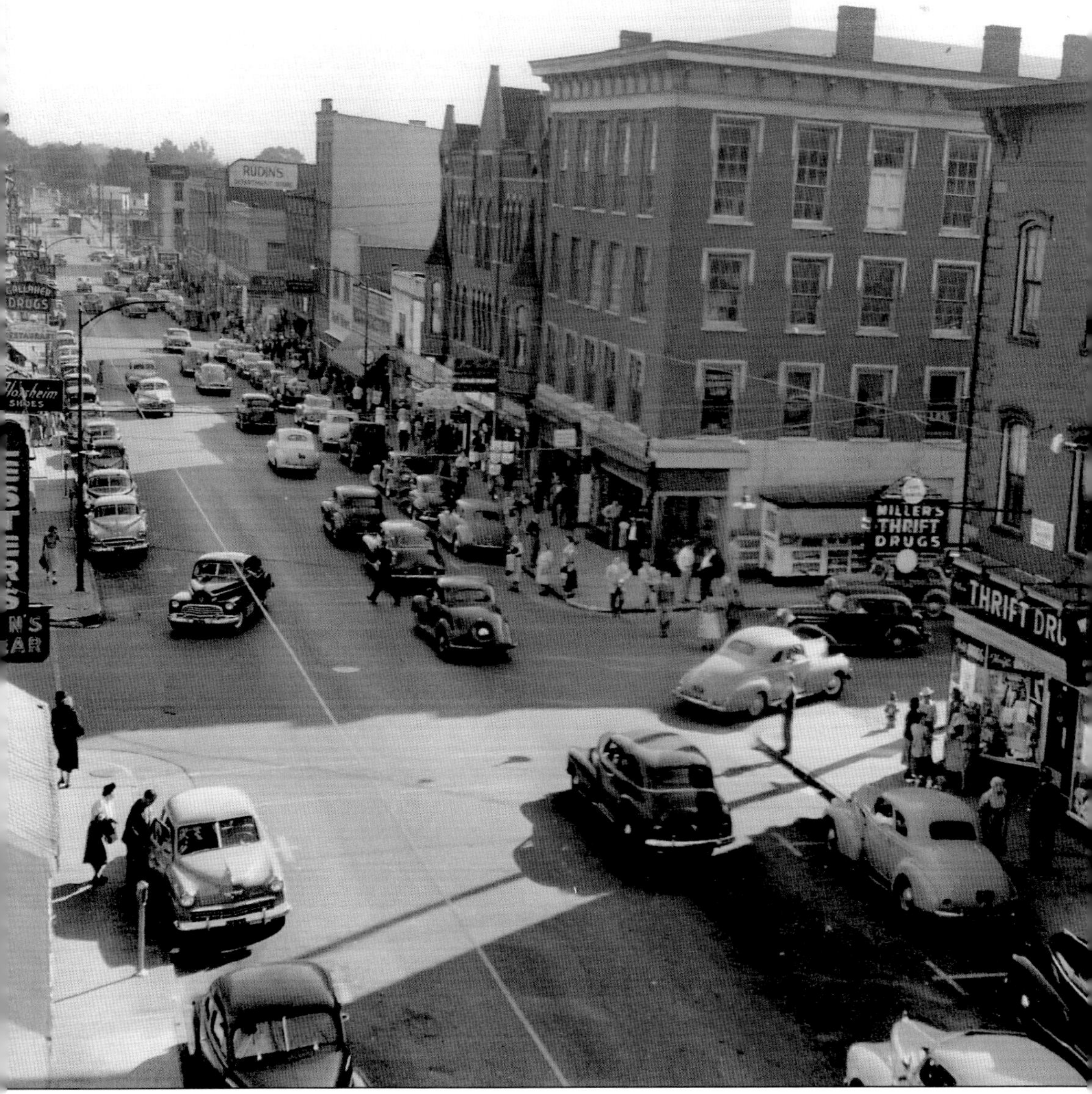


**South Main from Hotel Curtis.** The photographer shot this view of South Main Street from the upper floor of the Hotel Curtis in 1966. (Photograph courtesy of Sip's Coffee House in downtown Mount Vernon.)

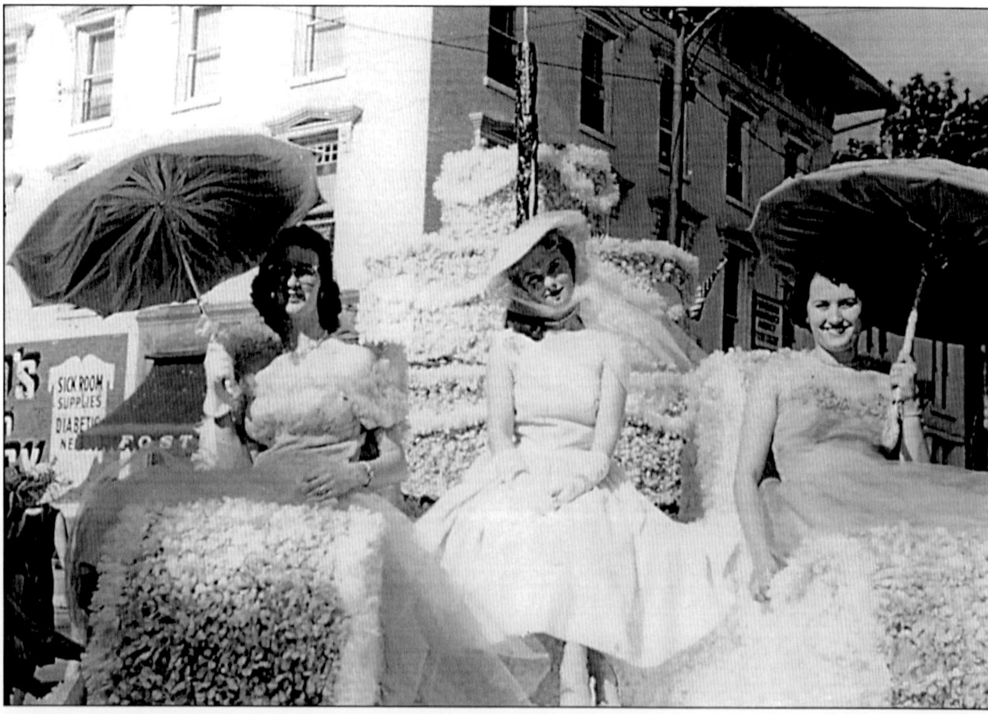


**SCHLAIRET FLOAT.** Family members and friends ride a float representing the trucking company in this *c.* 1960s parade in Mount Vernon. Left to right, they are: Diana DeWitt, Shirley Blubaugh, and Mary Spearman. (Photograph courtesy of Ken Blubaugh.)

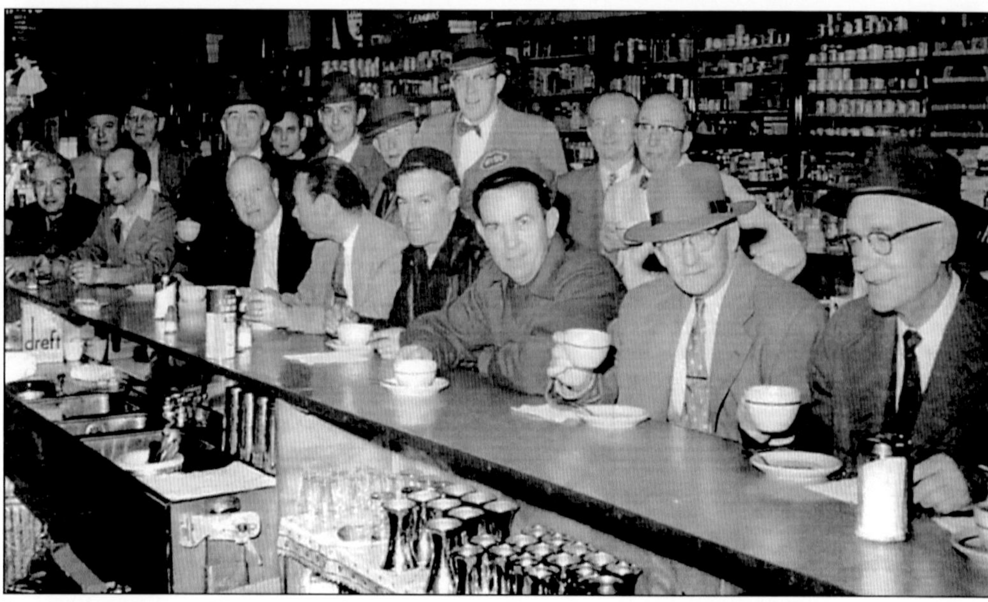


**LAST MEETING OF HECKLER'S COFFEE CLUB.** This photograph by Gary Hewitt was taken at the counter in Heckler's Drug Store *c.* 1965, just before the buildings on the southwest side of the Mount Vernon Square were razed for a new bank building. (Photograph courtesy of Sip's Coffee House in downtown Mount Vernon.)

# *Seven*

# People, Places, and Events

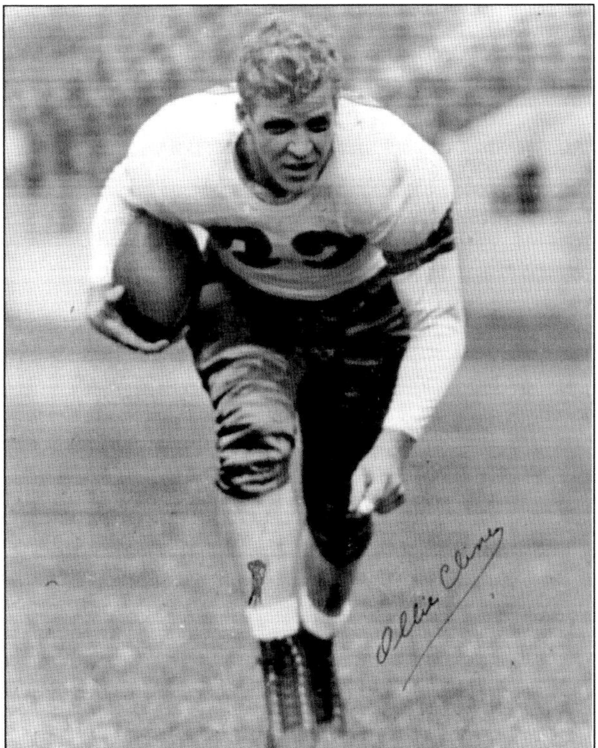


**All-American Ollie Cline.** Cline graduated from Fredericktown High School in the spring of 1944 and played that fall at the Ohio State University—the year they went undefeated. Cline was named an All-American in 1945. He held the most yards per game record until Archie Griffin broke it. (Photograph courtesy of the Fredericktown Historical Society.)

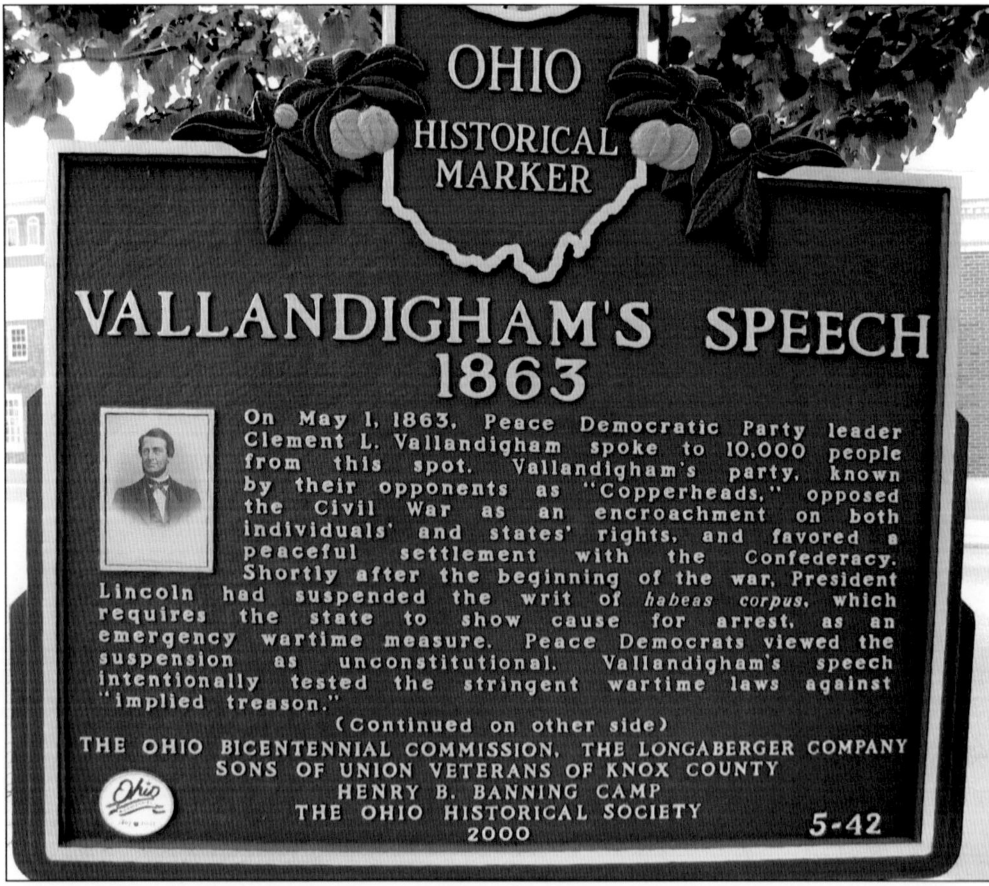


**VALLANDIGHAM'S SPEECH.** On May 1, 1863, Peace Party candidate Clement L. Vallandigham spoke to 10,000 people gathered on the Square in Mount Vernon. He spoke from a special platform arranged on the west side of the Square. Mount Vernon was reputed to harbor numerous opponents to the Civil War, then in progress. They were called "copperheads" by those who supported the Civil War. Mary Ann Ball was born in Mount Vernon in 1817 and at age 20 began her career as a nurse. "Mother Bickerdyke," as Ms. Ball was called, was a great favorite of the troops from both sides during the Civil War. Her plaque is on the Square near the one for Vallandigham. Dr. Lorle Porter, Mount Vernon native and noted historian, was instrumental in getting several historical markers, such as this one, posted in Mount Vernon. (Photograph by D.E. Boyd.)

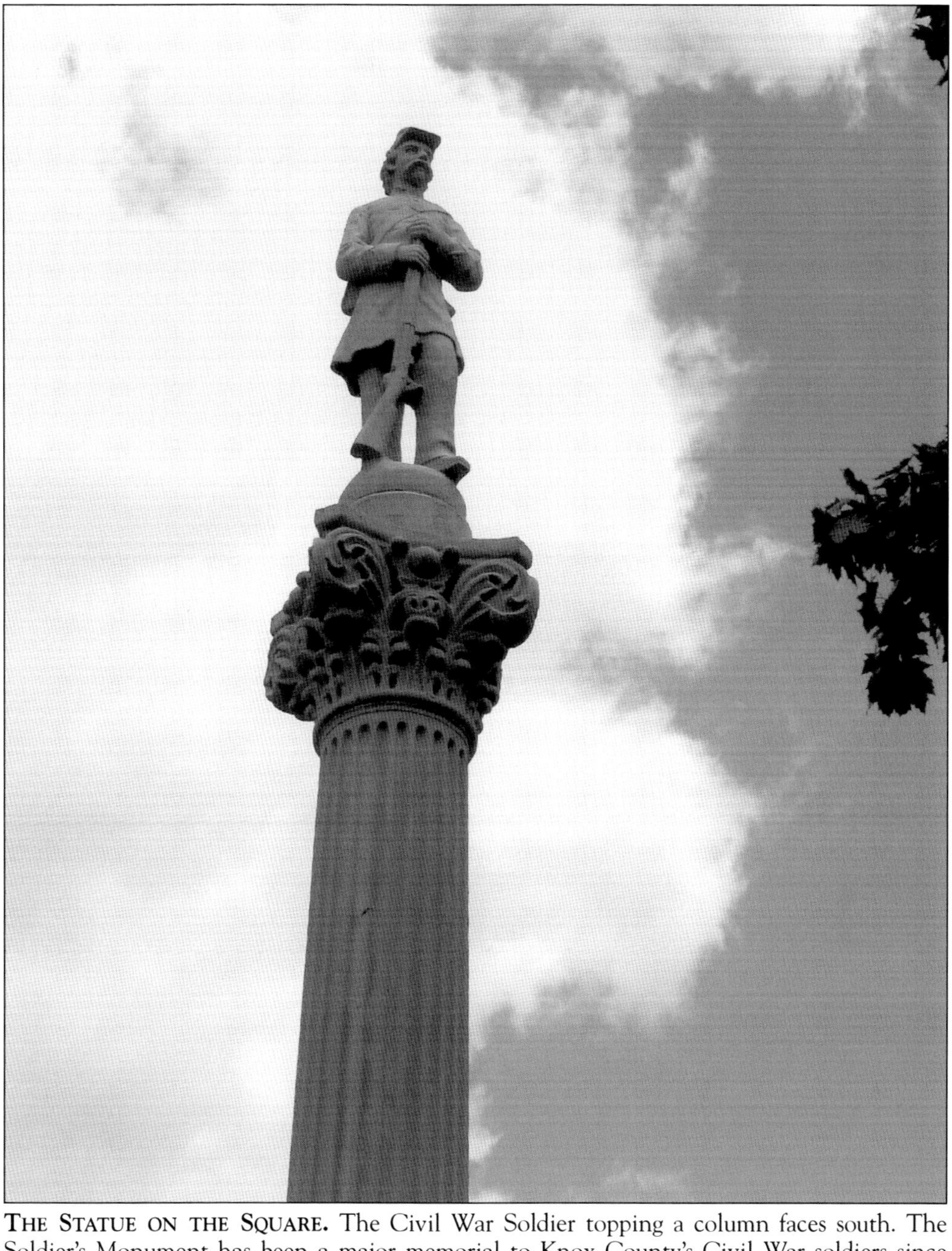

**THE STATUE ON THE SQUARE.** The Civil War Soldier topping a column faces south. The Soldier's Monument has been a major memorial to Knox County's Civil War soldiers since 1877. (Photograph by Andrew Lane.)

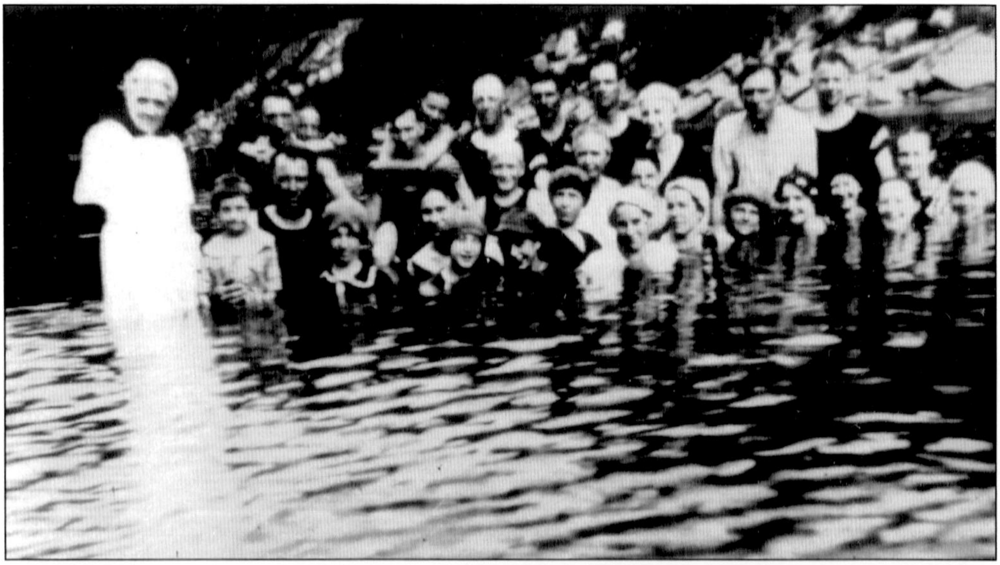

**BAPTISM.** This is a large-group baptism representative of many in the area. One of America's greatest preachers was Dr. Ralph Sockman of Fredericktown, who had a radio broadcast from New York City for much of the first half of the 20th century. (Photograph courtesy of the Knox County Agricultural Museum.)

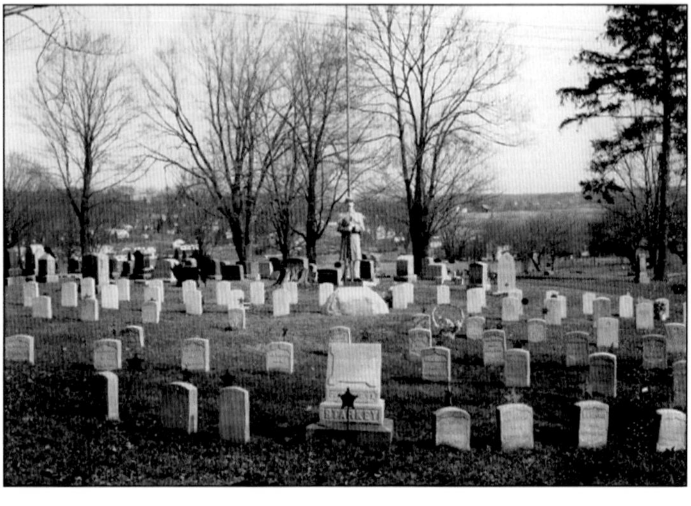

**CIVIL WAR PLOT.** This 1966 photograph shows Civil War graves in Mount Vernon's Mound View Cemetery north of Gay Street and State Route 3. (Photograph courtesy of Anita V. Lahmon.)

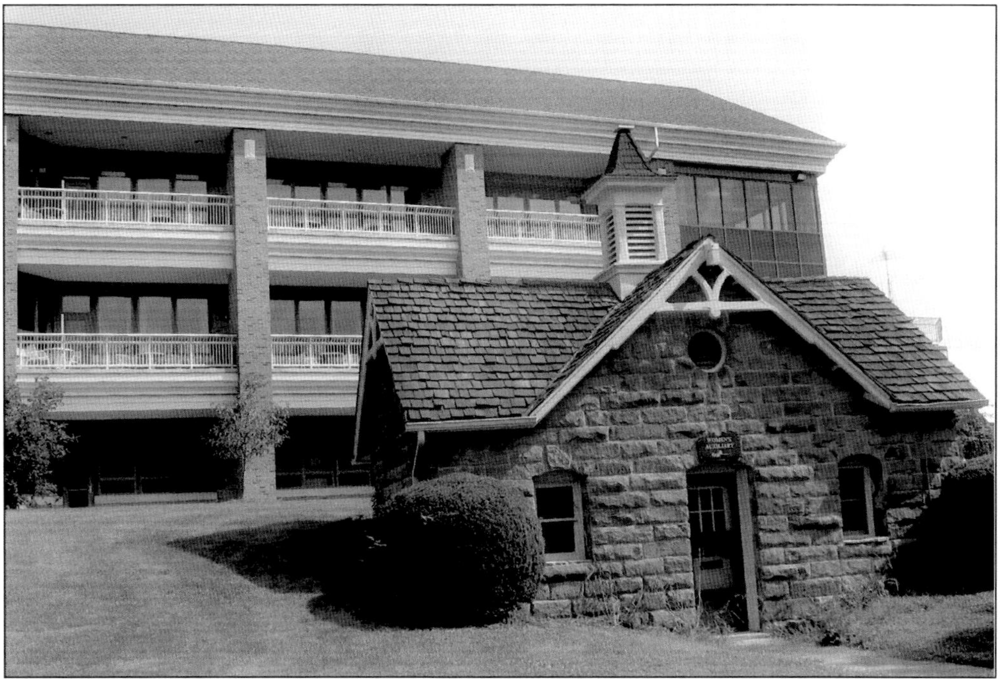

**THE OLD AND THE NEW, JUXTAPOSED.** In front, at the right of this photo is the original icehouse for Lake Home Farm, which dates from 1871 and is made of sandstone. Dominating the background is the Thorne Library/Learning Resource Center for the Mount Vernon Nazarene University, which was built in 1996. (Photograph by D.E. Boyd.)

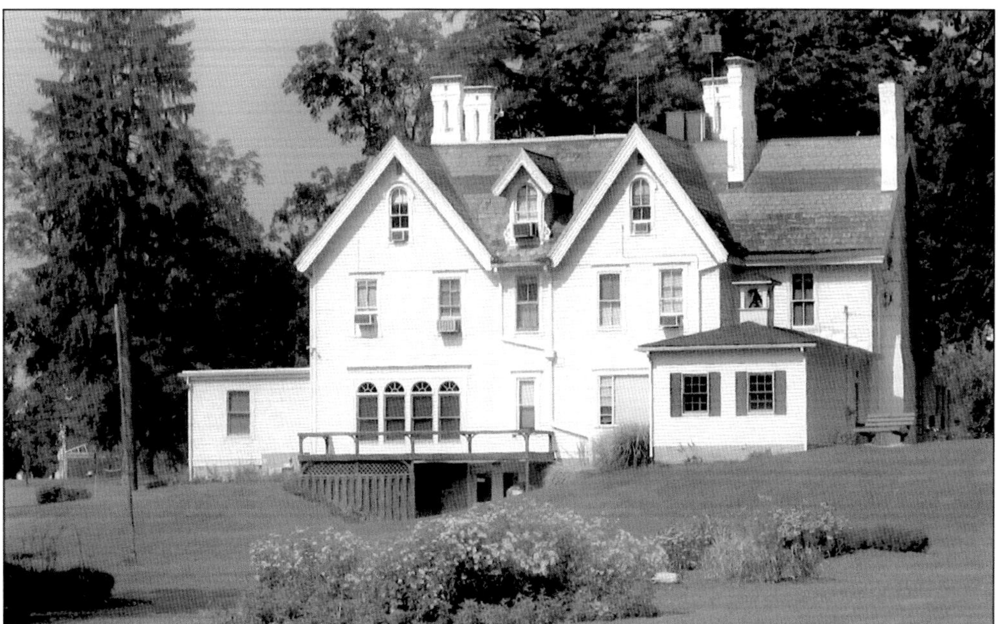

**THE UPDATED MOUNT VERNON NAZARENE UNIVERSITY ADMINISTRATION BUILDING.** This building was built in 1871, but it has been adapted to serve as administrative offices and a welcoming center since early 1967. (Photograph by D.E. Boyd.)

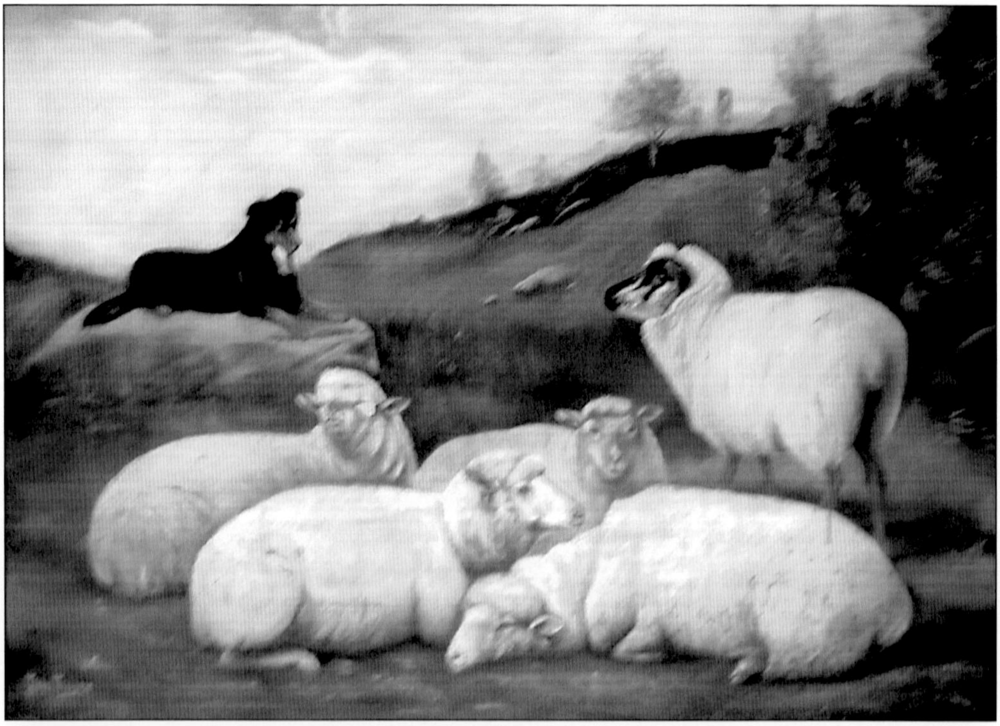

**A Pastoral Scene.** This painting dates from the early 1900s and is signed "J.B. Foote." (Photograph of painting in the Fredericktown Historical Society by D.E. Boyd.)

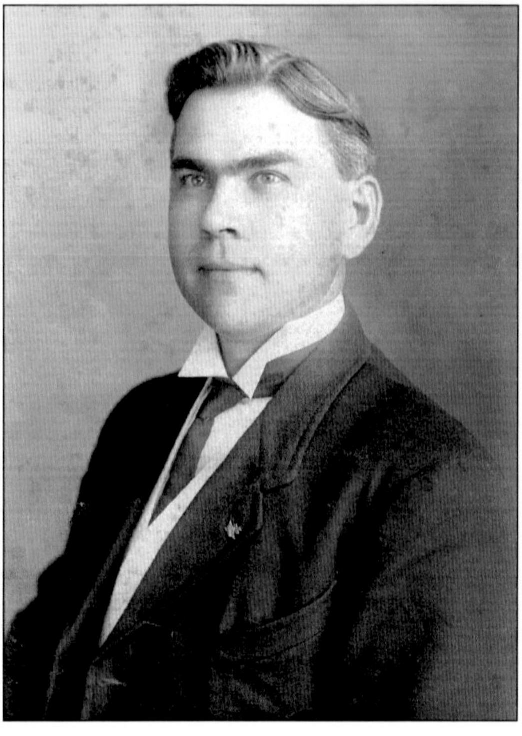

**J.B. Foote.** The Foote Foundry was established in 1856. J.B. took over in 1900 and built it into a nationally known concern. He is also known as a popular painter of local scenes and portraits. (Courtesy of the Fredericktown Historical Society.)

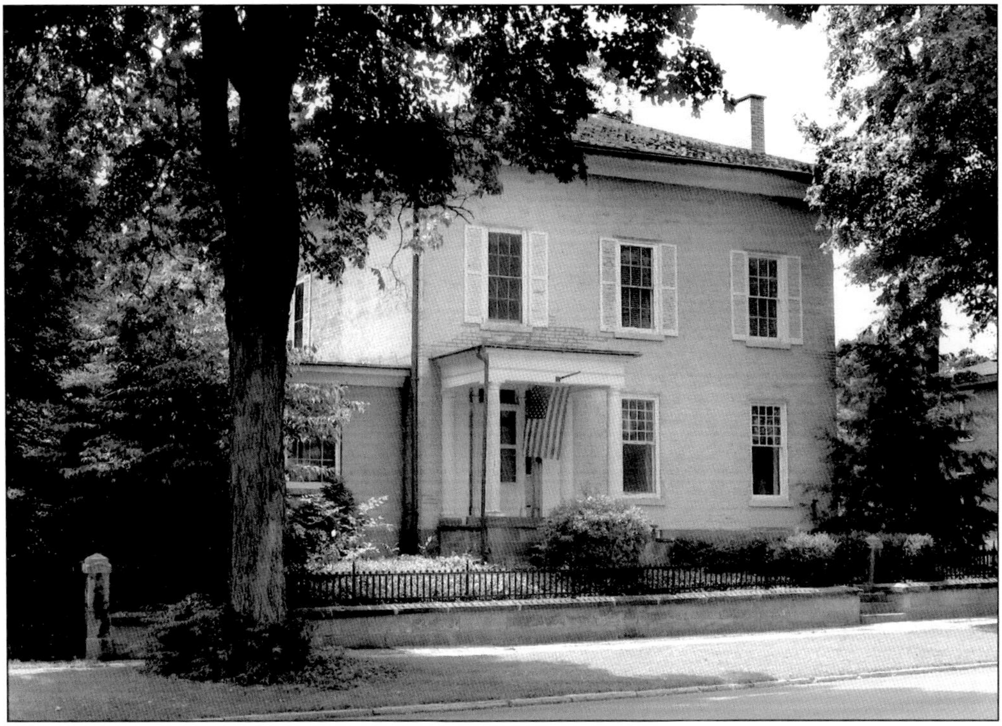

**THE SEMPLE-UPHAM HOUSE, 200 EAST HIGH STREET.** Built in 1855 by Matthew Mitchell, this house was occupied somewhat later by Dr. William F. Semple, who first patented a rubber-based chewing gum. In 1908, James and Mabelle Upham moved into the home when James started working for the Upham Gas Company. (Photograph by D.E. Boyd.)

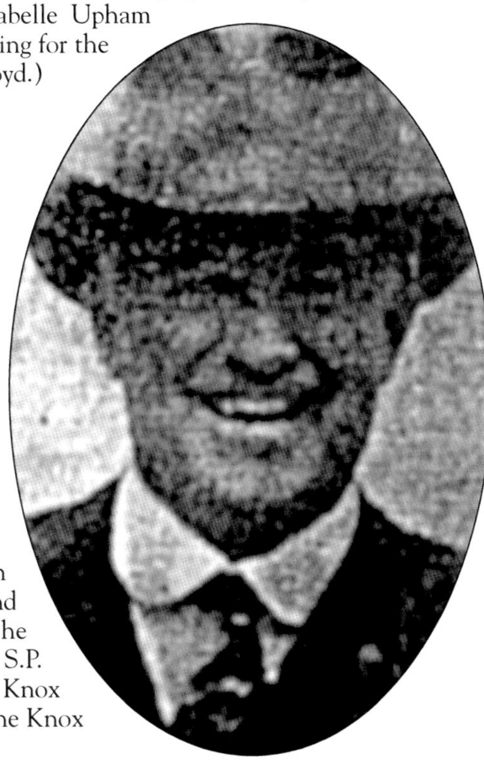

**DAVID A. UPHAM, GAS AND OIL PIONEER.** David Upham was involved in laying the first gas line in America in a wooden pipe in Pennsylvania. He moved to Mount Vernon in 1905 to found the Upham Gas Company. In 1917, he moved to Mineral Wells, Texas, and further developed his gas business. In 1926, he sold his company to two of his sons, J.A. and S.P. of Mount Vernon. The Uphams supplied gas to Knox County for 40 years. (Photograph courtesy of the Knox County Agricultural Museum.)

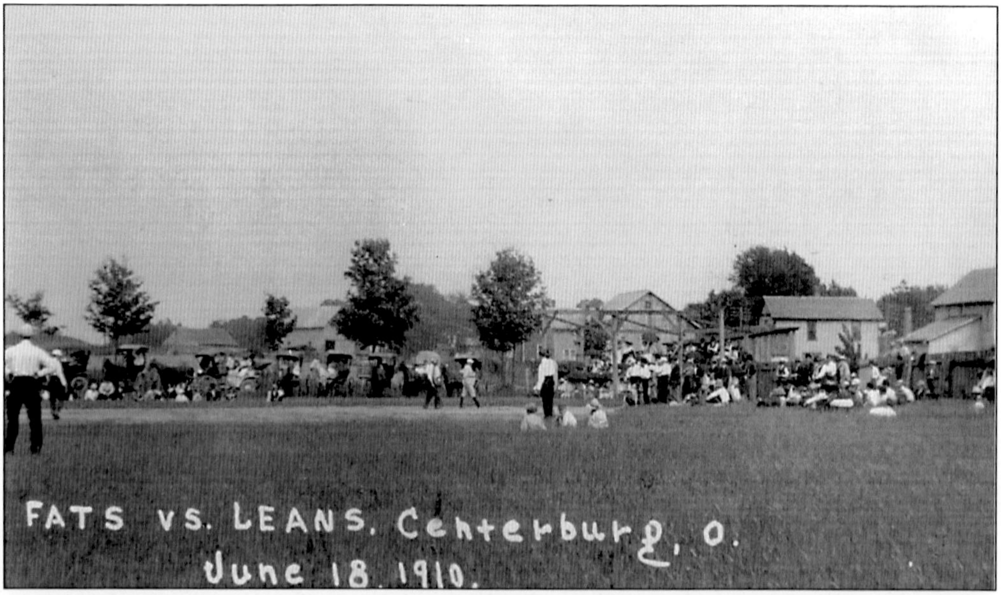


**FATS VS. LEANS.** We may not know who won the game, but the photograph is clearly labeled. (Photograph courtesy of the Knox County Agricultural Museum.)

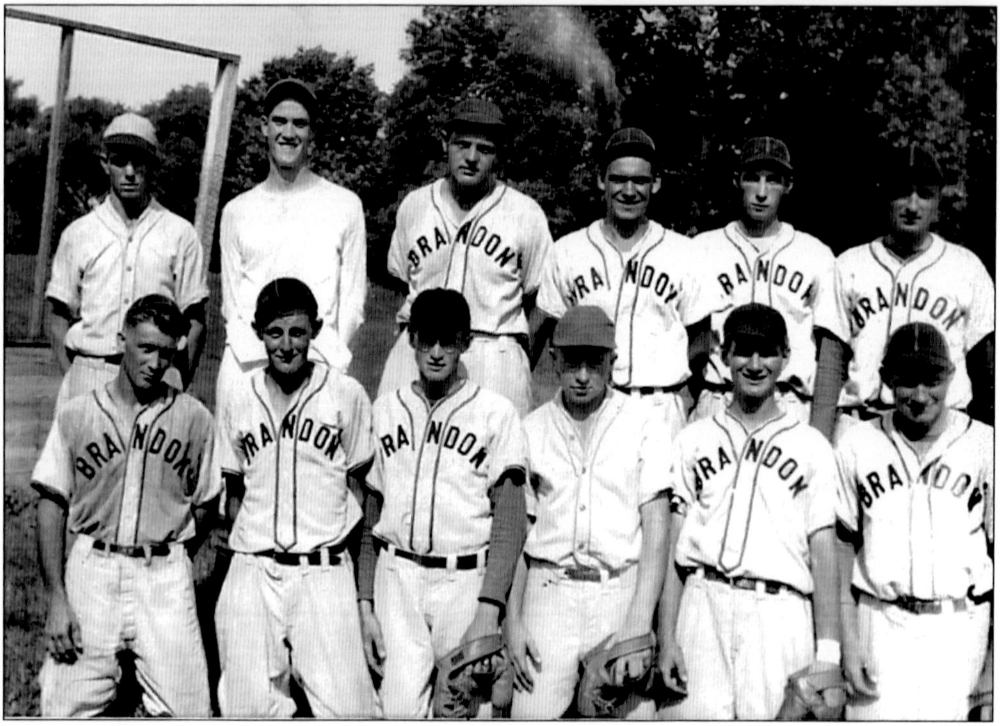


**A LATER VERSION, THE BRANDON BLUES.** The winners of the Mount Vernon City League in baseball in the 1950s were, left to right: (front row) Gordon Gore, unknown, Paul Rowe, Henry Tharp, Harry Wilson, and Fred Hayes; (back row) Early Thompson, Harry Chadwick, Rodger Spearman, and the others are unknown. (Photograph courtesy of the Knox County Agricultural Museum.)

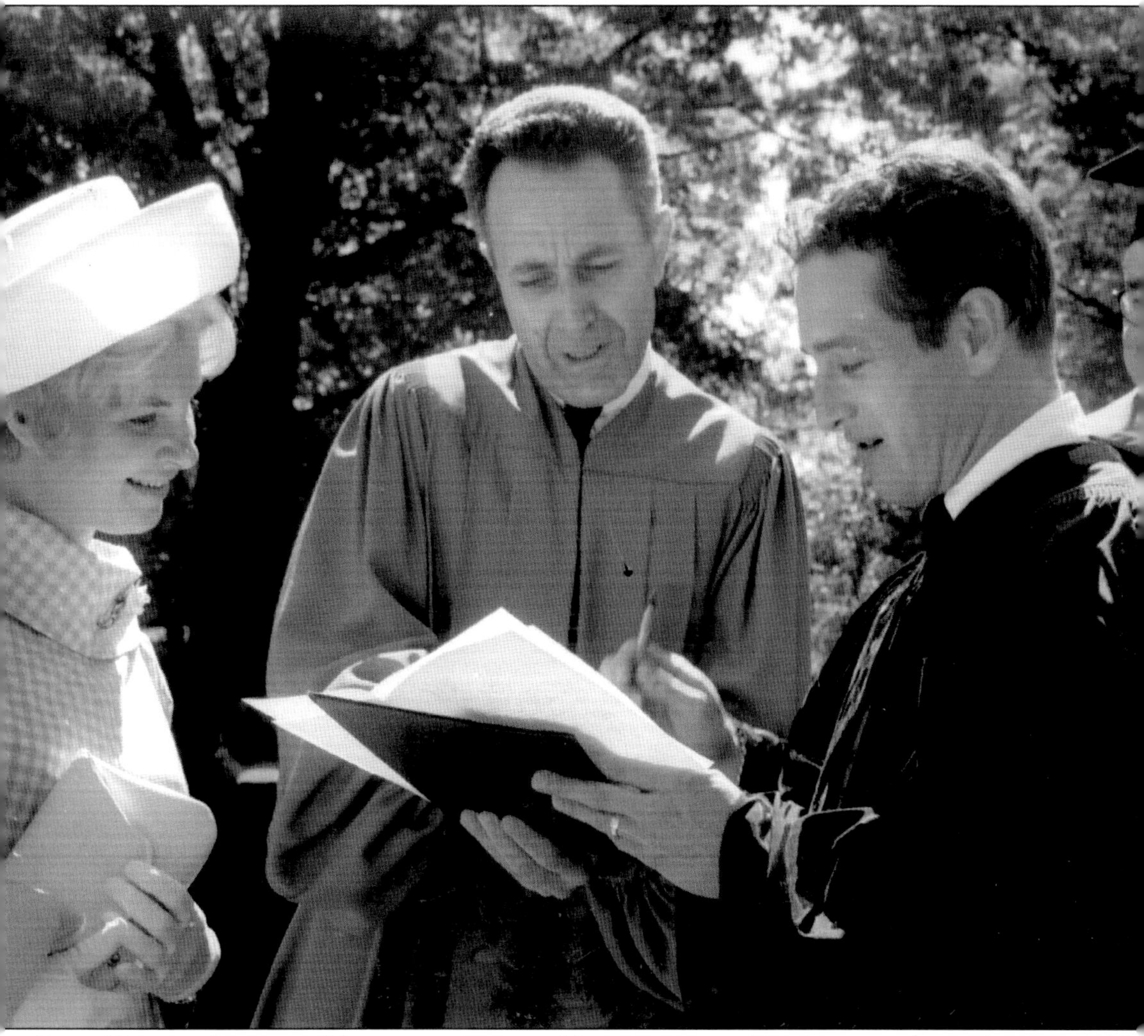

**PAUL NEWMAN RECEIVES HONORARY DEGREE.** Newman received an honorary degree from Kenyon college at the 1961 commencement: (left to right) Joanne Woodward, Professor of Music Paul Schwartz, and Paul Newman, a Kenyon graduate of 1948. (Photograph by D. Garverick Studio, Mount Vernon, courtesy of Olin Library, Kenyon College, Greenslade Special Collections and Archives.)

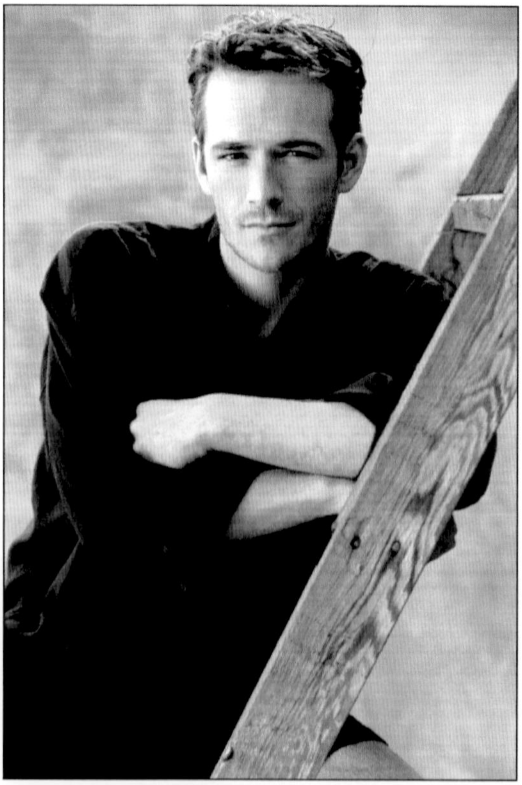

**LUKE PERRY, STAR OF THE STAGE, SCREEN, AND TELEVISION.** Luke graduated from Fredericktown High School and was known for always having fun. His earliest interest in TV was apparent when he began trying to figure out how those little people got in the television set. He wanted to be one of them! (Photograph courtesy of Mrs. Ann Bennett, Luke's mother.)

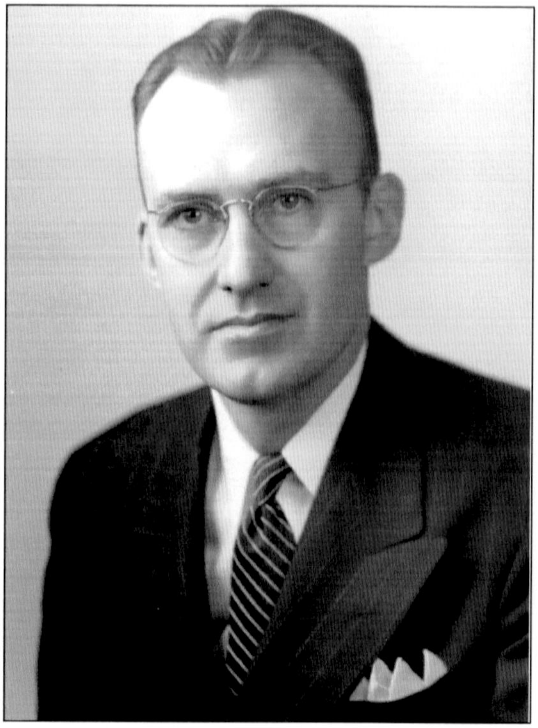

**NOVICE FAWCETT, EDUCATOR.** Novice grew up on a farm near Gambier, Ohio. At six foot four inches, he received a scholarship to play basketball at Kenyon and graduated in 1931, fulfilling his father's dearest wish. He became the president of the Ohio State University in 1956 and served until 1972. (Photograph courtesy of the Olin Library, Kenyon College, Greenslade Special Collections and Archives.)

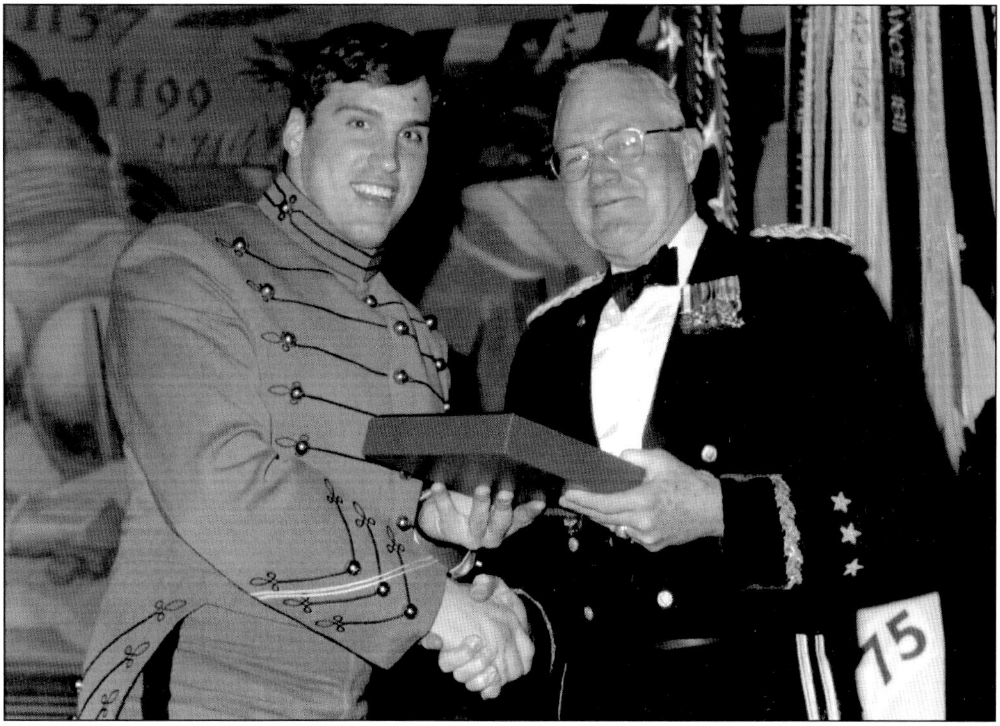


**DON SMITH RECEIVES THE ALL-AMERICAN AWARD.** General Scott, commandant of West Point, presents Don Smith of Fredericktown with his All-American Award in football in 1985. In 1984, the Army beat the Navy, and Smith played opposite his high school rival from Highland (13 miles west of Fredericktown in Morrow County). (Photograph courtesy of Don's father, Mr. Jesse Smith.)

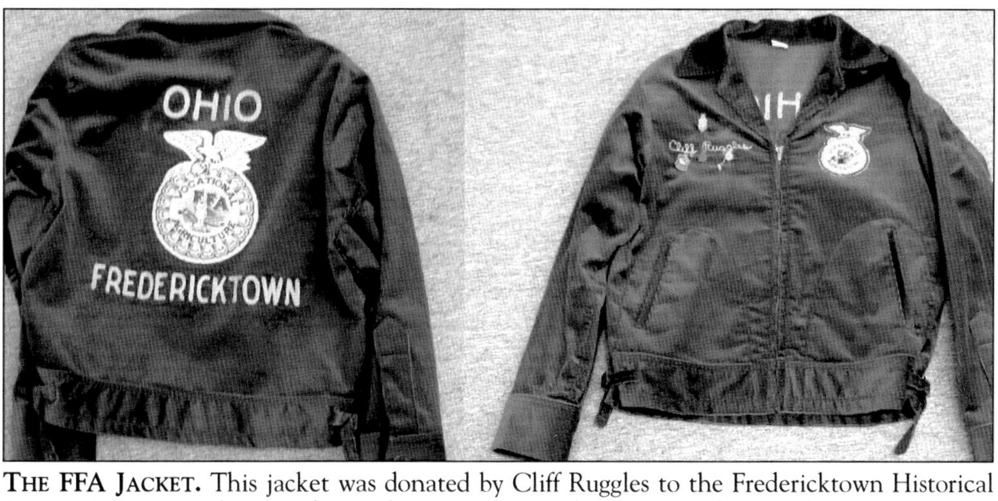


**THE FFA JACKET.** This jacket was donated by Cliff Ruggles to the Fredericktown Historical Society. The original jacket design, by Gus Lintner, the Vocational Agriculture Instructor in 1933, had what looked like the end of an ear of corn with "FFA" and a walking plow in the center. The eagle was added to the top later. (Photograph by D.E. Boyd.)

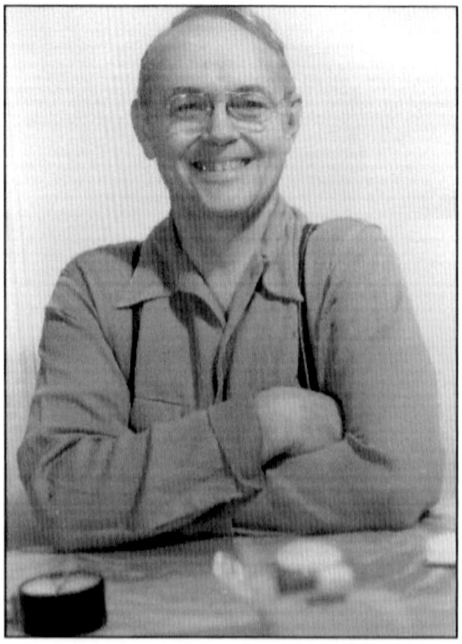

**GEORGE CRISE, INVENTOR.** George Washington Crise II grew up on a farm near Danville. He had a saying: "Those who don't use their brain have to use their back." He studied electrical engineering at the Ohio State University and manufactured and sold radios in Mount Vernon in the late 1920s and early 1930s. His first patent was for a furnace thermostat and regulator motor in 1935. The family sold the business, Patented Products, Corp. in 1997. (Photograph courtesy of Bob and Mary Crise.)

**WOOLSON'S OF NORTH MAIN STREET.** In April 2000, Woolson's won the Attraction Category in the Knox County Convention and Visitor's Bureau promotion. William A. Woolson came to town on the 7th of July 1897 and walked uptown to find a place to start a business. Larry Woolson runs the store now, and his son, Michael, has been in Hollywood films. (Photograph by D.E. Boyd.)

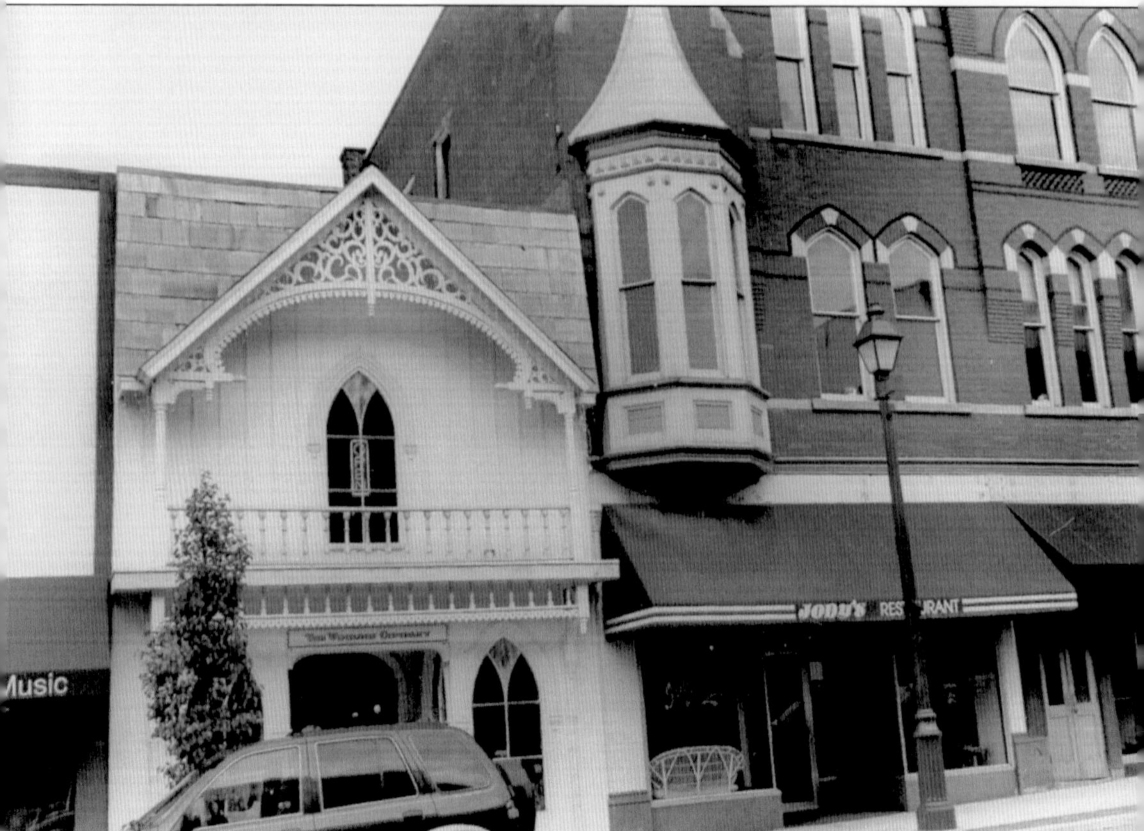

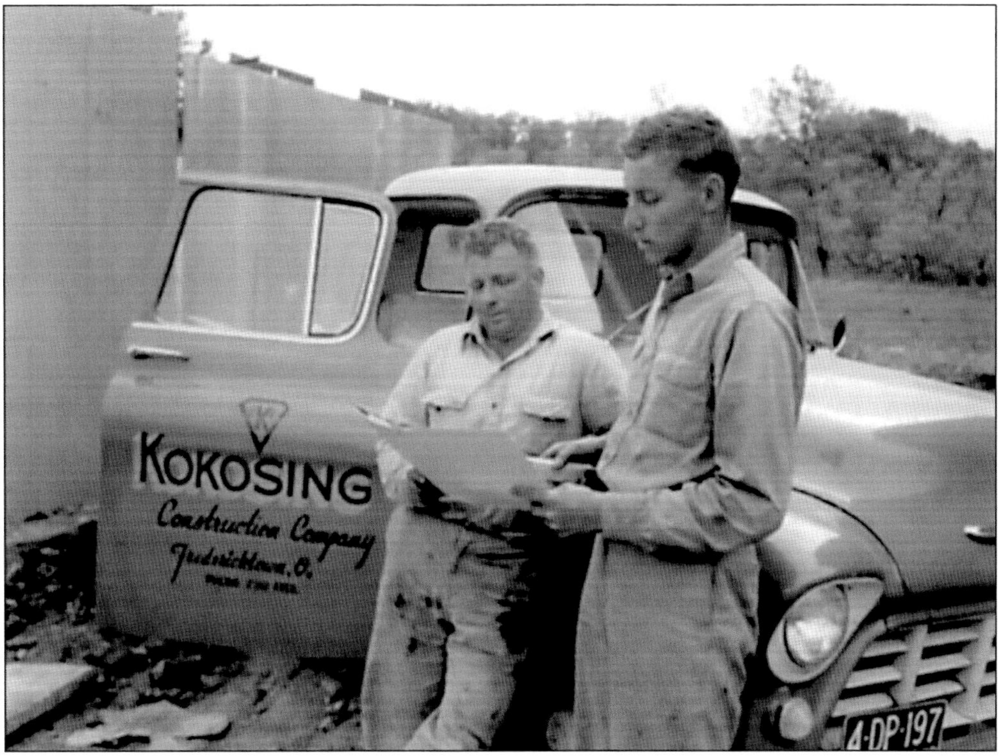


**BURGETTS DISCUSS PLANS.** Sam (left) and Bill Burgett discuss plans for making a pre-cast, concrete panel, milking parlor for Sam Burgett in 1957. Bill and Lester Rinehart started doing construction work together in 1951. Their company was called William Burgett Construction at first. The name changed to Kokosing Construction in 1954 and has grown to be one of the finest and largest construction firms in Ohio and the region. (Photograph courtesy of Kokosing Construction Co.)

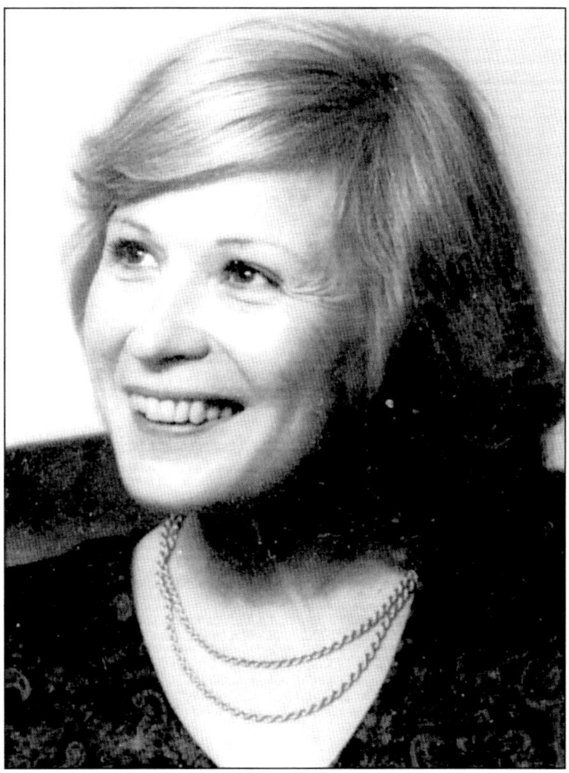

**FREDERICKTOWN NATIVE.** Betty Boyd Caroli graduated from Fredericktown High School. Her mother taught in the system for many years, and her father and brothers operated a trucking business in the area. Betty authored *First Ladies* for Oxford University Press in 1987. She now lives in New York City. (Photograph from Oxford University Press.)

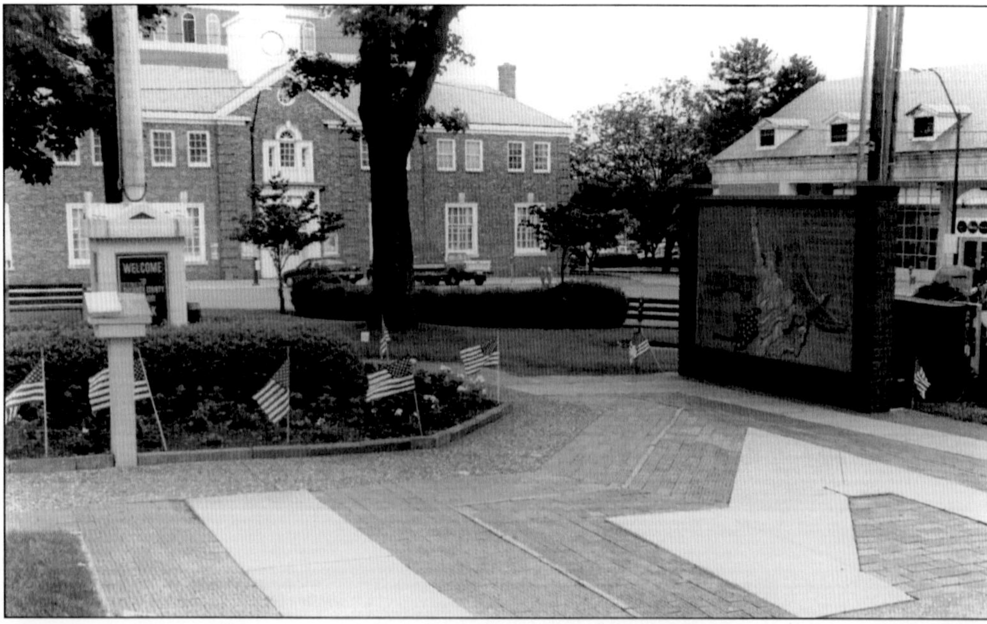


**VETERAN'S HONOR ROLL ON THE SQUARE.** A recent addition to the southwest corner of the Square is a carved brick wall and a walk paved with bricks with the names of servicemen or women on them. The walk commemorates those who served in WWII and later wars. One hundred twenty-three persons from Knox County lost their lives in WWII, and 18 persons from Knox County died in the Korean War. (Photograph by D.E. Boyd.)

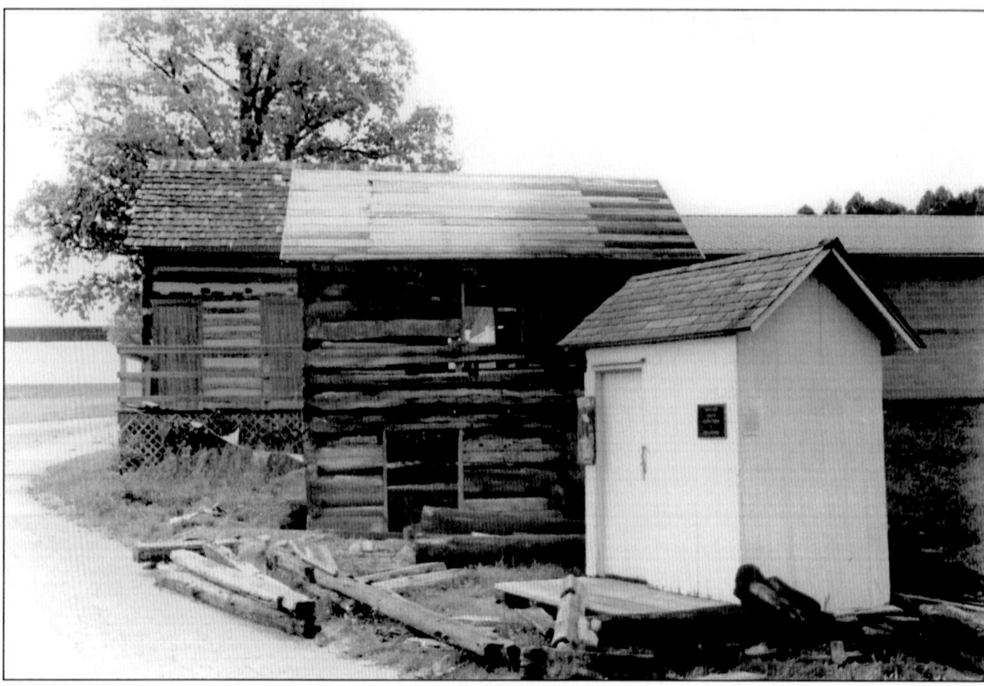

**BUILDINGS ADDED.** From left rear is a restored log cabin, a log springhouse in progress in 2004, and a privy, recently moved in as exhibits at the Knox County Agricultural Museum. (Photograph by D.E. Boyd)

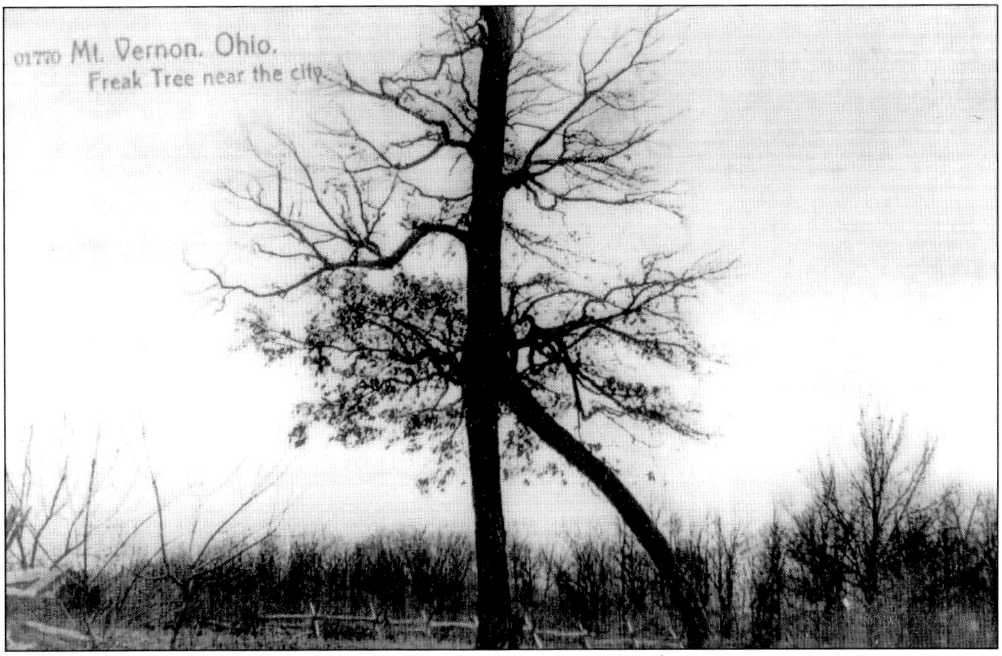


**TWIN OAKS.** This tree is really two trees that have grown together. They grew atop a hill south of Mount Vernon until the 20th century. There is still a Twin Oak Orchard near where they grew. (Photograph courtesy of the Knox County Agricultural Museum.)

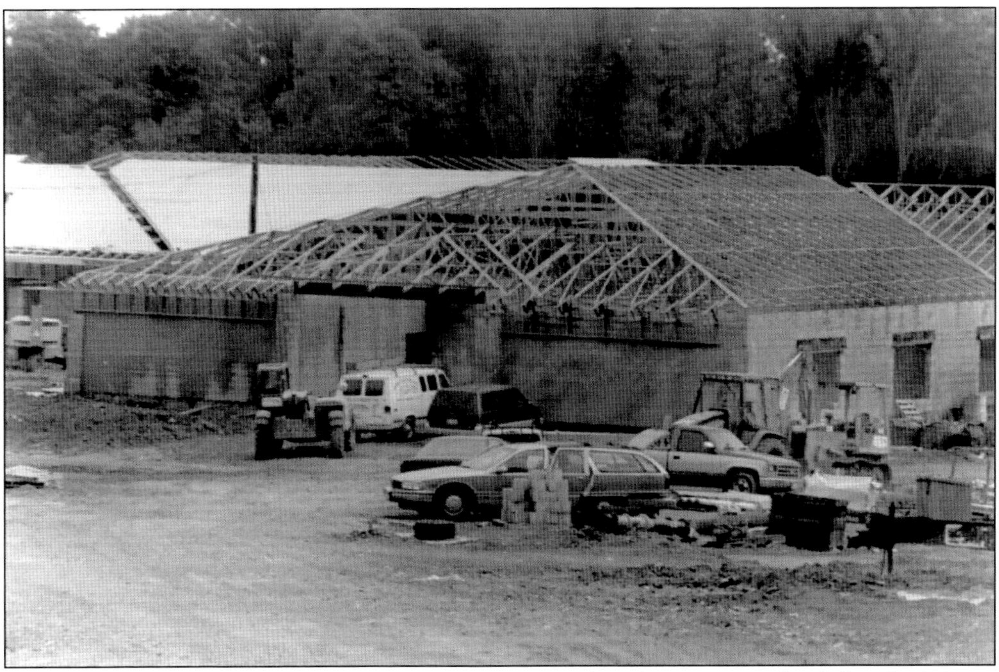

**THE NEW TWIN OAKS SCHOOL.** The new Twin Oaks Elementary School for the Mount Vernon School system is under construction in 2004. The school is built on a hill near where the trees pictured above once grew. (Photograph by D.E. Boyd.)

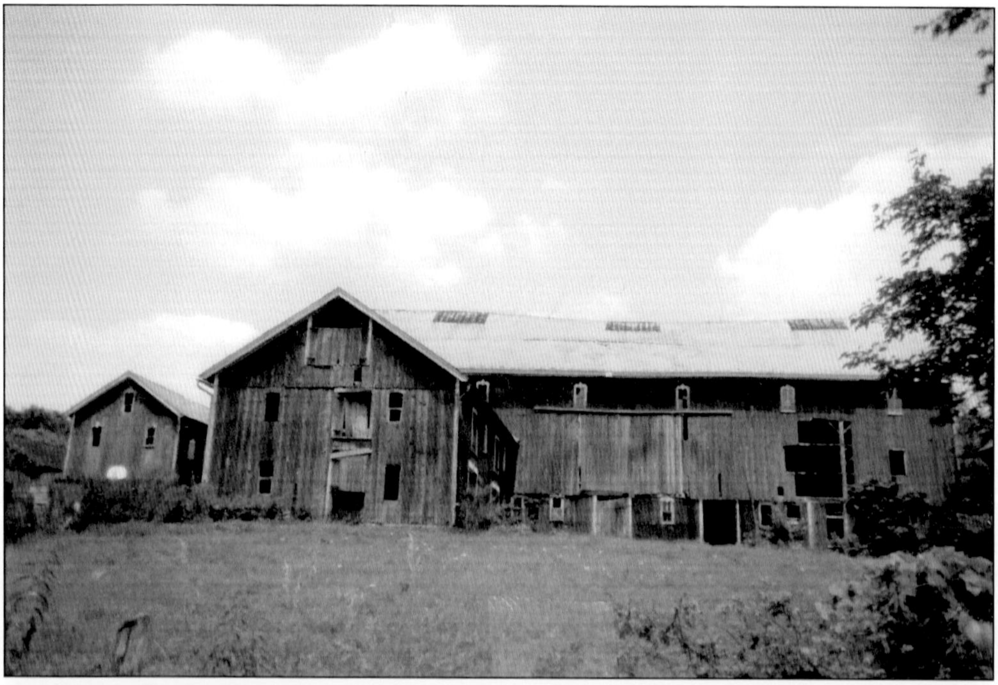

**THE EWERS BARN.** The image of a horse can barely be seen in colored slate on the roof of this barn in Fredericktown. The barn was taken apart and moved to an historic village near Cleveland in 2003. (Photograph courtesy of the Fredericktown Historical Society.)

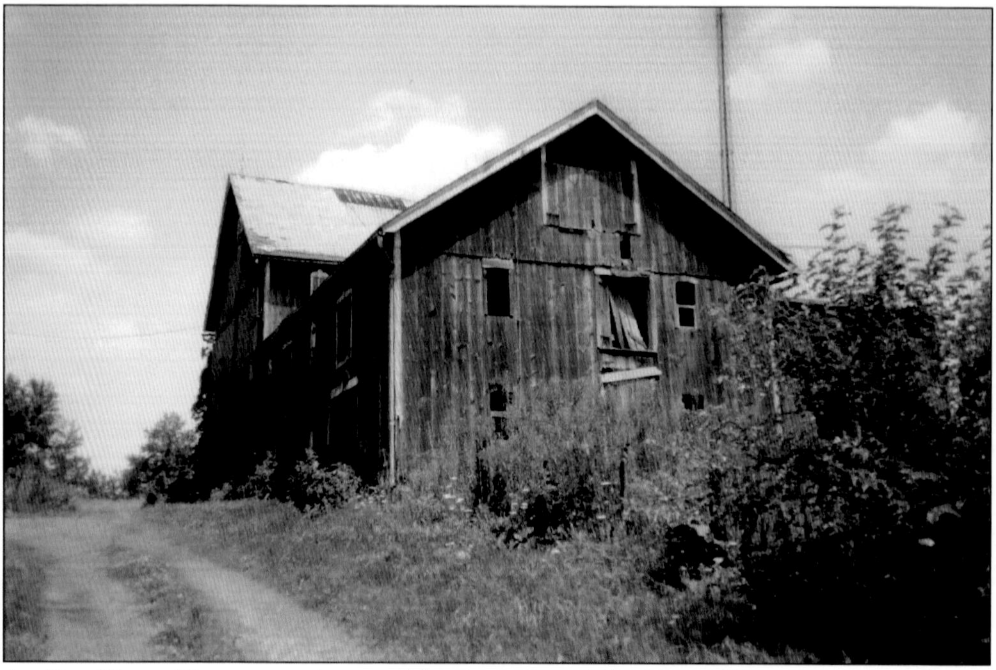

**AN END VIEW.** This is an end view of the Ewers Barn. The barn will be somewhat smaller in its new location. (Photograph courtesy of the Fredericktown Historical Society.)

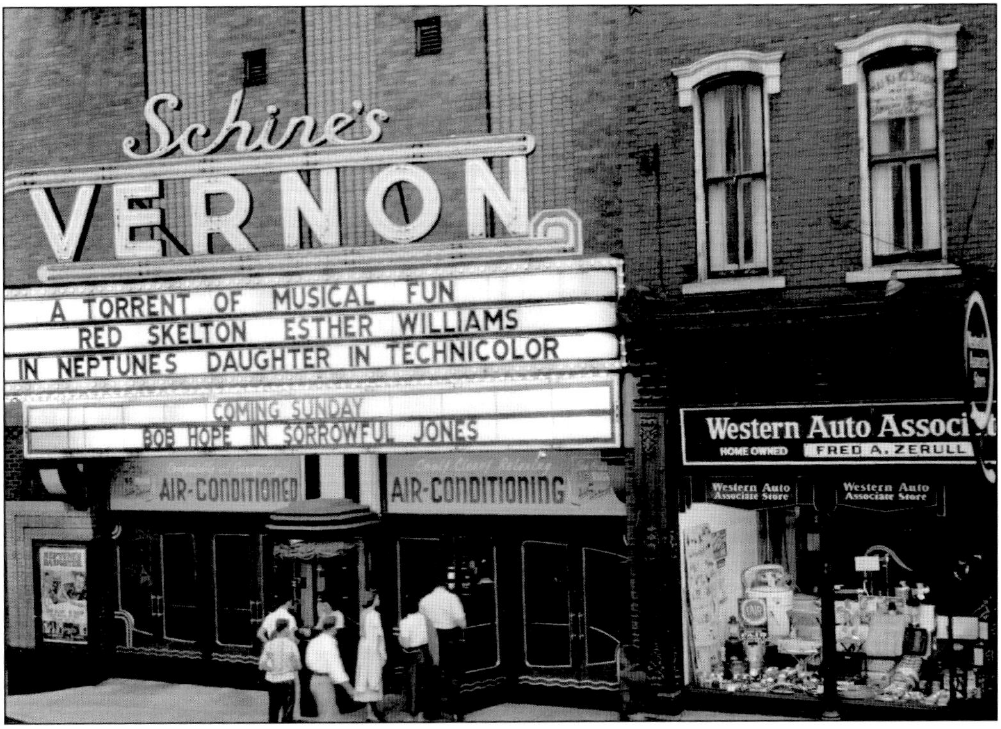


**SCHINE'S VERNON THEATER.** This is a close look at what was for many years Mount Vernon's most luxurious and popular theater. It was located on the southwest corner of the Public Square. (Photograph by the Ohio Department of State, courtesy of Sip's Coffee House in downtown Mount Vernon.)

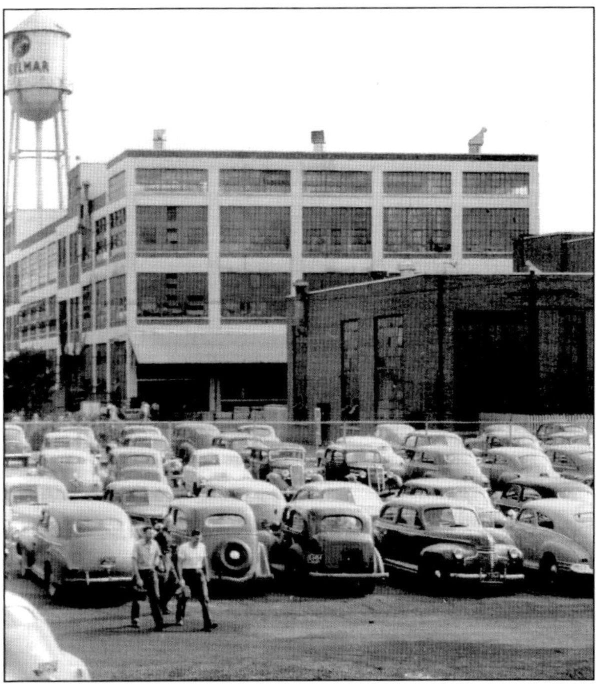

**THE SHELLMAR FACTORY, C. 1965–66.** This State of Ohio photo shows workers leaving the Mount Vernon plastic packaging factory. B.W. Martin and K. Shellaberger moved their operation from Wisconsin in 1935, and by 1939, it had doubled in size. (Photograph courtesy of Sip's Coffee House in downtown Mount Vernon.)

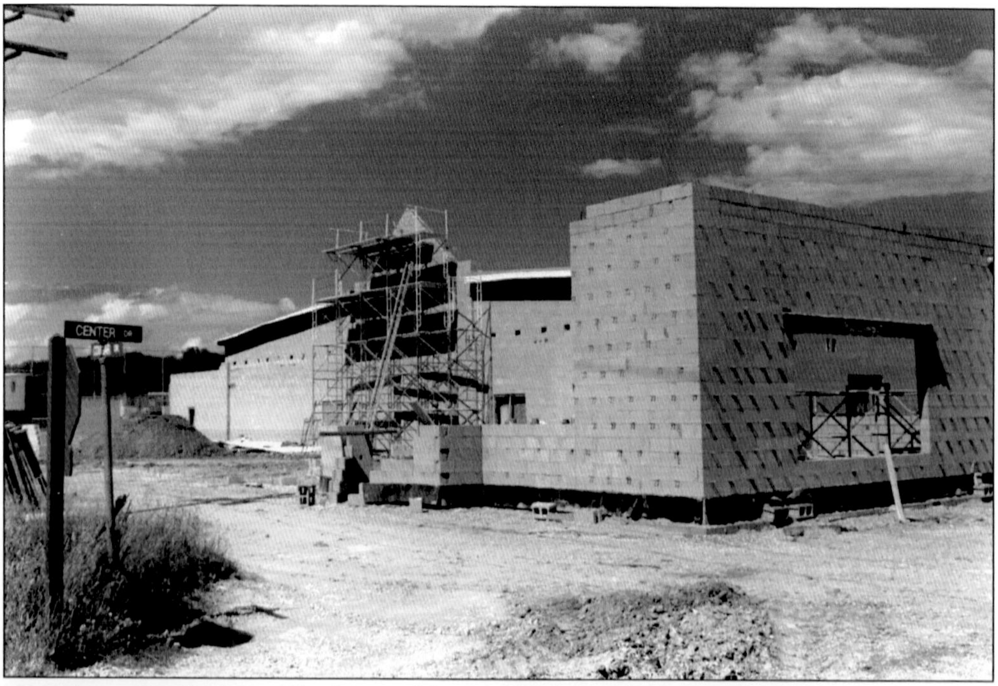


**NEW STUDENT CENTER.** The Mount Vernon Nazarene University is adding a new student center onto the west face of the Donoho Recreation Center. This photograph shows the progress up to date in 2004. (Photograph by D.E. Boyd.)

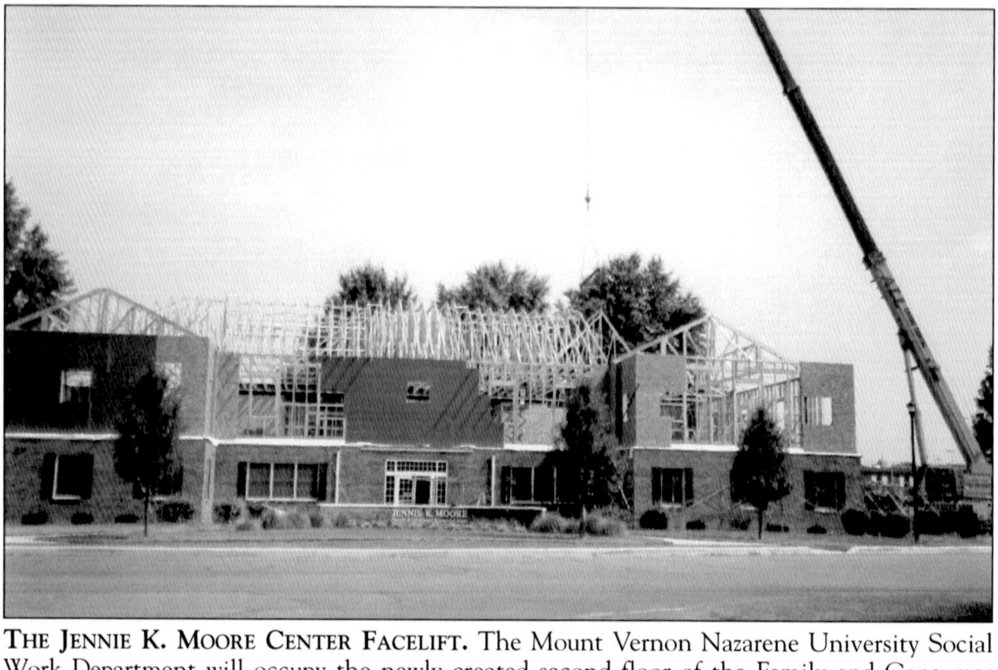

**THE JENNIE K. MOORE CENTER FACELIFT.** The Mount Vernon Nazarene University Social Work Department will occupy the newly created second floor of the Family and Consumer Sciences Building in the first semester of 2005. Work is being done in 2004(Photograph by Karen S. Boyd.)

# ACKNOWLEDGMENTS

This book would not have been possible without the passionate efforts towards preservation made by the earlier photographers and residents of Mount Vernon, who contributed to the archives from which I have drawn. Living historians, Tim McKee and Ken Arthur continued the tradition by encouraging me to write this book. Melissa Basilone, editor at Arcadia Publishing, has been very helpful, along with the entire Arcadia support staff who are needed to create a book. Current contributors, such as Janet Wacker, provided help in finding sources in the Mount Vernon and Knox County Public Library Reference Room and through her publication of a historical timeline. Tom House and Carol Marshall of the Olin Library, Kenyon College, Greenslade Special Collections and Archives, were thoroughly expert in researching and providing images from their collection. David H. and Marilyn Carter, Janice Ruggles, Dale and Margaret Beheler, Gordon and Vickie Beheler, Doris Brown, and the entire Fredericktown Historical Society went out of their way to help me with this project. Richard Morey, Paul Goossens, Joyce Selby, and others of the Knox County Agricultural Museum staff allowed me access to their valuable files. Mr. Jesse Smith, father of Don Smith, brought photographs and articles about his son. Ann Bennett loaned me a copy of a photograph of her son, Luke Perry, and supplied information about his career. Valuable technical assistance was provided by Crispin Webb, Andrew Lane, and Steve Werner—all computer whizzes—and by Andrew Johnston at the Mount Vernon Nazarene University General Computer Laboratory.

The people who responded to an article in the Mount Vernon News and loaned me numerous photographs and clippings or provided information include: Norma Laughrey; Margie and David Grubaugh; Richard A. Cochran; Anita V. and Robert Lahmon; John and Vivian Lahmon; Ken Blubaugh; Margene Ward; Jack and Donna Martin; Edward Blackburn, M.D.; John R. Fowler, DDS; Robert and Mary Crise; Charles W. Whitney; Mary-Anne K. Promputius, president of the Knox County Renaissance Foundation; Ronald L. Linson; Usher Levering; Russ McGibney of Sip's Coffee House in downtown Mount Vernon; and Jeff Boucher of Flapper's Bar & Grille.

Thanks to my family for their wonderful support: beginning with my wife, Karen; my children, Bentley, Laura, and Jonathan, all history buffs; my son-in-law, Bob Robertson; Karen's daughter, Beth Rainey; and my grandchildren, for allowing their parents to assist me. Thanks also goes out to members of my extended family: my brother, Walter H. Boyd, and my cousins, Ralph Watson and his sister, Bess Watson-Rhoades, Betty Boyd Caroli, and the Burgetts.

So many other people have contributed, I hope I will be forgiven if I mistakenly left someone out. I really appreciate all the help I have been given.

# BIBLIOGRAPHY

Hill Jr., N.N. *History of Knox County, Ohio, 1803–1881*. (Mount Vernon, Ohio: A.A. Graham & Company, 1881).

Levering, Robert W. *Horror Trek*. (Dayton, Ohio: Hurstman Printing Company, 1948).

Lorey, Frederick N., editor. *History of Knox County, Ohio 1876–1976*. (Evansville, Indiana: Unigraph Corporation for Knox County Historical Society, 1976).

Mayle, Dr. Paul. "Mount Vernon Nazarene College: The Miracle on the Kokosing," *Cradles of Conscience*. (Kent, Ohio: Kent State University, 2002).

Norton, A. Banning. *A History of Knox County Ohio from 1779 to 1862 Inclusive*. Columbus, Ohio: Richard Nevins, printer, 1862.

Porter, Dr. Lorle. Historical Markers and lectures. Mount Vernon, Ohio.

Price, Robert. *Johnny Appleseed*. Urbana, Ohio: Urbana University Press, 1954, reprinted in 2001.

Rinhart, Floyd and Marion and Robert Wagner. *The American Tintype*. Columbus, Ohio: The Ohio State University Press, 1999.

Wacker, Janet, compiler. *Countdown to Mount Vernon's 200th Birthday*. Mount Vernon, Ohio: Public Library of Mount Vernon and Knox County.

Williams, Albert B., editor. *Past and Present of Knox County, Ohio, Volume II*. Indianapolis, Indiana: B.F. Bowen and Company, 1912.

Wintermute, H. Ogden. *Daniel Decatur Emmett*. Columbus, Ohio: Heer Printing Company, 1955.

Numerous Fredericktown Historical Society publications
and one video by members of the Society were also referred to.